Hiking

the Selway-Bitterroot Wilderness

Scott Steinberg

FALCON®

GUILFORD, CONNECTICUT

An imprint of The Globe Pequot Press

Library of Congress Cataloging-in-Publication Data

Steinberg, Scott.
    Hiking the Selway-Bitterroot Wilderness / by Scott Steinberg.— 1st ed.
        p. cm. — (A Falcon guide)
    Includes index.
    ISBN 1-56044-962-4
    1. Hiking—Selway-Bitterroot Wilderness (Idaho and Mont.)—Guidebooks. 2. Selway-Bitterroot Wilderness (Idaho and Mont.)—Guidebooks. I. Title. II. Series.

GV199.42.S45 S74 2001
917.86'80434—dc21   2001023942

Manufactured in the United States of America
First Edition/First Printing

Contents

"From this place we had an extencive view of these Stupendous Mountains principally Covered with Snow like that on which we stood; we were entirely Serounded by those mountains from which to one unacquainted with them it would have Seemed impossible ever to have escaped...."

—Captain William Clark
June 27, 1806

ACKNOWLEDGMENTS

Thanks are due first to Lucas Thompson for introducing me to backpacking and the Bitterroots during our 1993 trip to Kerlee and Tin Cup lakes. In addition to accompanying me on several forays into the Elk Summit country and elsewhere, Dick Haines provided logistical support and added to my enjoyment of the trails with his camaraderie and good humor. Friend and fellow guidebook author Morton Arkava deserves special recognition for fielding my never-ending list of questions and for his constructive criticism of the draft manuscript. His 1983 guidebook *Hiking Trails in the Bitterroot Mountains* was a major source of inspiration when I set about writing my own book a dozen years later.

That this book contains the most accurate and up-to-date information for the Selway-Bitterroot Wilderness is due to the participation of the USFS wilderness rangers and trail specialists with whom I had the pleasure of dealing: Maria Bott, Greg Brown, Bill Goslin, Cheri Jones, Nick Hazelbaker, and Gene Thompson. Their on-the-ground familiarity with the wilderness and its trails answered many of my lingering questions and helped refine this book for the better.

I am grateful for the support and encouragement of friends and family who watched the book progress from wistful musings to a finished manuscript over a period of six years. In particular I appreciate the efforts of my father, Mike Steinberg, and my grandmother, Lee Steinberg, who accompanied me on some of my most memorable summer trips into the mountains.

As for my friends at Falcon Publishing, thanks go first to Randall Green for taking the risk of signing the Missoula kid for this project back in 1995. Thanks also to associate editor Jay Nichols and all the others at Falcon whose contributions and professionalism helped bring this book to life.

Enjoy the mighty Bitterroot Mountains. I sure have.

—Scott Steinberg
Missoula
April 10, 2000

Map Legend

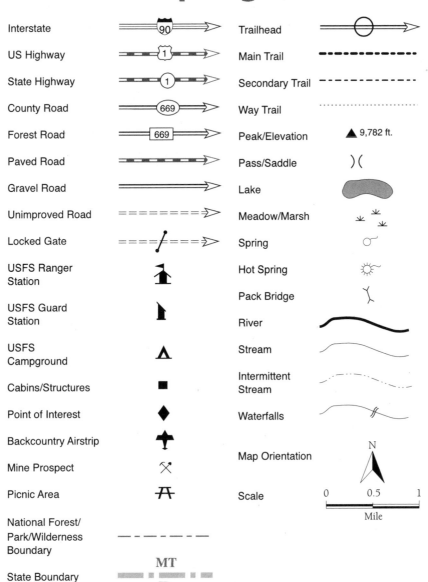

Interstate	Trailhead
US Highway	Main Trail
State Highway	Secondary Trail
County Road	Way Trail
Forest Road	Peak/Elevation
Paved Road	Pass/Saddle
Gravel Road	Lake
Unimproved Road	Meadow/Marsh
Locked Gate	Spring
USFS Ranger Station	Hot Spring
USFS Guard Station	Pack Bridge
USFS Campground	River
Cabins/Structures	Stream
Point of Interest	Intermittent Stream
Backcountry Airstrip	Waterfalls
Mine Prospect	Map Orientation
Picnic Area	Scale
National Forest/ Park/Wilderness Boundary	
State Boundary	

Topographical Map

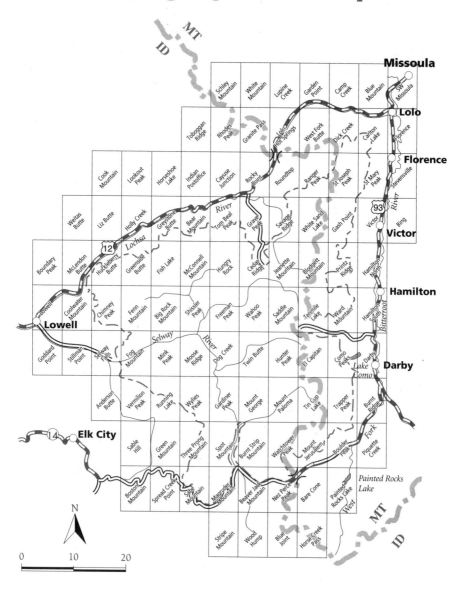

Overview Map

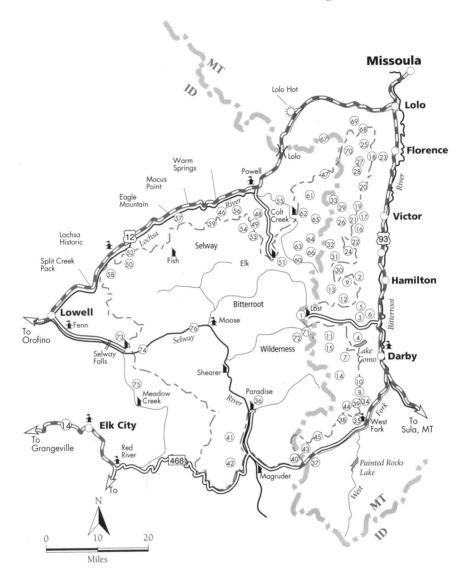

Introduction

The Selway-Bitterroot Wilderness is a vast and magnificent domain. Established by Congress with passage of the Wilderness Act of 1964, the wilderness encompasses more than 2,000 square miles of rugged Idaho and Montana backcountry. Its 1,340,681 acres are managed by the United States Forest Service (USFS) and are divided among six ranger districts on four national forests. Burned-over ridges, rushing waterfalls, rustic lookouts, and steaming hot springs scattered throughout the wilderness complex enhance its unique and subtle qualities.

Early trappers and prospectors found the Selway-Bitterroot hinterland enormously rich in natural beauty but essentially devoid of mineral wealth. Its stark isolation and rugged topography so discouraged human settlement that only five homesteaders ever staked their claim as permanent residents. Even by modern standards large tracts of the backcountry are far removed from the trappings of the industrialized world—several private inholdings, irrigation dams, and USFS outposts are the only lasting emblems of civilization within its boundaries.

Elevations within the wilderness range from 1,780 feet along the Selway River to the 10,157-foot summit of Trapper Peak. Topographically, much of the landscape consists of deep drainages and tapered ridgelines centered on the wild and scenic Selway River and building east toward the Bitterroot Divide. To early settlers, the Bitterroot Divide presented a nearly impassable

Wooden signs and windswept peaks greet visitors to the Selway-Bitterroot Wilderness.

Irrigation dams such as this one at Fish Lake are among the few reminders of civilization inside the wilderness boundaries.

barrier to westward migration, and quite justifiably so: This formidable physiographic feature defines the most rugged boundary between any two states in the Union. Stand atop any of the higher Selway-Bitterroot peaks and you gaze upon a mountain realm almost too large to comprehend.

At one time the Bitterroots reached heights approaching those of the present-day Andes, but downcutting by the Bitterroot, Lochsa, and Selway rivers over the millennia has reduced their average elevation to but a third of the original. Decomposing granodiorites, gneisses, and quartz monzonites of the 70-million-year-old Idaho batholith underlie much of the wilderness. Hard rock and placer ore deposits associated with this intrusive igneous body led to the development of mining districts elsewhere in central Idaho during the late 1800s, but the mineral-depleted Selway-Bitterroot never boasted any paying mines. The fiery genesis that created the Idaho batholith still drives a far-flung system of backcountry hot springs, however, bleeding primordial heat at temperatures ranging from lukewarm to scalding. The advance of alpine glaciers during the Pleistocene epoch (ending about 12,000 years ago) gave the higher terrain of the Selway Crags and Bitterroot Divide its present sculpted appearance, straightening and deepening canyons and excavating many of the cirques that now contain lakes.

Vegetation types found in the wilderness reflect its considerable climatic variability. Mosaic forest patterns in the lower Lochsa and Selway river watersheds are largely the result of major wildfires in 1910 and 1934; hardwoods and heavy brushfields have since colonized thousands of acres the original conifers have yet to reclaim. Douglas-fir and western ponderosa forest types predominate in the relatively dry Selway River breaks while immense old-growth grand fir and western red cedar—among the Selway-Bitterroots' greatest treasures—occupy wet microclimate habitats along certain Lochsa and Selway river tributaries. Scattered stands of lodgepole pine, Douglas-fir, and Engelmann spruce inhabit the intermediate and higher canyons and basins.

A combination of whitebark pine, subalpine fir, and the rare alpine larch take root along the highest ridges.

The wilderness supports a diversity of wildlife, with nearly 270 mammal and avian species identified to date. Forage created in the aftermath of the 1910, 1918, and 1934 wildfires sustains large wintering populations of elk and deer found on the Idaho side of the Bitterroots. Common on both sides of the Bitterroot Divide, moose are especially abundant in the rolling uplands and wet meadows of the Elk Summit country, home to the largest population in northern Idaho. Of equal interest are the genetically pure bighorn sheep indigenous to the Watchtower and Sheephead Creek drainages at the far southern periphery of the wilderness. Black bears and mountain lions are well dispersed throughout the wilderness complex, while grizzlies have been notably absent since their disappearance in the early 1950s. Many of the larger Lochsa, Selway, and Bitterroot river tributaries harbor both resident and anadromous fish. Most backcountry lakes support fisheries as well, with cutthroat and rainbow trout being the two most widespread species.

Due to its climatic and topographic complexity, there is no uniform "best season" for hiking the Selway-Bitterroot Wilderness. Precise calendar dates for snow-free hiking vary from one year to the next, but groups of trails do tend to open in a predictable sequence each summer. Trails along the lower Selway River are among the first to shed their snow and are usually passable by early April, whereas the intermediate draws and ridges are typically free of snow in late June. The last trails to open are those crossing the highest passes along the Bitterroot Divide; even in early August, patches of snow may remain on the north-facing slopes.

A hiker surveys the Bitterroot Divide near Packbox Pass.

Although the Bitterroots rank among the Northern Rockies' most rugged peaks, they feature a surprisingly extensive trail network offering access to some of their least-visited quarters. Even so, compared with many other big-name wildernesses and national parks, newcomers to the Selway-Bitterroot will find that its trails very seldom cater to those seeking instant gratification. It takes time and determination to reach many of the most worthwhile destinations. There are no boardwalks. There are no interpretive signs. Bridges are scarce. But if you do your homework and are willing to go without these bells and whistles, the Selway-Bitterroot Wilderness offers some truly unforgettable hiking.

USING THIS GUIDEBOOK

By any measure, the trail network of the Selway-Bitterroot Wilderness is immense: Approximately 2,000 miles of USFS trails crisscross the canyons and ridges of the wilderness and adjacent roadless areas. Of that total this guidebook describes some 600 miles in detail and provides cursory descriptions of another 300 miles of backcountry routes not otherwise featured. The zone of coverage includes all or portions of six USFS ranger districts on four national forests. These include the following:

Bitterroot National Forest
    Darby Ranger District
    Stevensville Ranger District
    West Fork Ranger District

Clearwater National Forest
    Lochsa Ranger District

Lolo National Forest
    Missoula Ranger District

Nez Perce National Forest
    Moose Creek Ranger District

ORGANIZATION

The 76 hikes featured in this guide are listed by USFS ranger district in order of increasing round-trip distance. (In the event that a trail overlaps two or more ranger districts, the narrative is generally included with the district encompassing the majority of its mileage.)

Trail descriptions begin with an at-a-glance hike profile designed to help backpackers select trails and plan trips according to their desires and abilities. A mile-by-mile breakdown of key points and notable landmarks follows this introductory section. Elevation profiles and photographs provide a schematic and visual preview of the trail. Special considerations, pertinent trailhead information, and a detailed narrative round out the remaining elements of each hike description. A suggested itinerary is provided for the longer hikes to give you an idea of trip-planning possibilities; side trips or optional variations of the main route are sometimes included as a supplement.

TRAIL CLASSIFICATION

This guidebook recognizes a four-tier trail classification system based on the criteria outlined below.

- **Mainline Trails (ML):** These trails are primary wilderness thoroughfares. Mainline routes sustain the heaviest recreational traffic, receive the most frequent maintenance, and tend to follow stream-bottom courses on well-defined treads leading into the backcountry. Tread condition generally ranges from excellent to fair due to heavy use and other factors.

- **Secondary Trails (S):** Secondaries include those routes with maintenance rotations ranging from two to five years. Secondary trails vary considerably in overall appearance, ranging from wide, easy-to-follow grades to severely eroded treads with poorly defined segments and lots of blowdowns. Stock parties should be prepared to cut out any trees downed across the route.

- **Way Trails (W):** These primitive routes are among the faintest and least traveled of wilderness trails, receiving maintenance on a four- to nine-year rotation. Blowdowns, faint tread, and other various factors provide an element of challenge very different from that of most mainline and secondary routes. Most such manways are impassable to stock; indeed, some are barely passable to those traveling on foot!

- **Relict Trails (X):** These nonsystem trails appear on various maps of the Selway-Bitterroot Wilderness, including old forest maps and quadrangles. Most of them last saw maintenance or reconstruction during the days of the Civilian Conservation Corps (CCC) in the 1930s. Many were subsequently abandoned for lack of maintenance and have since been dropped from USFS maps and trail inventories.

TYPE OF HIKES

All featured trails are classified according to the following three categories:

- **Loop:** This includes those trails that start and finish at the same trailhead with minimal retracing of your steps. This definition also includes "lollipops," trips requiring a short walk (typically five miles or less) via road to return to your vehicle at the end of the hike.

- **Shuttle:** This is a point-to-point trip that requires two vehicles (one left at each end of the trail) or a prearranged pick-up at a designated time and place. Many of the Bitterroots' finest backpacks involve trips of this type. One effective way to manage the logistical difficulties of shuttles is to arrange for a second party to start at the other end of the trail. The two parties then rendezvous at a predetermined time and place along the trail, trade keys, and drive to each other's home upon returning to the trailhead.

- **Out and back:** Such hikes involve traveling to a specific backcountry destination (typically a lake or peak) and retracing your steps to the trailhead. This is by far the most prevalent type in the Montana portion of the Bitterroots.

DIFFICULTY RATINGS

Each introductory section includes a subjective difficulty rating that takes into account a variety of factors such as trail length and condition, elevation profile, and overall degree of challenge. The ratings described below serve as a relative gauge and not an absolute benchmark with which every hiker will necessarily agree.

- **Easy:** Suitable for hikers of all abilities, these easy-to-follow trails are without substantial elevation gain or serious route-finding difficulty.

- **Moderate:** Suitable with novices with some outdoor experience and at least an average level of fitness, these trails may include poorly defined segments, minor fords, a few large hills, or a variable elevation profile.

- **Difficult:** Suitable for experienced hikers in excellent physical condition, these demanding trails typically include serious elevation gain and may involve swift stream fords or cross-country travel along exposed ridgelines. They are not for the faint of heart. Stamina and faint-trail skills are the necessary prerequisites.

- **Strenuous:** Suitable for none other than the most diehard backpackers, these routes will test the physical limits of the most Herculean individuals. Long trail mileages, next-to-nonexistent tread, and/or a variable elevation profile with considerable vertical relief are among the major contributing factors.

DISTANCES

Distance estimates cited throughout this book are an attempt to reconcile firsthand experience on the trail with sometimes conflicting information drawn from USGS topographic maps and USFS signs posted throughout the wilderness. Even so, these estimates are somewhat more conservative than those found in other guidebooks and stated on USFS signs. Keep in mind that distance is often of secondary importance to difficulty; on the whole, the latter provides a better overall indication of how demanding a hike is likely to be because it relies on several key factors instead of a single measurement.

ELEVATION PROFILES

Elevation charts accompany each trail description in this guidebook. They are intended to provide a visual representation of the elevation ranges you will encounter relative to certain prominent landmarks and other key points along the trail. The *cumulative* elevation gain and loss figures are tallied for reference in the at-a-glance section of each description.

MAPS

The maps in this book serve as a general guide only and under no circumstances are intended to substitute for the appropriate USGS quadrangles. The three types of maps available for the Selway-Bitterroot Wilderness include the following:

- **Selway-Bitterroot Wilderness Map (1:63,360):** depicts 100-foot contours and portrays the general configuration of landforms throughout the wilderness and contiguous roadless lands at a useful scale. Coverage at this scale requires two maps—one each for the northern and southern halves of the wilderness. Many minor inconsistencies and omissions present in the 1999 revision were carried over from earlier printings. These discrepancies are noted in this guidebook.

- **USFS Forest Maps (1:126,720):** lack contours but depict cultural features (especially roads) that other maps may portray inaccurately or omit altogether. The up-to-date forest road and closure information is useful for locating trailheads and scheduling your trip. But keep in mind that topographic detail at this scale is too sparse to provide any meaningful assistance beyond the trailhead.

- **USGS 7.5' Quadrangles (1:24,000):** far and away the most desirable maps for backpacking in the Bitterroots. Depicting the terrain in 20-, 40-, or 80-foot contour intervals, topographic maps are ideal for use in conjunction with a compass, altimeter, and/or Global Positioning System (GPS) receiver. But because these maps draw no distinction between the various classes of trail, there is a tendency to assume that all trails are maintained to the same standard when in fact they are not. *Caveat emptor!*

I cannot overemphasize the importance of taking the appropriate maps, particularly USGS quadrangles, and consistently referring to them during your travels. Doing so will enhance your routefinding expertise and foster a greater appreciation of the earth's landscapes. Local sporting goods stores and blueprint shops are a good source of USGS maps for the Bitterroot Mountains. The maps may also be ordered direct from the USGS or via the Internet at the following addresses:

Map Distribution
U.S. Geological Survey
Box 25286, Federal Center
Denver, CO 80225
http://mapping.usgs.gov

BACKCOUNTRY SAFETY AND HAZARDS

BACKCOUNTRY SAFETY

The Boy Scouts of America have long been guided by what is perhaps the single best piece of safety advice—Be Prepared! Being prepared includes carrying survival and first-aid materials, proper clothing, compass, and topographic maps—and knowing how to use them. When hiking the Bitterroots, have the following on hand and ready to use at all times:

- **First-aid kit:** This should include the following items: aspirin; adhesive strips (8); adhesive tape; antibacterial ointment; antiseptic swabs (2); butterfly bandages (2); codeine tablets; CPR shield; gauze pads (4); 3-inch gauze roll (1); inflatable splints (2); rubber gloves; Moleskin and Second Skin (for blisters, before and after); sewing needle (1); snakebite kit (1); triangular bandages (2); and lightweight first-aid instructions.

- **Survival kit:** This should include the following items: aluminum foil, candle, cigarette lighter, compass, fire starter, flare, flashlight (with extra batteries), matches (in waterproof container), signal mirror, space blanket, water purification tablets, and whistle.

For your own peace of mind and that of your family, *always* tell someone where you're going and when you expect to return. Aviators must file a flight plan before every trip, and anyone venturing into the backcountry of the Selway-Bitterroot Wilderness should do the same. Be sure to file your "flight plan" with a friend or relative before heading out. And stick to it.

Close behind carrying proper equipment and filing a flight plan lies physical preparedness. Know and respect your limitations. Physical readiness adds tremendously to your enjoyment of the surroundings; selecting a trail appropriate to your level of conditioning allows you to focus on the natural splendor instead of the mechanics of hiking itself. Be flexible enough in your trip planning to adapt to changing conditions should your original plans prove too ambitious.

There are a number of excellent references available for those interested in learning more about backcountry safety and survival. Falcon Publishing's *Wild Country Companion* and *Wilderness Survival,* for instance, cover these topics in depth.

TRAIL ETIQUETTE

The Selway-Bitterroot Wilderness attracts a wide variety of users, ranging from mountaineers setting out for some remote summit or long pack trains headed to hunting camps deep in the backcountry. As increasing numbers of recreationists head into the mountains for a perfect wilderness outing, so, too, the likelihood of conflict between users increases. Highlighting the potential for user conflict is the long-standing tension between backpackers and horsemen. Backpackers justifiably cringe at the sight of a long pack string, knowing that they will likely be slogging through the horse-churned mud and feces with their own two hooves—often for hundreds of yards or even miles at a time. The USFS spends millions of dollars annually to repair or reroute trails damaged by horse use in the Northern Rockies. Yet any regulations to further restrict stock use in the Selway-Bitterroot Wilderness are not forthcoming.

During your travels in the Selway-Bitterroot Wilderness you will be sharing most wilderness thoroughfares with stock users, *especially* if your trip originates at the Wilderness Gateway, Elk Summit, Twin Lakes, Bear Creek Pass, or Paradise trailheads. When you encounter a stock party, politely step off the trail on the *downhill side* and let the pack string pass. To prevent spooking the animals, avoid any sudden movements and speak to them in gentle, reassuring tones. Continue on your way once the stock party is well past. In the event that two stock parties meet, it is the longer and more heavily laden pack string that has the right-of-way.

THE SILENT KILLER

All backcountry travelers should be wary of hypothermia—a decrease in core body temperature that results when internal heat dissipates faster than it is replaced. In most cases this dangerous condition develops in air temperatures ranging from 30 to 50 degrees F. Dehydration, fatigue, and degree of exposure to the elements induce hypothermia and contribute to its progression. Mental and physical exhaustion and collapse result as the effects of hypothermia deplete the body's energy reserves. Death may follow unless the victim receives prompt medical treatment.

The human body employs a variety of mechanisms to maintain its optimal core temperature of 98.6 degrees F. Exposure to adverse conditions, such as wind-driven rain, promotes heat loss and forces your body to compensate by shivering and making involuntary adjustments to preserve the core temperature in vital organs. Both responses are energy-intensive and will soon exhaust your reserves; the only way to stop the drain is to reduce your degree of exposure.

The best defense against hypothermia is to stay dry. Water conducts heat away from the body 25 times faster than air alone, and when clothes get wet, they lose approximately 90 percent of their insulating value (wool is an exception). Wear layers of clothing for maximum versatility, adding or removing them as conditions dictate, with high-quality raingear forming a protective outer shell.

Watch for the developing signs of hypothermia if your party is exposed to cold, wet, and wind. When a member of your party has hypothermia, he or she may deny the problem. Believe the symptoms, *not* the victim. Even mild symptoms demand attention.

- **Mild hypothermia:** Seek shelter immediately. Strip off all wet clothes and provide energy foods such as hot liquids, sugars, and trail mix. Avoid alcohol, caffeine, and tobacco products as these are likely to increase the rate of dehydration and heat loss. Then get the victim into dry clothes and a warm sleeping bag. Build a campfire or fill well-wrapped hot water bottles to provide an external heat source.

- **Severe hypothermia:** Seek shelter immediately and attempt to keep the victim awake (to lose consciousness is to die). Provide sugar water or other warm liquids. Prepare a "hypothermia wrap" of multiple sleeping bags, wool clothing, and/or space blankets to minimize additional heat loss. Strip off all wet clothes and place the victim inside with another person—both naked. Apply wrapped hot water bottles, warm rocks, towels, or chemical heat packs to transfer heat to the major arteries at the armpits, groin, neck, and palms.

WATER SUPPLIES

The pristine waters of the Selway-Bitterroot Wilderness are cold and refreshing—or so a visual inspection would seemingly suggest. Yet even the most remote of wilderness backwaters may harbor harmful microorganisms. The most prevalent offender is *Giardia lamblia,* a single-celled pathogen that arrives in backcountry waterways via the feces of mammals such as beavers, packstock, and humans. Common disinfectants are ineffective against *Giardia;* research has demonstrated the cysts to be far more chlorine resistant than most bacteria and viruses. Drinking untreated surface water greatly improves your chances of exposure to *Giardia.* To reduce your risk of contracting the unpleasant symptoms associated with this water-borne parasite, you have three options.

- **Water-purification tablets:** By far the least attractive option, the tablets' active ingredients dissolve slowly in waters drawn from cold mountain lakes

This old bunkhouse still stands at Hauf Lake.

11

and have been derided by generations of backpackers for the objectionable off-taste they impart. This purification method is generally considered ineffective and an option of last resort.

- **Boiling water:** Being the most fuel-intensive method, boiling water is often impractical for longer backpacking trips since it consumes fuel that could otherwise be used for cooking. The minimum recommended boiling time varies somewhat, with the consensus ranging anywhere from five to ten minutes.

- **Water filters:** Despite their initial expense, a quality water filter is a must-have if you prefer long-distance backpacking. Prices and specifications vary depending on the manufacturer, but most employ a celluloid membrane or porous ceramic element designed to screen out the offending microbes. The only drawbacks are their up-front cost, slow throughput, and laborious operation. I recommend using your filter in conjunction with a collapsible plastic bucket from which water may be drawn; filtering water directly from a fast-moving stream is more difficult than most people realize.

FORDING STREAMS AND RIVERS

With the exception of trails along the major river corridors, bridges of any standard are uncommon in the Selway-Bitterroot Wilderness. Crossing swift mountain streams without the benefit of hewn footlogs or other bridges can be a risky proposition, but when done correctly you should suffer no ill effects.

Most drainages in the Bitterroots reach their seasonal crests in early June, when the combined effects of rainfall and snowmelt render many crossings impassable. Water levels also fluctuate as melting snowpack responds to the heating of the day—some of the larger Lochsa and Selway tributaries are known to rise a foot or more by late afternoon. Stream stages usually taper off by early July and reach their lowest ebb as Labor Day approaches, although passing rainstorms and irrigation demand skew this generalization somewhat.

When you come to a major stream crossing, shuck your pack and take a look around. Carefully assess the situation. Tricky fords are not always unavoidable and by surveying the upstream and downstream conditions, you may even turn up a better location at which to cross.

Stream fords sometimes seem innocuous at first glance, but even shallow crossings are deceptive and conceal a frigid, uneven channel of algae-covered cobbles. Most knee-deep fords are straightforward affairs, whereas progressively deeper water causes problems as the water's buoyant effect and the increased force of the current act in tandem against you.

Rather than fording a cold stream barefoot, use separate footwear—a pair of river sandals or canvas sneakers, for instance—to protect your feet and provide superior traction. Before sauntering into the current, stow all essential equipment (matches, camera, wallet, clothing, and sleeping bag) in watertight bags and unclip your hip belt and other restrictive straps. Start across the channel and allow your feet to slide along the streambed and seek the lowest possible footing as protection against rollouts. Discipline yourself to move slowly and cautiously, taking short, deliberate steps. When possible choose a path perpendicular to the current—doing so will spare your legs its full force and thus reduce your chances of a mishap.

GHOST TRAILS

Various maps of the Selway-Bitterroot Wilderness depict old, abandoned trails whose whereabouts are suspect or nearly unrecognizable on the ground. They are sometimes referred to as *ghost trails*. In the case of such trails a little detective work is often all that is necessary to reacquire the route should it take a wrong turn, be covered by snowfall, or seem to peter out completely. And as any veteran of the backcountry will tell you, perseverance pays dividends in the Bitterroots.

Trails throughout the wilderness are marked in a variety of ways. The three most common means of marking a trail include blazes, cairns, and signs.

- **Blazes:** Cut into the bark of trees alongside the trail, USFS blaze marks take the form of an upside-down exclamation point. Fresh blazes are unmistakable evidence of a trail and provide useful clues when deep snow or heavy brush obscures the tread. When traveling the Bitterroots, beware of errant blazes marking abandoned traplines from the early 1900s. These red herrings are not always obvious and sometimes resemble the inverted exclamation point.

- **Cairns:** When a trail traverses open terrain or ventures above timberline for any distance, its location is usually defined by a series of markers known as cairns. Constructed of three or more stones placed atop one another—an arrangement that almost never occurs naturally—cairns are unobtrusive but easy to recognize. Due to their low profile, however, a moderate snowfall diminishes their usefulness.

- **Signs:** Wooden signs are scattered at trail junctions and atop mountain passes across the wilderness complex. They are inconspicuous by design—the inscribed wood fades to a pale gray with time and easily blends in among the many tree trunks of similar color. In many cases the signs are simply absent; mindless individuals (you know who you are) either remove them for souvenirs or riddle them with bullet holes for good measure. Several important junctions described in this book remain unmarked and may go unnoticed unless you pay close attention. Still others may evade detection altogether.

Progressively fainter ghost trails require proportionately greater skill to find and follow. Careful investigation and attention to detail are essential but are no guarantee of success. The following observations are helpful when looking for a long-vanished trail and may provide clues to its location:

- **Saw works:** Sawn blowdowns, chopped out brush, and hacked logs usually indicate that a long-lost trail is in fact close at hand. USFS maintenance specifications have required cuts be made to an 8-foot clearing standard for a number of years. In heavily timbered areas (particularly dense stands of lodgepole pine), this swath produces an unnatural-looking corridor through the forest. Sometimes referred to as the hall of trees effect, the narrow clearings remain long after trail crews were last in the area.

- **Route considerations:** Use open terrain to your advantage and survey the landscape through which the trail ahead is to pass. With map, compass, and binoculars in hand and the trail's source and destination in mind, you should be able to approximate its location. The routes most favored by USFS trail crews follow a subdued profile of the natural topography, contouring around hillocks and skirting talus and other obstacles to achieve a sustained grade without repetitive ups and downs. Switchbacks are frequently employed to moderate the effects of a straight-line ascent in steep terrain. Trails cutting across open hillsides are especially apparent in early summer, when lingering snow highlights their linear trends from a distance.

- **Triangulation:** If you are really lost, use basic route-finding skills to locate your position by taking compass bearings of three prominent landmarks. (Note: your compass *must* be adjusted to reflect the local magnetic declination.) Plot your compass readings on a suitable map to produce an "error triangle" formed by their intersection. You are located somewhere inside this triangle; the more precise your compass measurements, the smaller the triangle and more accurate your location. Then compare the error triangle with the ghost trail location shown on the map. Use this method in conjunction with an altimeter or GPS receiver for maximum effectiveness.

Following ghost trails is an acquired skill that develops over time as your eyes become accustomed to the telltale clues. It is usually to your advantage to employ a team approach for ghost trails since you can usually cover more ground in less time when an extra pair of eyes is on the lookout for signs of a long-lost route.

GRIZZLIES IN THE BITTERROOTS?

For many people the subject of special hiking and camping precautions in bear country drives a dagger of boredom deep, deep into the heart. This attitude is especially prevalent in the Selway-Bitterroot Wilderness, where the absence of grizzlies for over half a century has encouraged a sense of complacency on the part of many wilderness users. All the same, knowing the following five-part system for defensive hiking is the best way to minimize your chances of a confrontation on the trail.

- **Don't go alone:** Hiking in small groups has definite advantages in the wilderness, not the least of which being a reduced likelihood of encounters with bears—grizzlies or otherwise. Statistics indicate that large groups are seldom involved in bear attacks while a large percentage of hikers mauled or killed were hiking alone at the time.

- **Stay alert:** Actively survey your surroundings as you hike, watching both ahead and to the sides of the trail. Exercise your peripheral vision to combat the temptation of lapsing into "trail hypnosis"—the tendency of fixating on the trail 10 feet ahead. Using your knowledge of bear habitat, be especially alert in areas most likely to be frequented by bears such as avalanche chutes, berry patches, and stands of whitebark pine.

- **Sounds:** Perhaps the best way to avoid an unpleasant surprise is to make sure bears know you are coming. Many hikers hang bells or cans of pebbles from their belts and packs specifically for this purpose, although any noise loud enough to alert a nearby bear will soon grow maddening to most hikers. There is some speculation that metallic noise is superior to human voices, which are more readily muffled by natural conditions.

- **Stay on the trail:** Through generations of associating trails with people, bears probably expect to find hikers on trails and seldom venture near major thoroughfares in broad daylight. On the other hand, hikers planning off-trail excursions are far more likely to cross paths with a traveling bear.

- **Sleeping late:** Like most wildlife, bears are more active around dawn and dusk than they are during the middle of the day. Hiking early in the morning of into late afternoon generally increases your chances of seeing wildlife while hiking during early afternoon greatly reduces the likelihood of an encounter.

As this book goes to print, efforts are under way to reintroduce grizzlies to their former range in the central Idaho backcountry, including the Selway-Bitterroot, Gospel Hump, and Frank Church–River of No Return wildernesses. A 1997 study by the U.S. Fish and Wildlife Service concluded that the Salmon-Selway ecosystem may eventually support as many as 280 grizzlies; reintroduction could begin as early as 2002. But ongoing political controversy may delay or even halt these efforts.

BACKCOUNTRY CAMPING

By following a few basic suggestions, overnight camping in the backcountry is no more risky than sleeping out in your own backyard. The following guidelines will help ensure a trouble-free stay.

Campsite selection: Unlike many national parks, overnight camping in the Selway-Bitterroot Wilderness is not subject to any cumbersome permit or reservation requirements. There are no designated campsites. It would be a mistake, however, to conclude that camping is permissible wherever there is room to place a tent. Some potential sites are more fragile than others—streambanks, lakeshores, and subalpine meadows are the most sensitive to disturbance and should be avoided whenever possible.

When scouting for a campsite, take care to select a sheltered location with a durable, well-drained surface at least 200 feet from the nearest trail or water source. Using preexisting campsites is almost always preferable to establishing new ones. Likewise, restrict your tents, campfires, and foot traffic to "hardened" areas where vegetation is either compacted or the ground already bare from previous use.

Keep in mind that many of the more accessible camping areas in the Idaho portion of the wilderness are reserved for outfitter use in September—wall tents and other gear usually occupy these sites by Labor Day. Note also that USFS personnel sometimes cordon off heavily used campsites (such as those around the Big Creek Lakes and in the Seven Lakes area) to promote their revegetation and recovery. Some overused areas may be subject to stock closure only; others may be razed or "iceberged" entirely.

Storing your gear and rations: Aside from clothing and sleeping gear, keep only valuables such as cameras and binoculars in your tent. Also have your flashlight and pepper spray close at hand in case an animal ventures into camp and wakes you up.

Experts recommend storing food in a bearproof manner at least 100 yards from your tent site. (Keeping your rations near the cooking area is usually preferable since doing so localizes food smells to a single location.) All food should be kept in resealable plastic freezer bags to prevent food odors from circulating through the forest. Double seal these individual bags by placing them inside larger ones to minimize leakage—this keeps food smells out of your pack and off your other camping gear and clothes.

For maximum bear-proofness, suspend your rations at least 10 feet above the forest floor and 5 feet from the nearest tree trunk. Place everything with any food smell—cooking gear, eating utensils, food storage bags, and incombustible garbage—in a sturdy "dry bag" (available at most outdoor specialty stores) and hoist it into the trees with a length of nylon rope or parachute cord for overnight storage. A steel pulley, available from most hardware supply stores, reduces friction between branch and rope, allowing you to lift much heavier loads. The illustrations on the following page depict three popular methods of storing your rations.

The Big Creek Lakes unfold in this view from the slopes below Packbox Pass. Mike Steinberg photo

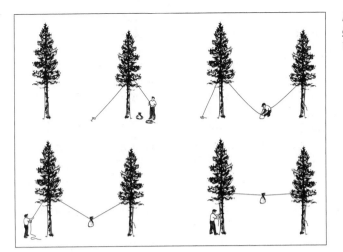

Hanging food and garbage between two trees.

Hanging food and garbage over a tree branch.

Hanging food and garbage over a leaning tree.

17

Cooking in camp: The overriding principle of backcountry cooking is to create as little odor as possible. In every sense what food you have along is much less critical than *how* you handle it, cook it, and store it. Remember that a distance of at least 100 feet should always separate your tent and cooking areas. Be careful not to spill on yourself while cooking—if you do, promptly change clothes and hang those with food odor with your rations as explained previously. Wash your hands thoroughly before retiring to the tent.

Campfires provide the best way to eliminate any lingering scents, but they also cause headaches for USFS wilderness rangers. These backcountry stewards spend much of their time removing unburned material (aluminum foil, refried beans, plastic utensils, etc.) from campfire rings each summer. Incinerating incombustible packaging such as aluminum foil is especially objectionable since the metallic oxide residue left behind permanently poisons the soil below—plants cannot grow again on the site. Burning large quantities of plastic packaging fouls air quality due to the inversion effects common in mountain canyons. Under such conditions you may smell a single plastic cup burning more than one-quarter mile away.

The best way to deal with this dilemma is to thoroughly rinse food or beverage containers after use and place them in double-sealed plastic bags for overnight storage. Any food particles and extra cooking or dish water can then be dumped along the edge of a campfire to burn off the smell. Pack out the plastic and foil when you break camp.

Minimize food scents by using as few dishes as possible. Dispose of "gray water" in a cathole at least 200 feet from your tent and the nearest water source. Wash dishes immediately after eating to ensure that any remaining food odors will quickly dissipate.

MOUNTAIN LIONS

Compared with bears and other wildlife, mountain lion sightings are rather uncommon in the backcountry of the Selway-Bitterroot Wilderness. The media have a tendency to sensationalize mountain lion encounters, particularly those in suburban areas of the Missoula and Bitterroot valleys, but sightings in the wilderness itself are surprisingly rare. In most cases, the big cats exhibit avoidance, indifference, or curiosity that never results in human injury.

But should you happen to cross paths with a mountain lion, resist the temptation of running—as doing so may trigger a predatory response. Maintain eye contact to demonstrate your awareness of its presence and move slowly and deliberately away while keeping the animal in your direct line of sight. If attacked, fight back and try to remain standing. Do not feign death. Pick up a branch or rock; pull out a knife or brandish your pepper spray. Individuals have successfully fended off mountain lions with blows from rocks, tree limbs, and even cameras.

For an in-depth discussion of lion behavior and tips for safe outdoor recreation in mountain lion country, pick up a copy of Falcon Publishing's *Mountain Lion Alert.*

RATTLESNAKES

Backpackers traveling the Selway River breaklands and surrounding country must contend with a hazard seldom encountered on the Montana side of the Bitterroots: rattlesnakes. Geographic names such as Bad Luck Creek and Rattlesnake Bar allude to the presence of these poisonous vipers; their habitat in the Selway-Bitterroot is largely restricted to the Selway River and surrounding terrain below 6,000 feet elevation. Stay alert and watch your step when backpacking in these low-lying areas. The rattlers are most active in temperatures between 75 and 90 degrees F and tend to lie low during the hottest hours of the afternoon. If small children or the family dog is along for the hike, take care to keep them from venturing out of sight ahead or from wandering very far from the trail. Always carry a snakebite kit and familiarize yourself with its use.

SEASONS AND WEATHER

The best time for backpacking the Selway-Bitterroot Wilderness is from early July to late September, with the latter half being by far the most enjoyable portion of this 12-week period. The three months preceding the prime season are traditionally the Bitterroots' wettest, with frequent cloudiness and rainstorms. Extensive snowfields and cornices drape the high country along the Bitterroot Divide until warmer weather arrives in July and August. (Even at the height of summer, snowfall remains a distinct possibility.) Snow typically returns to the higher ridges and passes in late September and then reclaims lower drainages in the weeks that follow. In some cases the snow-free window extends well into October, but autumn weather is notoriously fickle and subject to change from one minute to the next.

Weather patterns over the high-altitude topography of the Bitterroot Mountains are prone to sudden and unexpected changes. Water vapor rises, cools, and condenses as prevailing westerly winds carry moisture inland and over the higher peaks of Northern Rockies. The resulting thunderstorms occur at all hours of day or night but generally reach peak intensity in late afternoon, dissipating only as they lose the heating of the day. High winds, heavy precipitation (rain and snow), hail, and lightning may accompany their arrival.

Daily high temperatures within the wilderness vary according to elevation and degree of cloudiness. An average of 70 to 85 degrees F is fairly typical. Lower-elevation canyons achieve significantly hotter temperatures, especially along the Selway River, where furnacelike conditions routinely send the mercury toward 100 degrees F. Conversely, nighttime low temperatures generally hover in the 40s and upper 30s but may plunge into the upper 20s under clear skies.

Checking the forecast is always helpful for any outdoor pursuit and is especially useful for longer excursions into the backcountry. Up-to-the-minute forecasts such as those from the Weather Channel are also available online (http://www.weather.com). I personally prefer carrying a NOAA pocket radio to keep abreast of changing conditions on the trail. Compared with GPS and cellular phones, pocket radio reception is surprisingly good throughout the many deep canyons of the Selway-Bitterroot. Such gadgetry is compact, lightweight, and available for less than $50.

BACKCOUNTRY ESSENTIALS

ROAD AND TRAILHEAD ACCESS

In general, the road system leading to dozens of major Selway-Bitterroot trail-heads is well maintained. USFS signs clearly show the way to many of the more popular jumping-off spots, and, with forest maps in hand, you should have little trouble finding the others. The trailheads themselves vary wide-ly in terms of the available amenities and parking space, ranging from no-frills pullouts to full-blown USFS campgrounds.

The Montana portion of the wilderness features numerous canyon por-tal entry points reached via county and USFS roads extending west from U.S. Highway 93 and the Bitterroot Valley. Commercial services, groceries, and gas are available throughout the valley.

U.S. Highway 12 provides important all-season access to the northern pe-riphery of the wilderness. Several important trailheads are located right along the highway itself, where a series of four pack bridges offers dry passage over the Lochsa River. End-of-the-road trailheads at Beaver Ridge, Colt Creek, Tom Beal Park, and Elk Summit are reached via forest roads extending south and east from the highway corridor—these are generally navigable by mid-July each summer. Other points of entry at Wilderness Gateway and Race Creek serve as popular staging areas for parties venturing into the Sel-way Crags country at the extreme western margin of the wilderness. Sec-ondary trailheads at Big Fog Saddle, Coolwater Ridge, and Indian Hill provide additional trip possibilities.

The far southwestern expanse of the Selway-Bitterroot ranks as the least accessible portion of the wilderness. The Magruder Corridor Road (468) be-tween Elk City (Idaho) and Darby (Montana) is your primary means of ac-cess to this remote and lightly used area. Low-clearance vehicles and motorhomes are strongly discouraged from traveling the steep, winding, one-lane road west of the Selway River crossing. Heavy snowpack and high el-evations generally limit through-traffic to the 12-week period from late July to early October. The Magruder Corridor is so remote that no commercial services (food, gas, and lodging) are available for more than 120 miles!

Most trailheads in the Bitterroot Mountains are accessible via passenger sedans after the roads open up in July. However, your travels may require a four-wheel drive vehicle at some point. Be prepared, carry extra water, and have a jack and good spare tire on hand. Tire chains are useful if you expect to encounter snow or when the weather threatens. Remember that a shovel and bucket are required for all campfires built in nondesignated roadside campsites.

PLANNING YOUR TRIP

Any outing is more enjoyable if you do your homework and have at least some idea of what to expect. Reviewing maps and guidebooks such as this one beforehand allows you to anticipate potential trouble spots, such as stream fords, well before you leave the trailhead. It is always a good idea to contact the USFS district offices with any specific questions you may have. The USFS can provide up-to-date information on trail conditions as well as status reports on any road or trail closures due to forest fire activity.

Your itinerary is determined to a large extent by the length of trail you can reasonably expect to cover in a day's time. This varies according to trail conditions, individual stamina, and familiarity with the country. A daily range of between 8 to 10 miles is a good beginning guideline. Except in cases of emergency, enjoying the surrounding natural beauty should always supplant the desire for breakneck speed.

Most summer weekends see dozens of hikers and horsemen on the most popular trails; chronic overcrowding of trailhead facilities is typical during the summer holidays. It is always best to avoid these peak use periods and schedule a trip during the week whenever possible. You will frequently find that even the most overcrowded weekend spots seem deserted by midweek. There is no guarantee that you will have the trail entirely to yourself, but hiking on weekdays is the best way to improve your chances of relative solitude short of striking out cross-country.

WILDERNESS REGULATIONS

Thankfully the Selway-Bitterroot Wilderness is not subject to many of the frustrating regulations and permit systems that complicate and even discourage use of public lands elsewhere. The few restrictions that do apply are common sense and meant to ensure a quality wilderness experience. (Special stock and camping regulations apply to the popular Seven Lakes and Jerry Johnson Hot Springs areas. Further details are posted at their respective trialheads or are available upon request from the Lochsa Ranger District on the Clearwater National Forest.) Backpackers and horsemen are subject to the following wilderness-specific restrictions:

- All motorized vehicles and mechanical equipment (including mountain bikes and game wagons) are prohibited inside designated wilderness.

- Camping is limited to 14 days at one site.

- Twenty (20) head of stock is the maximum.

- Stock users should use only certified weed-seed-free feed.

- Party size is limited to 20 people.

- Please observe the voluntary USFS campfire prohibition at all campsites above 7,000 feet.

ZERO IMPACT

Like many other wilderness areas, the Selway-Bitterroot has a large capacity for human use. It is hard not to be struck by the sense of permanence and durability this mighty mountain range conveys as you travel among its many canyons and peaks or simply view them from afar. Yet for their rugged and enduring qualities the Bitterroots are surprisingly delicate and susceptible to damage from careless individuals.

Most wilderness users have little objection to following zero-impact camping techniques. All too often, however, the inconsiderate actions of a few people impact the natural environment at the expense of those who follow. Often their activities are dictated by the misguided habits of a past generation of backcountry campers who cut green boughs for evening shelters, built campfires with fire rings, and excavated drainage ditches around their tents. But as our national parks, national forests, and wilderness areas are loved to death by an increasing number of recreationists, we must all take care to put zero-impact ethics into practice—even when doing so imposes a modest inconvenience.

One recurring source of concern is the lasting effects of campfires in the backcountry. USFS wilderness rangers ask that you refrain from building campfires above 7,000 feet in the Selway-Bitterroot Wilderness. Compliance is voluntary. But by observing this restriction you can help prevent the kind of long-lasting damage that is becoming ever more prevalent in the backcountry. Beyond the scars left by campfires themselves are those made as campers remove limbs from slow-growing alpine trees and mutilate picturesque standing snags in their search for firewood. At this elevation it takes *hundreds* of years for a single whitebark pine to grow to the thickness of an adult's wrist, but only *minutes* to burn it in a campfire.

Although there are a number of sources for zero-impact information, Falcon Publishing's *Leave No Trace* is one of the best for updated tips and techniques. The following guidelines are adapted from this publication and from those adopted by the USFS.

Unnamed peaks such as the 9,883-foot Shard rise throughout the wilderness.

PLAN AHEAD AND MAINTAIN A LOW PROFILE

- Know the regulations, special considerations, and inherent risks for the area(s) you intend to visit.

- Visit the backcountry in small parties of no more than 10 individuals.

- Avoid popular areas during periods of peak use, such as summer holidays.

- Bring your cellular phone if you must, but please, use it only for emergencies. And keep in mind that reception in the deep canyons of the Selway-Bitterroot is unreliable.

ON THE TRAIL AND AT CAMP

- Stay on designated trails as much as possible in areas of high use. Never shortcut switchbacks.

- Control your pet(s) at all times.

- When traveling cross-country, select the most durable surfaces available—rock, gravel, dry grasses, and snow are the best choices. Avoid delicate wetlands and streambanks.

LEAVE WHAT YOU FIND

- Treat our natural heritage with respect. Always leave native plants, rocks, archaeological relics, and historical artifacts as you found them for others to discover and appreciate.

- Avoid damaging trees and plants by cutting boughs or removing brush. It is unlawful to cut down living trees within a designated wilderness.

- Allow sounds of the natural world to prevail. Minimize loud voices and noise, which carry across lakes and cirques.

PACK IT IN, PACK IT OUT

- Consume or pack out everything that you bring into the backcountry. *Never* bury refuse such as plastic packaging or aluminum foil; frost heave and scavenging wildlife will cause it to reappear.

- Protect wildlife and food by securely storing your rations in reusable plastic containers.

- Pick up all spilled foods to reduce the likelihood of an encounter with scavenging wildlife.

- Pack out all plastic or metal food packaging and containers. *Keep them out of the campfire.*

PROPER DISPOSAL OF WHAT CANNOT BE PACKED OUT

- Bury human waste in individual catholes at least 6 inches deep and 200 feet from the nearest water source and campsites. Cover and disguise when finished.

- Minimize soap use to keep the backcountry free of chemicals. Use biodegradable soap and wash dishes at least 200 feet from nearby water sources. Dispose of gray water outside the same 200-foot limit.

- Burn fish viscera well away from trails and camps. Never dispose of food scraps or entrails in backcountry waterways.

MINIMIZE THE IMPACT OF CAMPFIRES

- Be aware of current regulations and weather patterns specific to your area of travel. It may be dangerous or even illegal to build campfires during the summer wildfire season.

- *Always* carry a lightweight stove for cooking and enjoy a campfire *only* if it will not leave lasting scars.

- Never mutilate picturesque snags or other trees that contribute to the scenic value of a timberline environment.

- Please consider doing without a campfire if your camp is above 7,000 feet.

- Where fires are permitted, use established fire rings. Avoid fire-scarring exposed rocks, overhangs, or downed trees. If no fire rings are present, consider a simple mound fire or use a portable fire pan instead.

- Put out all campfires completely, thoroughly dousing the hot ashes. Scatter the cool ashes and charcoal over a large area well away from camp.

Bitterroot Trail Finder

	EASY	MODERATE	DIFFICULT
Short Day Hikes Less than 10 miles	1 Bailey Lake 2 Blodgett Overlook 3 Camas Lake 4 Lake Como Loop 17 Sweathouse Falls 19 Glen Lake 22 Fred Burr Reservoir 23 Larry Creek Complex 34 Baker Lake 46 Warm Springs Creek 67 Skookum Butte 71 Coquina Lake 73 Gedney Creek	6 Coyote Coulee 7 Little Rock Creek Lake 8 Trapper Creek 16 Bear Creek Overlook 20 Saint Mary Peak 37 Castle Rock 42 Flat Creek 47 Spruce Creek Lakes 48 Walton Lakes 50 Stanley Hot Springs 51 Diablo Mountain Lookout	5 Ward Mountain 9 Canyon Falls 18 Little Saint Joseph Peak 21 Gash Point 35 Boulder Point 36 Bad Luck Mountain 38 Nelson Lake 39 Trapper Peak 49 Grave Peak 52 Lone Knob Loop 68 Lolo Peak 72 Spruce Lake
Long Day Hikes 10 to 20 miles	55 Colt Killed Creek 60 Big Sand Lake 74 Cupboard Creek	10 Chaffin Creek Lakes 11 Lost Horse Lake 12 Roaring Lion Creek 24 Sheafman Creek 26 Bear Creek 27 Bass Lake 28 Kootenai Creek 29 South Fork Big Creek 40 Nez Perce Peak 44 Boulder Creek 63 Hidden Lake	25 Sweeney Ridge 41 Spot Mountain Lookout 43 Sheephead Creek Loop 45 Watchtower Creek to Sheephead Creek 53 Pouliot Loop 56 Cooperation Ridge 57 Mocus Point 58 Old Man Point 59 Bear Mountain Lookout 62 Dan Ridge Loop 64 Hidden Peak 69 Lantern Ridge 70 South Fork Lolo Creek to Bass Creek

Bitterroot Trail Finder (continued)

	EASY	MODERATE	DIFFICULT
Backpacking Trips 1 to 5 nights	55 Colt Killed Creek 60 Big Sand Lake 74 Cupboard Creek	10 Chaffin Creek Lakes 11 Lost Horse Lake 12 Roaring Lion Creek 15 Rock Creek 24 Sheafman Creek 26 Bear Creek 27 Bass Lake 28 Kootenai Creek 29 South Fork Big Creek 30 Blodgett Canyon 31 Mill Creek 44 Boulder Creek 54 Wind Lakes 63 Hidden Lake 65 White Sand Lake 75 Lower Meadow Creek 76 Selway River	13 Sawtooth Creek 14 Tin Cup Lake 25 Sweeney Ridge 32 Fred Burr Creek to Mill Creek 33 Big Creek to Bear Creek 43 Sheephead Creek Loop 45 Watchtower Creek to Sheephead Creek 53 Pouliot Loop 64 Hidden Peak 66 Hidden Creek Ridge 70 South Fork Lolo Creek to Bass Creek
Backcountry Lakes	1 Bailey Lake 3 Camas Lake 19 Glen Lake 34 Baker Lake 60 Big Sand Lake 71 Coquina Lake	7 Little Rock Creek Lake 10 Chaffin Creek Lakes 11 Lost Horse Lake 15 Rock Creek 24 Sheafman Creek 26 Bear Creek 27 Bass Lake 28 Kootenai Creek 30 Blodgett Canyon 31 Mill Creek 44 Boulder Creek 47 Spruce Creek Lakes 48 Walton Lakes 54 Wind Lakes 63 Hidden Lake 65 White Sand Lake	9 Canyon Falls 13 Sawtooth Creek 14 Tin Cup Lake 25 Sweeney Ridge 32 Fred Burr Creek to Mill Creek 33 Big Creek to Bear Creek 38 Nelson Lake 45 Watchtower Creek to Sheephead Creek 49 Grave Peak 53 Pouliot Loop 61 Siah Lake 66 Hidden Creek Ridge 68 Lolo Peak 70 South Fork Lolo Creek to Bass Creek 72 Spruce Lake

Bitterroot Trail Finder (continued)

	EASY	MODERATE	DIFFICULT
Fire Lookouts	67 Skookum Butte	20 Saint Mary Peak 47 Spruce Creek Lakes 51 Diablo Mountain Lookout	35 Boulder Point 41 Spot Mountain Lookout 49 Grave Peak 59 Bear Mountain Lookout 64 Hidden Peak
Canyon Overlooks	2 Blodgett Overlook	16 Bear Creek Overlook	18 Little Saint Joseph Peak 35 Boulder Point 36 Bad Luck Mountain
Waterfalls Rapids, riffles, and pools	4 Lake Como Loop 17 Sweathouse Falls 46 Warm Springs Creek 74 Cupboard Creek	7 Little Rock Creek Lake 8 Trapper Creek 10 Chaffin Creek Lakes 15 Rock Creek 26 Bear Creek 27 Bass Lake 28 Kootenai Creek 30 Blodgett Canyon 31 Mill Creek 44 Boulder Creek 76 Selway River	9 Canyon Falls 25 Sweeney Ridge 32 Fred Burr Creek to Mill Creek 33 Big Breek to Bear Creek 70 South Fork Lolo Creek to Bass Creek
Subalpine Country Ridges, passes, and plateaus	34 Baker Lake 60 Big Sand Lake 67 Skookum Butte 71 Coquina Lake	11 Lost Horse Lake 15 Rock Creek 16 Bear Creek Overlook 20 Saint Mary Peak 31 Mill Creek 37 Castle Rock 40 Nez Perce Peak 42 Flat Creek 47 Spruce Creek Lakes 51 Diablo Mountain Lookout 54 Wind Lakes	5 Ward Mountain 18 Little Saint Joseph Peak 21 Gash Point 25 Sweeney Ridge 32 Fred Burr Creek to Mill Creek 33 Big Creek to Bear Creek 35 Boulder Point 39 Trapper Peak 41 Spot Mountain Lookout 43 Sheephead Creek Loop

	EASY	MODERATE	DIFFICULT
Subalpine Country Ridges, passes, and plateaus (continued)			45 Watchtower Creek to Sheephead Creek 49 Grave Peak 53 Pouliot Loop 56 Cooperation Ridge 59 Bear Mountain Lookout 62 Dan Ridge Loop 64 Hidden Peak 66 Hidden Creek Ridge 68 Lolo Peak 69 Lantern Ridge 70 South Fork Lolo Creek to Bass Creek 72 Spruce Lake
Along Streams Lots of running water	17 Sweathouse Falls 22 Fred Burr Reservoir 55 Colt Killed Creek 60 Big Sand Lake 73 Gedney Creek 74 Cupboard Creek	7 Little Rock Creek Lake 8 Trapper Creek 10 Chaffin Creek Lakes 12 Roaring Lion Creek 15 Rock Creek 24 Sheafman Creek 26 Bear Creek 27 Bass Lake 28 Kootenai Creek 30 Blodgett Canyon 31 Mill Creek 44 Boulder Creek 50 Stanley Hot Springs 54 Wind Lakes 65 White Sand Lake 75 Lower Meadow Creek 76 Selway River	13 Sawtooth Creek 32 Fred Burr Creek to Mill 33 Big Creek to Bear Creek 45 Watchtower Creek to Sheephead Creek 61 Siah Lake 70 South Fork Lolo Creek to Bass Creek

Bitterroot Trail Finder (continued)

	EASY	MODERATE	DIFFICULT

Mountain Summits
 Peaks and points
	67 Skookum Butte	20 Saint Mary Peak
		 37 Castle Rock
		 40 Nez Perce Peak
		 51 Diablo Mountain
		     Lookout
			5 Ward Mountain
			 18 Little Saint Joseph
			     Peak
			 21 Gash Point
			 35 Boulder Point
			 36 Bad Luck
			     Mountain
			 39 Trapper Peak
			 41 Spot Mountain
			     Lookout
			 49 Grave Peak
			 57 Mocus Point
			 59 Bear Mountain
			     Lookout
			 64 Hidden Peak
			 66 Hidden Creek Ridge
			 68 Lolo Peak

Hazardous Fords
 Avoid until midsummer
	55 Colt Killed Creek
	 60 Big Sand Lake
		8 Trapper Creek
		 10 Chaffin Creek
		     Lakes
		 12 Roaring Lion
		     Creek
		 24 Sheafman Creek
		 50 Stanley Hot
		     Springs
		 54 Wind Lakes
		 63 Hidden Lake
			13 Sawtooth Creek
			 14 Tin Cup Lake
			 32 Fred Burr Creek to
			     Mill Creek
			 33 Big Creek to Bear
			     Creek
			 61 Siah Lake
			 64 Hidden Peak
			 66 Hidden Creek Ridge
			 70 South Fork Lolo
			     Creek to Bass Creek

Overcrowding Likely
 Hikers and horses by the handful
	2 Blodgett
	     Overlook
	 3 Camas Lake
	 4 Lake Como Loop
	 19 Glen Lake
	 22 Fred Burr
	     Reservoir
	 34 Baker Lake
	 46 Warm Springs
	     Creek
	 60 Big Sand Lake
	 71 Coquina Lake
	 74 Cupboard Creek
		15 Rock Creek
		 20 Saint Mary Peak
		 26 Bear Creek
		 27 Bass Lake
		 28 Kootenai Creek
		 30 Blodgett Canyon
		 44 Boulder Creek
		 48 Walton Lakes
		 50 Stanley Hot
		     Springs
		 51 Diablo Mountain
		     Lookout
		 63 Hidden Lake
		 76 Selway River
			9 Canyon Falls
			 14 Tin Cup Lake
			 25 Sweeney Ridge
			 33 Big Creek to Bear
			     Creek
			 68 Lolo Peak

Bitterroot National Forest

Darby Ranger District

1 Bailey Lake

Highlights:	A shallow subalpine lake well suited for an afternoon visit.
Type of hike:	Out-and-back day hike.
Total distance:	2 miles or 3.2 kilometers (round trip).
Difficulty:	Easy.
Best months:	July through September.
Elevation gain:	640 feet.
Maps:	Saddle Mountain and Tenmile Lake USGS quads.

Trailhead access: Take U.S. Highway 93 to its marked junction with Lost Horse Road, approximately 9 miles south of Hamilton. Turn west and follow this winding mountain road through the countryside and into the canyon beyond. This excellent road features numerous wide turnouts and reaches the Lost Horse Guard Station in 17.7 miles. Here the road forks; veer left to locate the signed Bailey Lake Trailhead after another 0.2 mile. This site offers only limited parking for three vehicles, either beside the road or in a small clearing opposite the take-off point. No formal facilities are available.

The hike: This hike takes you to a shallow mountain lake that lies within 45 minutes of its roadside trailhead and offers fair angling. The trail requires a short ascent as it traverses granite-strewn terrain and razed forest left over from the 1988 fire season. This is a nice place to spend a leisurely September afternoon.

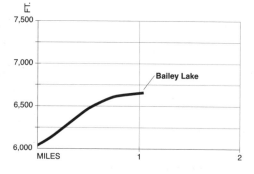

Beginning on a muddy, torn-up tread, the route ambles upslope and quickly leaves green bottomland forest and enters a burned-over landscape. The trail next dodges a number of downed trees as it switchbacks its way through the burn. Segments of the route are poorly defined, so watch carefully for cairns and old blazes on the dead trees to reacquire the trail should its location grows doubtful. An eerie quality so familiar to old burn areas permeates the surroundings as you continue through alabaster granite slabs and charred trees among which the fir and pine are gradually regrowing. With a parting southeast glance toward Bear Creek Pass, the trail bends west to follow the outlet stream past a gathering of shallow pools to its source at Bailey Lake.

Bailey Lake • Lost Horse Lake
Coquina Lake • Spruce Lake

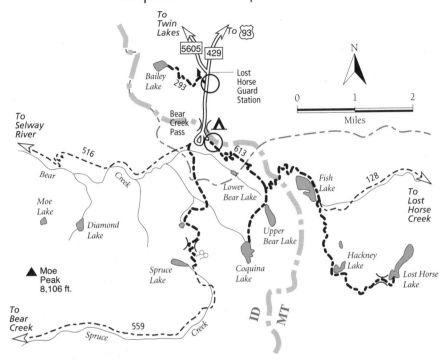

At first glance this lake may seem too shallow to sustain a fishery, but the mud-bottomed pool does indeed offer fair fishing for pan-sized rainbow-cutthroat hybrids. Burnished snags stand around its far margins with only a few select pockets of surviving timber scattered along the lakeshore. Its sheltered location and shallow waters often conspire to produce a stunning mirrorlike surface—a reflection as deep and flawless as any I can recall. Campsites are also available, but in all fairness they are too close to the trailhead to offer much seclusion.

2 Blodgett Overlook

Highlights:	A majestic vantage of the Bitterroots' flagship canyon.
Type of hike:	Out-and-back day hike.
Total distance:	3 miles or 4.8 kilometers (round trip).
Difficulty:	Easy.
Best months:	May through October.
Elevation gain:	540 feet.
Map:	Hamilton North USGS quad.

Blodgett Overlook • Canyon Falls

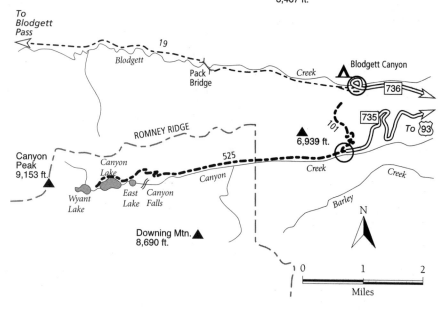

Trailhead access: Take U.S. Highway 93 to its junction with Bowman Road at the Donaldson Brothers cement plant 2 miles north of Hamilton. Turn here and follow hiking signs (located at most intersections) along Bowman Road for 0.6 mile, then turn south and follow Ricketts Road for 2 more miles to a four-way intersection. Continue straight on Blodgett Camp Road and watch for the marked intersection with Forest Road 735 after another 2.4 miles. Turn left and follow this dusty road for the remaining 2.8 miles. The small parking area doubles as the Canyon Creek Trailhead and can accommodate as many as 10 passenger vehicles, but offers no other facilities of any kind.

The hike: This short, well-maintained trail is suitable for hikers of all abilities. The route requires an unhurried 45-minute hike, crossing the crest of Romney Ridge to reach a collection of stony outcrops at the overlook area. Beyond the overlook unfolds a scene of rugged splendor, with talus-strewn couloirs and granite faces rising along the length of Blodgett Canyon and to the crest of Printz Ridge.

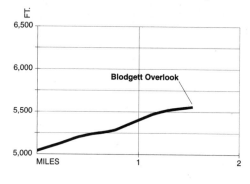

Beginning as the Canyon Creek Trail (525ML), the overlook trail veers right at a signed junction 20 yards from the trailhead. From here the wide, well-constructed tread negotiates rounded talus and a series of three switchbacks that traverse mostly open hillside with frequent exposures of mylonite bedrock. This distinctive geologic unit is well exposed in most of the Bitterroots' canyon portals and is distinguished by its unusual shear texture that developed as older Precambrian metasediments moved across underlying semimolten granite about 70 million years ago. Those ancient rocks, along with some of the younger igneous varieties, now reside in the Sapphire Mountains 20 miles or more to the east.

Benches placed at several locations along the trail provide respite with scenic views, although at no time is the trail sufficiently difficult to slow your progress. Views of Hamilton and the Sapphire Mountains continue for a time before the route turns northwest, enters a shady fir forest, and contours over the spine of Romney Ridge to reach its terminus overlooking Blodgett Canyon. A sign announces trail's end and warns of high cliffs located just out of sight ahead.

From any of the exposed rocks are sensational vantages into the canyon corridor, with 8,467-foot Mill Point and other peaks of Printz Ridge looming above the sheer faces and talus cones across the way. The influence of Pleistocene-epoch glaciers in this nearly east-west canyon is unmistakably rendered in the U-shaped geometry of its profile.

Mylonite bedrock plunges toward the Bitterroot Valley at the mouth of Blodgett Canyon.

3 Camas Lake

Highlights: A small mountain lake with good fishing.
Type of hike: Out-and-back day hike.
Total distance: 5.4 miles or 8.7 kilometers (round trip).
Difficulty: Easy.
Best months: July through September.
Elevation gain: 1,230 feet.
Map: Ward Mountain USGS quad.

Trailhead access: Take U.S. Highway 93 to the marked turnoff on Lost Horse Road, located some 9 miles south of Hamilton. Follow this paved country road west for 2.3 miles to a posted junction with Forest Road 496. Turn right, leave the pavement, and continue for an additional 6 miles to reach the trailhead loop—located at a spacious pullout just off the main forest road. (The USFS rebuilt this road during the summer of 1999, so it is now much smoother.) The no-frills trailhead offers parking for up to a dozen vehicles, and the trail starts north along a barricaded logging road.

Keypoints:
0.0   Inception of trail at the Camas Creek Trailhead.
0.1   Trail crosses Hayes Creek.
1.9   Trail crosses Camas Creek via a footbridge.
2.6   Unmarked junction to Kidney Lake.
2.7   Terminus of maintained trail below Camas Lake.

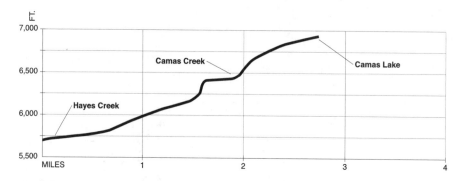

The hike: This fine day hike leads to a charming mountain lake nestled among gray talus and green forest just 9 miles southwest of Hamilton. The route is maintained only as far as Camas Lake, yet a determined hiker may pursue several other objectives as well, including rigorous cross-country journeys to Kidney Lake or several nameless lakes located in the upper reaches of Camas Creek. Any of these choices provides fine fishing possibilities and all three are quite scenic.

From its inception the trail enters a regrown clearcut, easily crosses Hayes Creek, and contours northeast as it follows an old logging grade. An occasional backward glance reveals the ragged outline of the Como Peaks and

34

Camas Lake • Coyote Coulee

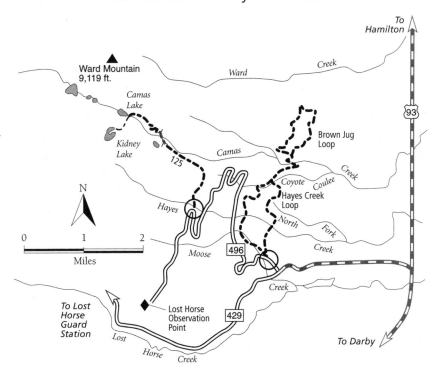

an assortment of higher summits behind them. After tracing the old road for the better part of a mile, the route abruptly veers northwest and enters untouched forest in the Camas Creek drainage. The well-constructed tread gains elevation as it proceeds along the shaded incline. A fir forest canopy effectively limits scenic views for the next mile. At one point the trail traverses a narrow talus field, then crosses Camas Creek and a tributary on sturdy footbridges a short time later. The trail renews its ascent beyond these bridges, with a series of well-constructed switchbacks that carry you through an open forest with views of the neighboring mountainsides. Entering the site of an old burn, the route makes its way across the uneven terrain that ultimately brings you to its terminus at Camas Lake.

Camas Lake occupies a small but deep canyon basin southeast of 9,119-foot Ward Mountain. The immediate shoreline consists of a heavy spruce-fir forest and perhaps an acre of aquatic reeds and other vegetation. Its cold waters harbor plenty of pan-size cutthroat trout and an assortment of sunken logs that have lain undisturbed on the bottom for decades. Campsites are not especially widespread, and those available are too overused and accessible to provide a pristine overnight camp.

Option: A potential extension of the trail involves a difficult and time-consuming scramble northwest from Camas Lake to reach a pair of nameless lakes farther upstream. The crosscountry effort is considerably more

Subalpine country above Camas Lake.

demanding than the trail to Camas Lake, but by carefully threading your way through the boulders and staying close to Camas Creek you will be amply rewarded. You first come across a rather small lake, sometimes referred to as Middle Camas, 0.5 mile upstream of Camas proper. This is a pretty lake with good fishing; there are a few nice campsites among the trees that grow along its shores.

A second and much larger body of water, located 1 mile upstream of Camas Lake, carries the echo of waterfalls across its mirrored surface. Twin pyramids overlook this high lake from west and northwest perspectives, providing a backdrop for the waters that bear their reflection. This Upper Camas offers good angling for small cutthroat—and a few larger ones as well.

Side trip: Kidney Lake, a must-see side trip, is a splendid pool cradled in a hanging cirque. Reaching it requires either following a faint blazed trail from its origins several hundred yards below Camas Lake or making a steep cross-county scramble up timbered talus slopes southwest from the lakeshore. Regardless of the approach, a 500-foot climb is necessary to reach the horseshoe-shaped tarn. Kidney Lake and its surroundings are positively spellbinding—black waters, boulder-studded shorelines, and a shredded cirque wall reinforce its allure. A wooded islet extends across the lake and nearly renders it in two as the water level recedes into late summer. The remains of an old irrigation dam are present.

4 Lake Como Loop

Special considerations: Between Memorial and Labor Day weekends all vehicles parked within the Lake Como Recreation Area must display a USFS day use recreation pass. The current cost is $2 per day; season passes carry a $20 charge. Passes are available at any Bitterroot National Forest office.

Trailhead access: Take U.S. Highway 93 to Lake Como Road, 12 miles south of Hamilton and 4 miles north of Darby. Follow this paved county road west from the highway, and keep right at a junction with Forest Road 550 after 2.9 miles. Continue for another 1.3 miles and pass the developed swimming beach to reach the trailhead near Kramis Pond. Outhouses and ample parking are available at this well-marked trailhead.

Keypoints:
- 0.0   Inception of the North Como Trail (502ML).
- 2.8   Junction with the Rock Creek Trail (580ML). Pack bridge over Rock Creek.
- 4.0   Trail crosses Little Rock Creek via a footbridge.
- 6.6   Trail reaches a boat launch at the eastern end of Lake Como.
- 7.5   Completion of loop via FR 1111.

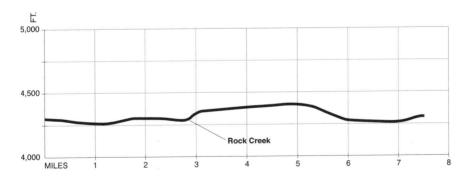

The hike: The Lake Como National Recreation Trail serves as either a convenient loop or as the first leg of a longer backpack into the Rock Creek drainage. Its minimal profile, low elevation, and fine views of the Como Peaks make it a good candidate for early season hiking in the Bitterroot foothills. You can hike the loop in either direction, but this description follows the

Lake Como Loop

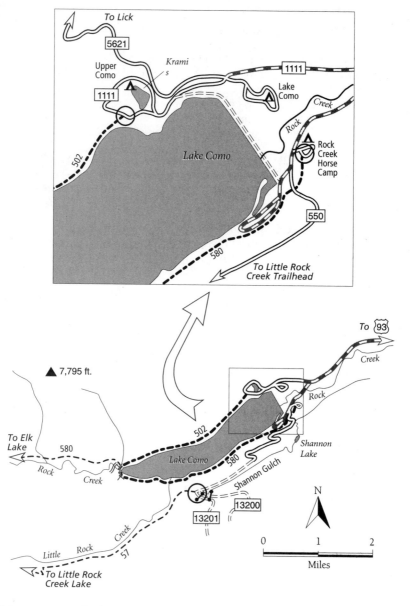

trail in a counterclockwise circuit originating from the USFS trailhead at the Upper Como Campground. Equestrians should note that the North Como Trail (502ML) is closed to all stock use.

Forest surrounds you from the outset, and the trail, paved for handicap access for the first 0.2 mile, is well maintained. The terrain undulates gently underfoot as the route follows a wide tread parallel with the lakeshore. Wildflowers and intermittent rivulets appear beside the trail every so often, and occasional breaks in the forest canopy allow views of the spectacular Como Peaks, whose high flanks remain snowbound well into July. Nearing the head of the lake, the trail enters a landscape still recovering in the aftermath of a 1988 wildfire. There is something disquieting about the scene as you walk among the blackened snags.

At the western estuary of Lake Como the route comes to a junction with the Rock Creek Trail (580ML). The inlet provides a fine stopover point, with Rock Creek rushing through its dropping, boulder-strewn channel beneath shady palisades and into the lake below. (A sturdy pack bridge spans this otherwise impassable torrent.)

The trail bends east and resumes its progress through the burn, passing well above several small embayments along the lakeshore. This southern portion of the National Recreation Trail sustains heavy traffic from stock parties headed into Rock Creek, so be prepared to yield and step off the trail should you encounter any. At 4 miles the route reaches Little Rock Creek, where a pair of ax-flattened log footbridges offer a dry crossing. There is surprisingly little shade for the remaining 2.6 miles as the route first leaves the burn and then follows the southern shoreline of Lake Como to the boat launch facilities at its lower end. Views of Ward Mountain and a few other Bitterroot peaks are available. To complete the loop, just continue from the boat launch along the crest of the dam and return to your starting point via FR 1111.

5 Ward Mountain

Highlights:	A lofty vantage running the entire length of the Bitterroot Valley.
Type of hike:	Out-and-back day hike.
Total distance:	8.4 miles or 13.5 kilometers (round trip).
Difficulty:	Strenuous.
Best months:	July through September.
Elevation gain:	4,850 feet.
Maps:	Hamilton South and Ward Mountain USGS quads.

Trailhead access: Take the Roaring Lion Creek Road from its marked junction with U.S. Highway 93—approximately 3.5 miles south of Hamilton—and continue west into the Bitterroot foothills. After 2.5 miles this dusty road arrives at a junction with Forest Road 1134. The Ward Mountain Trailhead, denoted with a simple wooden sign, is located at this intersection. Parking at this infrequently crowded trailhead consists of two informal pullouts that can accommodate up to four vehicles; additional parking is available at the Sawtooth Creek Trailhead loop to the immediate north.

Ward Mountain • Roaring Lion Creek • Sawtooth Creek

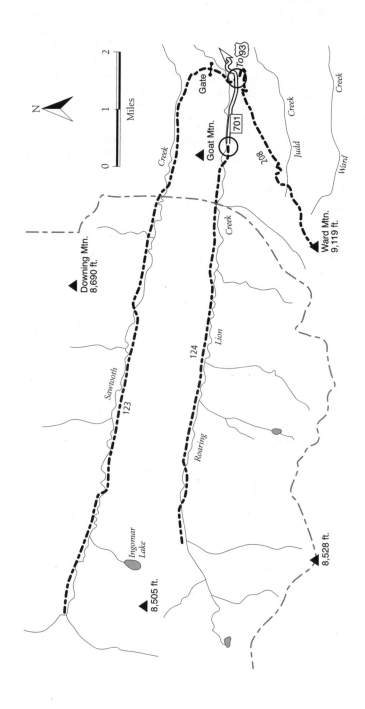

Keypoints:
- 0.0   Inception of trail along Roaring Lion Creek Road.
- 2.0   Overlook of the Roaring Lion drainage.
- 2.8   Trail crosses the upper reaches of Judd Creek.
- 4.2   Trail reaches the high crest of Ward Mountain.

The hike: Beginning at the outskirts of the Bitterroot Valley, the Ward Mountain Trail climbs 4,850 vertical feet in 4 miles to reach a former lookout site at the summit. An undertaking of nearly medieval brutality on a hot August afternoon, the Ward Mountain Trail is suitable only for those in reasonably good physical condition. Quite possibly it is the single most exhausting trail in the entire Bitterroot Range.

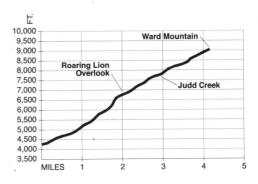

As if to lull the traveler into a false sense of security, the trail climbs a wooded bench and begins a gentle ascent across a south-facing foothill. This painless beginning is deceptive, however, and the grade increases dramatically as you enter an old clearcut, known unofficially as Molly Meadow. The ascent continues through a badly charred pole forest ahead, among stands of Indian paintbrush and fireweed. Although most of the trees involved in the blaze later died as a result, stately ponderosas along the perimeter of the fire survived by virtue of their thick, protective bark. From the low eastern flank of Ward Mountain, the trail zigzags steeply uphill and eventually returns to the canyon rim, where a rough footpath veers right to reach a good stopping-off spot. Here you have an excellent vantage of the Roaring Lion drainage, with summits such as 9,153-foot Canyon Peak and 8,690-foot Downing Mountain providing some background interest. Ward Mountain remains out of sight to the southwest.

Without any further delay, the trail summons a full head of steam and surges upslope toward the unseen summit. Intermittent views of the Hamilton area are available as you edge southwest into unburned timber and reach a shallow stream crossing at the head of Judd Creek. (Use of a filter is strongly encouraged for any drinking water obtained at this point.) The trail resumes its ascent above Judd Creek and soon enters a sparse alpine forest with fine northeast views of the Bitterroot Valley and distant Sapphire Mountains. After a time the tread levels slightly and affords a brief respite among a widely spaced alpine forest.

Without any landmarks or other indicators of progress, the trail meanders west while increasing altitude reduces the surrounding forest to hedges of ice-pruned trees and shrubs. Frustration begins to mount as the trail continues with almost painful deliberation toward the elusive summit. A final effort brings you to a wrecked lookout foundation atop 9,119-foot Ward Mountain. Views from this broad summit encompass virtually all of the Bitterroot Valley and peaks representing six major western Montana mountain belts—the Anaconda, Beaverhead, East Pioneer, Flint Creek, Mission, and Sapphire ranges. Closer at hand are nearly two dozen prominent Bitterroot peaks. Some are more outstanding than others, but all contribute to one of the Bitterroots' finest mountain vistas.

6 Coyote Coulee

See Map on Page 35

Highlights: A low-elevation trail offering pleasant foothill hiking and early season access.
Type of hike: Double loop.
Total distance: 8.8 miles or 14.2 kilometers (complete double loop). Distance and elevation figures were developed from a USFS trail proposal map dated March 1995. In comparison, measuring wheel estimates by Mort Arkava indicate a total distance of 9.2 miles for the entire double-loop hike.
Difficulty: Moderate.
Best months: April through October.
Elevation gain: 1,490 feet.
Elevation loss: 1,490 feet.
Maps: Darby and Hamilton South USGS quads.

Special considerations: Coyote Coulee's low elevation and accessibility make it ideal for early season hiking beginning each April. The trail was developed in cooperation with the Bitterroot Backcountry Horsemen, so you should expect to see lots of equestrians on the trail—and, since it lies outside the Selway-Bitterroot Wilderness, a few mountain bikers as well.

Trailhead access: Take U.S. Highway 93 to Lost Horse Road approximately 9 miles south of Hamilton. Follow the paved county road west for 2.3 miles and veer right onto Forest Road 496. Continue 0.2 mile to the trailhead for Coyote Coulee. Constructed in the fall of 1998, the new trailhead features stock facilities (unloading ramps and hitchrails) and ample parking space for as many as 10 or more vehicles.

Keypoints:
0.0   Inception of trail at the Coyote Coulee Trailhead.
0.1   Junction with the southern loop.
0.6   Trail vaults Hayes Creek.
2.0   Coyote Coulee and junction with the connecting trail.
2.7   Connecting trail crosses Camas Creek.
3.0   Junction with the northern loop.
5.6   Trail completes northern loop and returns to connecting trail.
5.9   Connecting trail crosses Camas Creek once again.
6.6   Connecting trail junction in Coyote Coulee.
7.8   Trail vaults Hayes Creek once again.

8.0 Trail reaches Moose Creek.
8.3 Second crossing of Moose Creek.
8.7 Trail completes southern loop.
8.8 Coyote Coulee Trailhead.

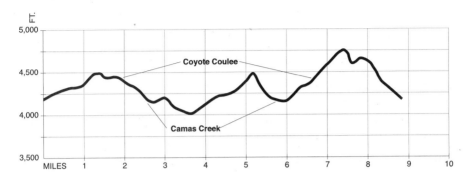

The hike: Located in rolling foothills along the western margin of the Bitterroot Valley, the Coyote Coulee Trail consists largely of the stitched-together segments of old orchard roads and spur railway grades. Its unusual configuration features southern (Hayes Creek) and northern (Brown Jug) loops of 4 and 2.6 miles, respectively, with a mile-long connecting trail in between. The entire route offers a varied course with lots of ups and downs and traverses land that was once privately held but has since returned to USFS ownership.

The trail starts along an old jeep road and quickly comes to a junction marking the start of the southern loop. You can take either fork, but this description follows the trail system in a counterclockwise fashion. A meandering course takes the trail through heavy coniferous forest punctuated with pockets of hardwoods to reach an easy crossing of Hayes Creek. North of this minor stream you cross several low draws and enter the vestiges of an extensive Bitterroot Valley apple orchard dating back to the early 1900s. The route meets and follows an old forest road through the area as a network of primitive side roads branch off to either side. (The entire Coyote Coulee Trail system is well marked with blue plastic tags, so there is almost no chance of getting lost.) Rounding a hillock, the trail descends into Coyote Coulee itself and arrives at a junction with the connecting trail to the Brown Jug Loop.

This connecting segment leads northeast as it makes a gradual descent to reach Camas Creek at 2.7 miles. Wet feet may be unavoidable in late spring unless felled logs or exposed boulders are present. Upon crossing the stream, a short climb carries you to a junction marking the beginning of the Brown Jug Loop at the 3-mile mark. Taking the right-hand fork once again, the trail ventures into open ponderosa forest with limited though pleasant views of the Bitterroot Valley. In at least one location the trail appears to follow the bed of an old spur railway whose cut-and-fill design is readily apparent.

The route continues through several shallow draws and maintains a generally northern bearing until it meets an abandoned logging road coming in from the east. Then veer left and continue along this wide "double lane," following the road as it contours across a hillside to the west. After crossing several wooded ravines, the trail shuffles downslope and soon returns to the connecting trail above Camas Creek. From here retrace your steps on the mile-long segment to the junction with the Hayes Creek Loop in Coyote Coulee.

The right-hand fork leads farther up the drainage and passes the remains of an early homestead. After leaving the coulee behind, you wander through an especially dim and overgrown stretch of forest and climb steadily uphill, only to make an equally gradual descent a short time later. The route crosses a long-abandoned irrigation diversion ditch on its way to Hayes Creek—this crossing 0.5 mile upstream of the first. Beyond Hayes Creek the trail passes an old stone foundation and descends alongside Moose Creek before returning to the roadside trailhead.

Options: You can hike the trail in a clockwise or figure-8 direction without any increase in difficulty. Hiking the Hayes Creek Loop by itself is another possibility, but doing so fails to take advantage of the especially pleasant open terrain found along the Brown Jug Loop.

7 Little Rock Creek Lake

Highlights:	An exceptionally scenic mountain lake with plentiful cutthroat trout.
Type of hike:	Out-and-back day hike or overnighter.
Total distance:	9.2 miles or 14.8 kilometers (round trip).
Difficulty:	Moderate.
Best months:	July through September.
Elevation gain:	1,780 feet.
Elevation loss:	360 feet.
Map:	Como Peaks USGS quad.

Trailhead access: Follow U.S. Highway 93 to its junction with Lake Como Road, 12 miles south of Hamilton and 4 miles north of Darby. Take this paved county road west from the highway and turn left at a junction with Forest Road 550 after 2.9 miles. Continue on FR 550 as it passes through cut-over timberland south of Lake Como and arrives at the signed Little Rock Creek Trailhead after another 4 miles (the final 2 miles are especially rough). Located below a locked gate on the high slopes overlooking Lake Como, this roadside trailhead has parking space for up to eight vehicles.

Keypoints:
0.0   Inception of trail at the gated terminus of FR 550.
1.2   Trail enters the Selway-Bitterroot Wilderness.
4.2   Old irrigation dam below Little Rock Creek Lake.
4.6   Trail terminus above the inlet of Little Rock Creek Lake.

Little Rock Creek Lake • Rock Creek

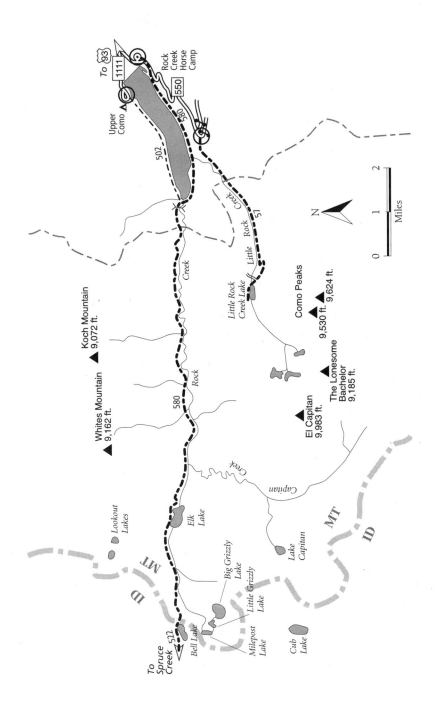

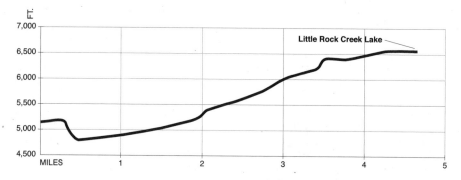

The hike: This dead-end trail leads to a delightful mountain lake featuring good cutthroat fishing and spectacular scenery. The route is not regularly maintained and is quite steep and rough in certain locations, with numerous rocks and roots exposed in the tread underfoot. Little Rock Creek Lake offers interesting base camp possibilities for mountaineers, as do a group of sites nestled near the base of El Capitan.

The trail initially saunters west from the trailhead, crossing lodgepole forest that burned in 1988 and is now in the early stages of recovery—with numerous green saplings having taken root. Upon reaching the canyon rim, the route makes an abrupt descent across an open hillside populated with ponderosa pines, and the Como Peaks rise above the drainage ahead. As Lake Como recedes out of sight to the northeast, you enter unburned woodland for the first time and begin a modest ascent at stream gradient. The shaded trail frequently crosses gray talus fields as it navigates an otherwise dark stream-bottom forest. After traversing a spooky-looking timbered pocket, the trail emerges on a granite apron and begins a series of stairstep climbs alternating between low bedrock ledges and spruce-fir forest. A short time later the route reaches several badly eroded segments in which the waters of invasive rivulets drain down the trail and elsewhere accumulate in pools of standing water. Additional climbing brings the trail to within 50 yards of Little Rock Creek, which tumbles within the narrow confines of its own bedrock channel. The route next ascends two steep rock ledges, then circles around to tackle a third and reaches a fine campsite in the forest just below Little Rock Creek Lake.

Impounded behind an abandoned irrigation dam overgrown with pygmy willows, Little Rock Creek Lake resides in a steep-walled, glaciated basin in partial view of 9,983-foot El Capitan—an immense granite leviathan towering some 3 miles to the southwest. Sheer bedrock ramparts provide a rugged backdrop north of the lake, their shredded facades stained with a purple patina that illustrates the temporary abundance of running water in spring. Forest and talus encircle the shoreline, while a graveyard of water-killed trees maintains a silent vigil near the inlet. Lakeshore access is straightforward and the waters provide excellent angling for small but lively cutthroat trout.

Option: Ambitious wilderness travelers may continue upstream to a group of three high tarns cradled directly beneath El Capitan and the 9,185-foot Lonesome Bachelor, approximately 2 miles southwest of Little Rock Creek

46

El Capitan rises beyond water-killed snags at the inlet of Little Rock Creek Lake.

Lake. All three are quite deep and offer a selection of secluded campsites—and reaching them is more a matter of resolve than expert routefinding.

8 Trapper Creek

Highlights: A lightly used stream-bottom trail with several creek crossings and cascades.
Type of hike: Out-and-back day hike or overnighter.
Total distance: 9.4 miles or 15.1 kilometers (round trip).
Difficulty: Moderate.
Best months: July through September.
Elevation gain: 1,620 feet.
Maps: Burnt Ridge and Trapper Peak USGS quads.

Trailhead access: Take U.S. Highway 93 to its junction with Montana Highway 473, 4 miles south of Darby. Turn south and continue along the West Fork Bitterroot River for just over 6 miles to reach the marked trailhead turnoff on the Tin Cup–Chaffin Road (374), whose junction appears 0.5 mile south of the Trapper Creek Job Corps Center. Follow this good gravel road northwest and keep left at the marked junction with the Trapper Creek Road (5628). From here follow the road for another 2.5 miles to reach its terminus in the logged-over lower reaches of Trapper Creek. The spacious trailhead can easily accommodate 20 vehicles and features a stock unloading ramp, hitchrail,

Trapper Creek

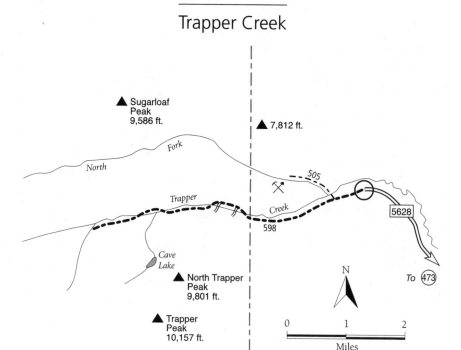

and its own attractive view of 9,801-foot North Trapper Peak. The trail originates beside a USFS information board posted nearby.

Keypoints:

- 0.0   Inception of trail at the Trapper Creek Trailhead.
- 0.6   Unmarked junction with the North Fork Trapper Creek Trail (505X).
- 2.0   Trail enters the Selway-Bitterroot Wilderness.
- 2.1   First crossing of Trapper Creek.
- 2.4   Trail passes waterfalls on Trapper Creek.
- 2.7   Second stream crossing.
- 3.5   Third crossing of Trapper Creek.
- 3.9   Fourth and final stream crossing.
- 4.7   Trail fades out above Trapper Creek.

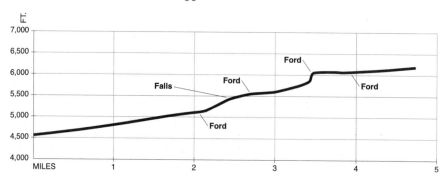

The hike: This stream-bottom route provides a relatively short out-and-back day hike into a forested canyon and alongside a clear mountain stream overlooked by towering granite spires. The trail is somewhat more challenging than other streamside trails in the Bitterroots: It makes four successive crossings of Trapper Creek, encounters numerous exposed roots and fallen trees, and negotiates several exposed bedrock segments with outsloping tread that may prove hazardous for stock travel when icy. The trail is not maintained on an annual basis but receives significant stock use.

From its bottomland beginnings, the trail follows a fair to poor tread and ambles west through cut-over forest for the first half mile. Excellent views of North Trapper Peak and the serrated prow that separates Trapper Creek and its north fork soon give way to limited glimpses of both as the route enters spruce-fir woodland and crosses several small talus fields. After a period of uneventful headway, the trail enters the Selway-Bitterroot Wilderness and crosses a substantial tributary stream, only to reach a wider crossing of Trapper Creek itself a short distance beyond. The tread intersects Trapper Creek at an oblique angle, crosses the stream via downed logs and an exposed boulder bar, and resumes its course on the opposite side about 20 yards upstream.

The trail forges ahead, passing beneath high rock faces looming overhead. After clambering up an outsloping rock ledge, you reach an overlook of a stairstep waterfall in which Trapper Creek drops some 30 feet into a narrow pool edged with broken boulders. Several smaller falls follow close on the heels of the first as you continue upstream to a second stream crossing. A more insistent ascent ensues beyond this easy boulder hop. The trail's

Trapper Creek cascades down sheaves of bedrock.

upslope surges seem carefully scripted to avoid considerable downfall that littered the forest understory at the time of its construction.

A poor trail eventually returns to Trapper Creek for its third and fourth crossings, neither of which are especially troublesome, except perhaps during peak runoff. Beyond the uppermost crossing, you soon reach a shallow woodland pond finned by small rainbow-cutthroat hybrids. It is not long before the trail fades out somewhere upstream, ascending steadily to its conclusion about 1 mile northwest of Cave Lake.

9 Canyon Falls

	See Map on Page 32

Highlights: A large waterfall and views of Canyon Peak from Canyon and Wyant lakes.
Type of hike: Out-and-back day hike or overnighter.
Total distance: 10 miles or 16.1 kilometers (round trip).
Difficulty: Difficult.
Best months: July through September.
Elevation gain: 2,820 feet.
Elevation loss: 200 feet.
Maps: Hamilton North, Printz Ridge, and Ward Mountain USGS quads.

Trailhead access: Take U.S. Highway 93 to its junction with Bowman Road at the Donaldson Brothers cement plant 2 miles north of Hamilton. Turn here and follow hiking signs (located at most intersections) along Bowman Road for 0.6 mile, then turn south and follow Ricketts Road for 2 more miles to reach a four-way intersection. Continue straight on Blodgett Camp Road and watch for the marked intersection with Forest Road 735 after 2.4 miles. Turn left and follow this dusty road for the remaining 2.8 miles. The trailhead can accommodate as many as 10 passenger vehicles, but offers no other facilities of any kind.

Keypoints:
  0.0 Inception of trail at the Canyon Creek Trailhead.
  1.6 Trail enters the Selway-Bitterroot Wilderness.
  3.2 Trail climbs steeply toward Canyon Falls.
  3.6 Overlook of Canyon Falls.
  4.1 Trail draws abreast of East Lake.
  4.3 Terminus of maintained trail at Canyon Lake.
  5.0 Earthen irrigation dam at Wyant Lake.

The hike: Three miles of tedious forest travel provide a rather monotonous introduction for the Canyon Falls Trail. The cataracts themselves do not possess the classic vertical plunge of Niagara Falls but instead feature an impressive 400-foot drop down a polished bedrock sluice. It should come as little surprise that the trail receives very heavy weekend use.

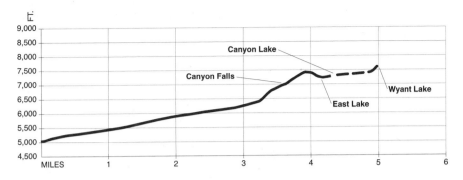

From its beginnings in a stately stand of ponderosa pine, the trail passes a marked junction to the Blodgett Overlook (101S) and follows Canyon Creek upstream through sun-dappled woodland. After 3 miles of uneventful travel, the trail turns north and begins a rather difficult ascent from the bottomland forest. Scenery continues to improve as you climb a furrowed trail whose gravel bed is frequently wet and slippery underfoot. The rhythmic din of Canyon Falls continues to intensify as the trail shuffles between whitewashed granite shelves. A short time later, the trail reaches a distant vantage of the previously unseen cataracts. Here the boiling waters of Canyon and Wyant lakes tumble fitfully down a tilted rock face before disappearing into the broken talus below.

The trail resumes its climb through open boulder fields and traverses patchy forest below the blackened battlements of Romney Ridge. Upon reaching a rocky knoll, the course bends south and follows cairns downslope to the location of East Lake at 4.1 miles. All that remains of this former irrigation

Canyon Peak and Canyon Lake.

reservoir are the bleached stumps and shallow stream channel that were once concealed by the lake; native grasses and lodgepole saplings are actively colonizing the emergent lakebed.

Returning to firm ground, the route continues west through open forest to Canyon Lake, a high glacial tarn surrounded by hardscrabble forest and late-season snowfields. With a surface elevation of 7,300 feet, Canyon Lake is home to a thriving fishery. The aesthetic qualities of the lake are tempered somewhat by a rockfill irrigation dam and spillway at the outlet. Although there are several suitable sites in the vicinity, the best campsites are located along the western shore.

From the upper end of Canyon Lake, a faint footpath climbs alongside the plunging inlet stream and peeling headwall cliffs to a quiet cove at Wyant Lake. Impounded by a concave earthen dam faced with fitted stones, this frigid pool is nestled in a glacial bowl at the very head of the canyon. Wyant Lake is set amid a Lilliputian forest in the shadow of 9,153-foot Canyon Peak, whose summit requires a semitechnical ascent. The contrived rectangular lines of the town of Hamilton are readily visible from this elevated vantage.

10 Chaffin Creek Lakes

Highlights:	Three beguiling lakes with select campsites, good fishing, and spectacular scenery.
Type of hike:	Out-and-back day hike or overnighter.
Total distance:	13.2 miles or 21.2 kilometers (round trip).
Difficulty:	Moderate.
Best months:	July through September.
Elevation gain:	2,720 feet.
Maps:	Burnt Ridge and Trapper Peak USGS quads.

Trailhead access: Travel U.S. Highway 93 to its junction with Montana Highway 473, 4 miles south of Darby. Turn right and continue to a signed junction denoting the turnoff for Chaffin Creek. Follow the Tin Cup–Chaffin Road west for 2.8 miles to an unmarked junction, keep right, and continue west for another 1.1 miles to reach the signed trailhead. This particular location amounts to little more than an unimproved switchback with room enough for six vehicles.

Keypoints:
- 0.0   Inception of trail at the Chaffin Creek Trailhead.
- 2.6   Trail enters the Selway-Bitterroot Wilderness.
- 4.6   Trail completes a perilous ford of Chaffin Creek.
- 5.3   Trail returns to the north bank of Chaffin Creek.
- 5.5   Terminus of maintained trail at Hart Lake.
- 6.0   Tamarack Lake irrigation dam.
- 6.6   End of description at Chaffin Lake.

Chaffin Creek Lakes • Tin Cup Lake

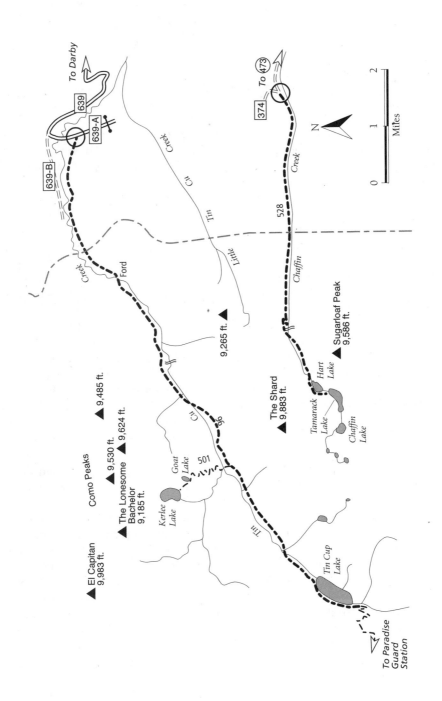

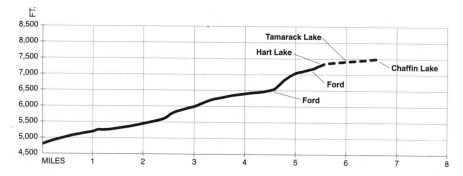

The hike: This trail leads to a lovely group of lakes offering a choice of campsites, excellent fishing, and spectacular mountain scenery. All of the rudiments for a memorable wilderness excursion await visitors in this outstanding Bitterroot drainage. One visit is all that is necessary to validate this statement.

The trail leaves civilization beneath the towering pines and follows a steady incline upstream, carefully threading a line between the wooded canyon floor and patchy rockslides that blanket its wall for the first 3 miles. At one point the trail breaks out of the trees and climbs a loose talus hillock, which allows views up the hall-like canyon corridor and hints at a lake-filled basin beyond. Be sure to note the dynamic appearance of the canyon walls as the lighting angle changes from dawn to dusk, revealing and revoking detail and depth in an intricate play of light and shadow.

The trail remains alongside Chaffin Creek for the duration of several more talus incursions before leaving the creek bottom for a steeper climb. The formidable bulwarks of 9,586-foot Sugarloaf Peak briefly appear across the way as the trail contours over an open hillside and once more returns to the tumbling watercourse. Here you must complete a difficult ford of Chaffin Creek—quite hazardous at high water—to proceed. Once on the opposite side the trail snakes upstream below looming igneous escarpments towering over lodgepole forest. The grade then fords dual channels of Chaffin Creek in rapid succession before proceeding along its northern bank for the soggy remainder. (A trail that appears on the outdated Trapper Peak quadrangle forgoes this second ford Chaffin Creek and later fades out in the company of rounded granite terraces southwest of Hart Lake.)

The official grade soon reaches Hart Lake and enters a well-established campsite area. Travelers with a late start should not plan on camping here because this site is frequently occupied by earlier arrivals. Hart Lake's mirrored depths dutifully reflect the scenic splendor of the surrounding mountain peaks, all of which exceed 9,000 feet. Here the trail splits—one branch parallels the northern shore and a second follows the lake's southern wooded waterfront. After reaching a log-strewn chute on the far side of the tarn, the trails splinter into a series of paths headed toward Tamarack Lake.

The route resumes a short climb and soon converges on Tamarack Lake, this time emerging below an old irrigation dam. This uninspired concrete-and-stone construct retains a long, cold lake in the shadows of an austere canyon. An indistinct footpath traverses rocky terrain and sparse timber to

Looking east from Tamarack Lake.

access campsites situated above the northern edgewater. Tamarack Lake provides good fishing for pan-size, silvery rainbow trout.

Chaffin Lake is found by tracing Tamarack's inlet stream west through heavy timber and past a gathering of green sloughs to the round body. A few dry campsites are located in the woods near a substantial logjam at the outlet. Cradled in a deep pocket below a plummeting waterfall, this tarn is immured by sheer cliffs on three sides, cliffs whose warranty against delamination has long since expired.

11 Lost Horse Lake

See Map on Page 31

Highlights: A splendid backcountry lake with plenty of campsites and good fishing. Exceptional scenery.
Type of hike: Out-and-back day hike or overnighter.
Total distance: 14 miles or 22.5 kilometers (round trip).
Difficulty: Moderate.
Best months: July through September.
Elevation gain: 2,180 feet.
Elevation loss: 1,240 feet.
Map: El Capitan USGS quad.

Special considerations: This trail traverses high country on both sides of the Bitterroot Divide, so have your raingear along and be sure to fish only those waters for which you hold a license. The route beyond Fish Lake is not officially sanctioned and has never been maintained to USFS standards; many segments are poorly defined and require faint-trail skills. Have your map and compass ready.

Trailhead access: Take Lost Horse Road (429) west from its junction with U.S. Highway 93, 9 miles south of Hamilton. Follow this recently improved gravel road west for 17.7 miles to the Lost Horse Guard Station. Here the road forks: Stay left and follow signs for Bear Creek Pass. The road continues south and crosses the Bitterroot Divide to reach the trailhead loop after another 1.2 miles. A USFS information board is posted at the trail's point of departure near the southwest end of the loop. Parking space is well distributed throughout the general vicinity, with both an outhouse and packstock amenities (hitchrails and ramps) located nearby. This is an extremely popular trailhead during the fall hunting season.

Keypoints:

0.0	Inception of trail at Bear Creek Pass.
0.9	Trail passes above Lower Bear Lake.
1.0	Trail enters the Selway-Bitterroot Wilderness.
1.6	Junction with trail to Upper Bear Lake.
2.6	Trail reaches the pass into Montana.
3.5	Trail reaches the head of Fish Lake.
4.0	Abandoned dam at the outlet of Fish Lake.
5.4	Trail rounds the western end of Hackney Lake.
7.0	End of description at Lost Horse Lake.

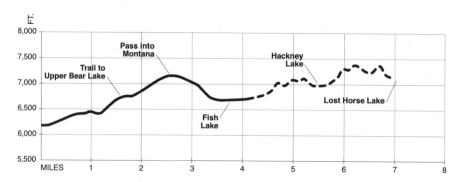

The hike: At first glance Lost Horse Lake might seem an improbable day hike. No USFS trail leads to within a reasonable distance of its shores, and most casual hikers, satisfied with the scenery and fishing at Fish Lake, see little pressing need to venture farther afield. But those who have done so seldom voice regret. Hearing of the old hunter's trail to the lake, I hiked there on a whim one September morning and thoroughly enjoyed my three-hour stay.

The trail heads southeast from Bear Creek Pass and traverses boulder-studded forest before emerging into open terrain below the wilderness boundary. Attractive views of distant granite peaks continue as you enter designated wilderness and continue across talus slopes well above Lower Bear Lake and its surrounding meadows. A downstream glance takes in the upper canyon of Bear Creek, with the rock-strewn prominence of Elk Ridge arrayed along its southern rim. As you continue southeast, the trail reenters green forest and tackles yet another series of switchbacks alongside Bear Creek. You arrive at an unmarked junction to Upper Bear Lake at 1.6 miles. Stay left for Lost Horse Lake.

The mainline route continues east on a series of well-constructed switchbacks. A slow ascent persists as the trail snakes its way across a relatively open hillside that still shows evidence of an old wildfire. Pleasant vantages of Upper Bear Lake and the length of Bear Creek are available from granite balconies situated alongside the trail. Among an increasing number of silver-gray snags, the trail reaches a wooded pass atop the Bitterroot Divide. A sign marks the pass for posterity. A jaunt southeast along the divide reveals the deep blue surface of Fish Lake, as well as several excellent campsites—a short but very scenic departure from the established trail.

Fish Lake remains unseen as the trail enters Montana and navigates a tedious 500-foot descent into the South Lost Horse drainage. Switchbacks draw the trail ever closer to its objective until at last the lake emerges before you. The route continues along the lakeshore for another 0.5 mile to reach an abandoned earthen dam at its outlet, beyond which the trail is no longer maintained. Fish Lake is an especially picturesque body of water nestled northwest and within sight of 9,162-foot Whites Mountain. Colorful and well-fed rainbow trout inhabit the tarn, whose glacial origin is readily apparent to the casual observer. Its wooded peninsula is likely a recessional moraine left by retreating Pleistocene-epoch glaciers at the close of the last ice age.

The trail becomes a route as it continues across the old dam below Fish Lake and cuts southeast at an obvious but unmarked junction. Follow the tread downhill between two swampy areas before starting a short ascent out of the stream bottom. The route traverses rocky timbered country, and often you must pause to reconsider its location after a false start. Cairns are helpful but not especially abundant. The route seesaws across the exposed granite, then reenters heavier forest on its way over to Hackney Lake. Hackney is a small, shallow body nestled among the granite shelves below the South Lost Horse–Rock Creek Divide. It lies in subalpine forest midway between Fish and Lost Horse lakes and is a real reprieve for late-starting hikers unable to reach the latter before nightfall. Some very attractive campsites are available.

Southeast of Hackney Lake the trail surmounts an open shelf and crosses a series of three high meadows, each nestled in a shallow, rubble-filled basin. At times the route grows a bit dim, but cairns and a few trees provide the necessary clues to stay on course. A brief final ascent takes the trail through a wooded saddle just southwest of Lost Horse Lake. Simply follow the remainder of the tread, which descends steeply into the stream bottom, as far as the head of the lake. Then shuck your pack and have a look around.

Lost Horse Lake occupies a long basin surrounded with a patchwork of talus and trees. Its outline is sinuous and irregular, with numerous small coves

Whites Mountain overlooks Hackney Lake.

and inlets providing ample seclusion and campsite possibilities. In many places there is good shoreline access; elsewhere, low bedrock ledges drop abruptly to the waterline. Once at the lake, you might want to stay awhile: Lost Horse is home to a thriving cutthroat fishery (the rest is self-explanatory).

12 Roaring Lion Creek

See Map on Page 40

Highlights: A glaciated drainage with good scenic value but without any obvious attraction.
Type of hike: Out-and-back day hike or overnighter.
Total distance: 15 miles or 24.1 kilometers (round trip).
Difficulty: Moderate.
Best months: July through September.
Elevation gain: 1,380 feet.
Maps: Hamilton South, Tenmile Lake, and Ward Mountain USGS quads.

Trailhead access: Take U.S. Highway 93 to Roaring Lion Creek Road—approximately 3.5 miles south of Hamilton—and drive west for 2.5 miles to reach the junction with Forest Road 1134 at the Ward Mountain Trailhead. Do not stop here; instead, continue west along the rocky FR 701 for one additional mile to reach the Roaring Lion Creek Trailhead. Space is available for up to six vehicles at the trailhead, located within a ponderosa grove due south of Goat Mountain.

Keypoints:
0.0   Inception of trail at the Roaring Lion Creek Trailhead.
0.2   Trail reaches its first crossing of Roaring Lion Creek.
1.4   Trail enters the Selway-Bitterroot Wilderness.
6.1   Second ford of Roaring Lion Creek.
6.8   Trail completes its third and final ford.
7.5   Trail peters out along the upper reaches of Roaring Lion Creek.

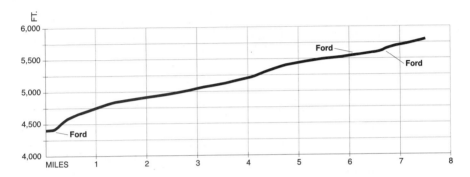

The hike: This out-and-back trail ascends a gentle, wooded canyon alongside Roaring Lion Creek. Over its length you encounter standard Bitterroot fare—a rushing mountain stream, extensive talus fields, lodgepole forest, and towering granite spurs—that is pleasing in a general sense but not outstanding in any particular respect. Since Roaring Lion Creek lacks any prime backcountry attraction, such as high waterfalls or mountain lakes, most recreational use tends to be light and limited to the lower 3 miles of the drainage.

A well-maintained trail sets out from the trailhead and traverses uneven terrain as it ambles west. After a short journey through shaded streambottom forest, you arrive at a makeshift log crossing of Roaring Lion Creek. Downed logs and boulders provided a dry crossing when I hiked this trail on August 24, 1996. Once across, the trail makes pleasant headway as cedar and grand fir shade the forest floor underfoot. The trail then saunters through drier pine forest and enters the first of many talus fields. Hereafter begins what is to become a familiar scenic refrain for the next 3 miles: lodgepole forest interrupted with interceding talus fans overlooked from the north by cleaved granite fins.

After drawing abreast of a large hanging cirque to the south, the trail advances streamside momentarily before retreating into the trees once more. A repetitive cycle of talus and forest are cause for tedious going as you close in on the second stream crossing, located some 6.1 miles from the trailhead. (A possible campsite is available at this location.) This shallow, stillwater crossing is hardly cause for concern in August. Colorado blue spruce and Douglas-fir provide some shade as the trail edges steadily northwest.

Upon completing its third and final stream crossing, the trail fades into a sketchy route that leads into a wide clearing lying at the foot of a brush-covered avalanche chute. A second and third such clearings follow close on the heels of the first. Often the route is difficult to follow through the encroaching native grasses. Southwest views from any of these openings take in the bright granite headwall and nameless peaks overshadowing it from the high Bitterroot Divide. The trail ventures into parts unknown beyond the third clearing and, with the stream close at hand, ultimately disappears in the remote upper basin of Roaring Lion Creek.

13 Sawtooth Creek

<table>
<tr><td>Highlights:</td><td>A long and lightly used streamside retreat, well maintained in its lower miles but very rough in its upper reaches.</td><td>See Map on Page 40</td></tr>
<tr><td>Type of hike:</td><td colspan="2">Out-and-back overnighter.</td></tr>
<tr><td>Total distance:</td><td colspan="2">22 miles or 35.4 kilometers (round trip).</td></tr>
<tr><td>Difficulty:</td><td colspan="2">Difficult.</td></tr>
<tr><td>Best months:</td><td colspan="2">July through September.</td></tr>
<tr><td>Elevation gain:</td><td colspan="2">1,870 feet.</td></tr>
<tr><td>Elevation loss:</td><td colspan="2">150 feet.</td></tr>
<tr><td>Maps:</td><td colspan="2">Hamilton South, Tenmile Lake, and Ward Mountain USGS quads.</td></tr>
</table>

Trailhead access: Take Roaring Lion Creek Road west from its marked junction with U.S. Highway 93, approximately 3.5 miles south of Hamilton. Follow this dusty road west for 2.5 miles into the Bitterroot foothills to reach the junction with Forest Road 1134. Veer right and continue for a very short distance to the Sawtooth Creek Trailhead. Parking at this infrequently crowded loop consists of several pullouts with some additional shoulder width that can accommodate up to six vehicles. A stock unloading ramp and hitchrail are also available.

Keypoints:
    0.0   Inception of trail at the Sawtooth Creek Trailhead.
    0.1   Footbridge over Roaring Lion Creek.
    0.5   Trail enters privately owned land at a steel gate.
    1.2   Trail reenters the Bitterroot National Forest.
    3.0   Trail fords Sawtooth Creek to reach its north bank.
    3.2   Trail enters the Selway-Bitterroot Wilderness.
    5.4   Second crossing of Sawtooth Creek.
    8.7   Third and final crossing of Sawtooth Creek.
    11.0   Trail peters out along the headwaters of Sawtooth Creek.

The hike: Most of the major Bitterroot canyons offer reasonably good trails leading to specific destinations and turnaround points. Not so with Sawtooth Creek. It is an unusually rugged trail beyond the first several miles, with

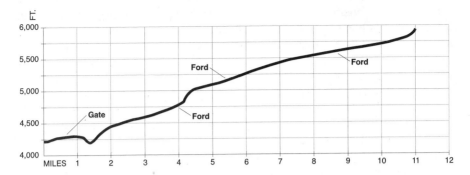

numerous rocks, roots, and brush crowding the trail. The upper reaches of the drainage are very lightly used and free of the crowds that tend to congregate elsewhere in the Bitterroots. The stream itself offers good fishing for small cutthroat trout in its many beaver ponds and pools.

The route begins by following an old roadbed downhill past a locked gate and to a good footbridge over Roaring Lion Creek located just downstream of the stock crossing. The roadbed then descends along Roaring Lion Creek before bending north into the foothills below Goat Mountain. You pass through a privately owned section at a steel gate after 0.5 mile; please remain on the trail, which travels through a "game preserve" that is posted against trespassing for the next 0.7 mile. The route alternately rises and descends, steeply at times, and turns northwest to enter the Sawtooth Creek canyon portal.

After several steep pitches, the trail crosses talus and passes a metal sign prematurely announcing the wilderness boundary. A good campsite appears beside the trail at the first creek crossing, some 3 miles into the hike. This ford presents a real hazard at high water, especially since the stream bottom is protected beneath an armor of heavy, angular cobbles that make for poor footing in the swift current. The trail parallels Sawtooth Creek above the ford, passing a series of shallow beaver ponds and traversing several open pine parks and rocky faces enroute to the second creek crossing. This crossing occurs in the vicinity of a wet meadow and can be a bit deceptive considering the marshy terrain and confusing game trails.

A progressively rougher tread continues along the south side of Sawtooth Creek for the next 3.3 miles, crossing rough talus with many small twists and turns. Encroaching brush will thoroughly thrash any exposed skin. The forest floor is so heavily laden with deadfall that any off-trail hiking would seem a hopeless cause. At 8.7 miles the trail passes an excellent streamside campsite just below the third and final crossing of Sawtooth Creek. A second trailside campsite follows closely on the opposite side of the stream, and the trail soon shuffles past a shallow pool of standing water occupied by dozens of lily pads and a few submerged logs.

From there the trail continues upstream to its terminus—growing dimmer by the mile—until it at last disappears near the confluence of Sawtooth Creek's twin headwaters forks below the Bitterroot Divide. There are some nice views, mostly from the toes of open avalanche slopes, interspersed over these final miles.

Side trip: Most visitors to the Sawtooth Creek area follow the trail upstream for a short distance—usually no more than a few miles—and retrace their steps to the trailhead. Some expeditious hikers venture to the trail's terminus near the head of the drainage. But only a select few souls successfully tackle the rugged cross-country scramble up the south wall of the canyon to reach Ingomar Lake. The attempt is physically demanding and requires considerable routefinding expertise. Ingomar Lake lies in a narrow cirque overlooking the upper reaches of the Sawtooth Creek drainage 3 miles southwest of Canyon Peak. As seen from the vicinity of Sawtooth Creek, the canyon terrain is rather deceptive; backpackers must resist the temptation of leaving the trail too early for any number of similar-looking (but lakeless) cirques east of Ingomar's true location. Once at the lake, take pride in your accomplishment. Then break out the fishing rod—for the scenic treasures above the water are only a hint of what lies below!

14 Tin Cup Lake

<table>
<tr><td align="right">Highlights:</td><td>A deeply glaciated canyon and several mountain lakes with excellent fishing.</td></tr>
<tr><td align="right">Type of hike:</td><td>Out-and-back overnighter.</td></tr>
<tr><td align="right">Total distance:</td><td>22 miles or 35.4 kilometers.</td></tr>
<tr><td align="right">Difficulty:</td><td>Difficult.</td></tr>
<tr><td align="right">Best months:</td><td>July through September.</td></tr>
<tr><td align="right">Elevation gain:</td><td>2,090 feet.</td></tr>
<tr><td align="right">Elevation loss:</td><td>90 feet.</td></tr>
<tr><td align="right">Maps:</td><td>Como Peaks, Darby, Tin Cup Lake, and Trapper Peak USGS quads.</td></tr>
</table>

See Map on Page 53

Trailhead access: To reach the Tin Cup Trailhead, follow Tin Cup Road southwest from Darby for 1.5 miles and turn left onto Singing Pines Road at the T intersection. Follow this washboard-and-pothole county road for another 2 miles before turning left yet again on Forest Road 639-A at a marked intersection. An undeveloped trailhead is located just south of a bridge spanning Tin Cup Creek. Adequate parking is available, but no other facilities are present.

Keypoints:

0.0	Inception of trail at the Tin Cup Creek Trailhead.
1.7	Junction with an abandoned inlead trail.
2.3	Trail enters the Selway-Bitterroot Wilderness.
3.2	Trail fords Tin Cup Creek.
5.2	Large talus field offers spectacular canyon scenery.
6.2	Trail makes its second crossing of Tin Cup Creek.
7.5	Unmarked junction with the Kerlee Lake Trail (501X).
9.4	Trail completes its final ford of Tin Cup Creek.
10.2	Irrigation dam at the foot of Tin Cup Lake.
11.0	Trail leaves the head of Tin Cup Lake.

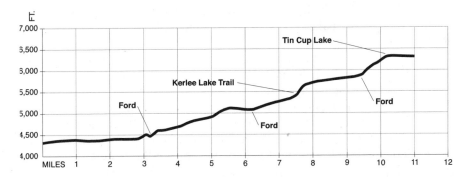

The hike: This trail provides access to Tin Cup Lake, a huge blue body nestled below the Bitterroot Divide. It should probably be avoided altogether following a prolonged spell of wet weather, when the excess moisture converts long segments of trail to an unpleasant quagmire, and rain-swollen Tin Cup Creek hampers stream crossings via slippery footbridges. The Kerlee Lake Trail offers backpackers access to exceptional angling and scenery set among the Como Peaks—at the cost of strenuous physical effort.

After leaving its undeveloped trailhead, the trail ambles along some distance south of Tin Cup Creek and eventually enters the canyon. The easy grade and lack of scenery encourage a rapid pace as the trail first assimilates a derelict road coming in from the north and then continues upstream through bottomland forest to reach a wide crossing of the stream. (A single log spanned the channel in 1999.) Beyond this crossing you follow a gentle incline upstream for 2 additional miles, emerging alternately below large brushfields and alongside deep fishing holes. Closing in on the 5-mile mark, the grade steepens substantially in anticipation of an incoming talus field. In one of the Bitterroots' finest canyon scenes, the surrounding forest at last surrenders what only moments before was hidden—a spectacular glacial canyon from which a crown of peaks rises toweringly nearly *1 mile* overhead. Such dramatic vertical relief ranks among the steepest uplifts found anywhere in the Northern Rockies.

For another mile the trail continues upstream toward several meltwater rivulets—good stopovers to replenish empty canteens—and then completes a slow descent to stream level for a second log crossing over the rushing waters. After traversing a long aisle of greenery below moss-covered escarpments, the trail files below a conical glacial spur covered with peeling granite and reaches an unmarked but obvious junction with the Kerlee Lake Trail (501X). Several excellent campsites are available here.

Uneventful forest travel persists for some time while the grade continues to gain altitude for its final encounter with Tin Cup Creek. Although no convenient boulders or fallen trees are available at this calf-deep ford, the current is passable even at high water. Upon completing the ford, the trail continues southwest through virgin forest while openings in the canopy permit views of the surrounding mountainsides. A rather tiresome ascent heralds the final approach to Tin Cup Lake.

63

Some 10.2 miles after leaving the trailhead, you reach the sprawling blue expanse of Tin Cup Lake. The lake boasts excellent fishing for a mixed bag of pan-sized trout—indeed, it would be difficult *not* to catch your limit on any given afternoon. In 1998, the Tin Cup Water Company began emergency repairs to stem reservoir leakage along the outlet pipe, lowering the water level and flying in heavy equipment to complete the work. Campsites below the irrigation dam are uniformly poor due to chronic overuse, a situation similar to that at the far southern end of the lake. From there the trail makes a prolonged ascent to the Bitterroot Divide and eventually enters the immense White Cap Creek drainage on the Idaho side of the Bitterroots.

Side trip: An unmarked junction to Goat and Kerlee lakes appears approximately 7.5 miles from the trailhead, immediately below Tin Cup Creek's confluence with its only sizable tributary. Here a granite apron leads down to the mortised watercourse of Tin Cup Creek, which can be crossed by means of a makeshift pole bridge (there is also a good ford 100 yards upstream). Shortly after this crossing the course begins its lung-burning 1,800-foot switchbacked climb in earnest. Once the trail draws to within a few hundred yards of Goat Lake it abandons a successful strategy of switchbacks in favor of a brutal straight-line ascent over loose dirt. Goat Lake is a mud-bottomed affair whose barren waters occupy a slight depression in the woods. There is little to be said for the lake in terms of campsites given the wider selection available at nearby Kerlee Lake.

Multiple routes to Kerlee Lake proceed in a northwestwardly direction through woodland littered with the rotting wreckage of its predecessors. With an elevation of 6,996 feet, Kerlee Lake harbors an excellent cutthroat fishery. North of this cobalt blue jewel towers an assemblage of Bitterroot behemoths, including the Como Peaks and 9,185-foot Lonesome Bachelor.

Looking south from Kerlee Lake.

Inspection through binoculars reveals a granite silhouette from which the Bachelor earns its namesake.

15 Rock Creek

See Map on Page 45

Highlights: Mountain scenery and angling at any of five trail-accessible lakes.
Type of hike: Out-and-back backpacking trip.
Total distance: 29.4 miles or 47.3 kilometers (round trip).
Difficulty: Moderate.
Best months: July through September.
Elevation gain: 2,680 feet.
Elevation loss: 200 feet.
Maps: Como Peaks, Darby, El Capitan, and Hunter Peak USGS quads.

Special considerations: You can shorten the Lake Como segment of the trail by arranging for water transport to and from the upper end of the lake, a savvy strategy that reduces the overall round-trip distance by nearly 8 miles.

Trailhead access: USFS signs along U.S. Highway 93 mark the junction to Lake Como Road some 12 miles south of Hamilton and 4 miles north of Darby. Follow the paved Lake Como Road west from the highway and turn left at a junction with Forest Road 1111 after 2.9 miles. A paved turnout to the Rock Creek Horse Camp appears 0.5 mile beyond this point—horse ramps, hitchrails, restrooms, and generous parking are available. A slightly shorter route along the north shore of the lake begins at an alternate trailhead near Kramis Pond, but packstock are forbidden from using the North Como Trail (502ML). All vehicles parked at either trailhead are required to display the USFS day-use recreation pass between Memorial and Labor Day weekends. The current cost is $2 per day; season passes carry a $20 charge. Passes are available at any Bitterroot National Forest office.

Keypoints:
0.0   Inception of the Rock Creek Trail (580ML) below Lake Como.
2.8   Two log footbridges span Little Rock Creek.
4.0   Pack bridge over Rock Creek and junction with the North Como Trail (502ML).
4.6   Trail enters the Selway-Bitterroot Wilderness.
10.7   Unmarked junction to Lake Capitan.
11.9   Trail reaches the foot of Elk Lake.
13.4   Trail draws abreast of One Horn Basin.
14.6   Trail enters Idaho atop the Bitterroot Divide.
14.7   Terminus of maintained trail at Bell Lake.

The hike: The Rock Creek drainage is home to a relative abundance of wildlife—moose, elk, and white-tailed deer. Yet the drainage and its many

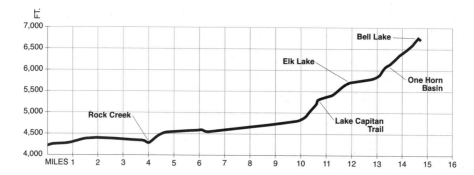

lakes draw heavy recreational traffic, including long pack strings and large backpacking parties, well before hunters converge on the area each September. Expect to see lots of stock on the Rock Creek Trail. Returning to the trailhead on July 27, 1997, I passed a total of 27 horses and mules bound for Belt Lake. Such popularity has degraded much of the tread into a semicontinuous mud wallow. This prompted the USFS to undertake a massive trail reconstruction and water diversion project completed in September 1998.

Upon leaving the trailhead loop, the trail crosses Forest Road 550 before wandering past the boat launch area and along the wooded southeastern shore of Lake Como. Views of Ward Mountain soon disappear as you continue west and enter the site of a recent forest fire, where lodgepole pine that once overlooked the lakeshore from surrounding hillsides now float in nearby embayments. As it approaches the head of the lake, the trail comes to a pair of ax-flattened log crossings over Little Rock Creek. An additional mile of burned-over trail takes you to the confluence of Rock Creek with Lake Como. An excellent pack bridge spans Rock Creek and its roaring chasm just south of the junction with the North Como Trail (502ML).

At this point the trail turns west once more and climbs a series of burned lodgepole benches that offer good views of Rock Creek and parting glimpses of Lake Como. After entering designated wilderness a short time later, the route returns to unburned fir-hemlock forest and makes casual headway as it continues upstream. Although infrequently seen from the trail, Rock Creek itself is a wide, swift watercourse with numerous deep holes, riffles, and gravel bars. You will encounter no fewer than six major tributaries of this stream over the next 5 miles; several of these rivulets drain right across the trail; while others require treacherous log crossings and boulder hops. As the canyon narrows into a deep defile ahead, the trail ascends more rigorously to reach an informal junction with a hunter's trail leading into the Capitan Creek drainage and to an outfitter's camp at Lake Capitan. The main trail meanders upstream; the granite prow of 9,983-foot El Capitan thrusts into view 3 miles to the southeast. An intervening ridge abruptly conceals this peak, however, and there is little to see as you complete the next mile of trail to Elk Lake.

Surrounded by heavy timber and impounded behind a massive moraine, Elk Lake is a broad and relatively shallow body of water. The lake supports large numbers of rainbow trout, including a few hefty specimens. Of equal interest are the elk and deer that forage in marshy meadows at the head of the lake; watch for moose as they patrol the shallows. Campsites near the foot of the lake tend to be overused and of very poor quality, while those at the midpoint—halfway along the northern shore—are the former site of an outfitter's camp that was abandoned due to numerous blowdowns.

After leaving Elk Lake, the trail climbs at stream gradient through an old fir forest and arrives at a badly waterlogged segment where waters from Lookout Lake claim the trail's course for their own. With this nuisance out of the way, a poor tread takes you across several brush-filled avalanche chutes and soon draws abreast of One Horn Basin. This rather large, lakeless cirque is guarded by a single glacial horn whose form and proportions bear a striking similarity to those of Glacier National Park. Emerging in mud-wallow meadows every so often, the trail begins its final push toward the Bitterroot Divide and reaches the first of several broad hillside clearings just in advance of the pass into Idaho. Views from these clearings reveal the high mountain basin harboring the Grizzly Lakes, as well as the nameless summits that loom overhead. A brief traverse brings the trail to a wooded pass on the state line divide and continues to Bell Lake, while a de facto trail veers south from the divide to reach the Grizzly Lakes.

Bell Lake is a delightful place. With granite blocks the size of boxcars poised along its shores, this tranquil pool is nestled in full view of 8,472-foot Hunter Peak. First-rate campsites are located at the northeast end of the lake, but an outfitter frequently occupies them. If this is the case, some careful sleuthing of the lake basin may be necessary to turn up an alternate site. The rainbow trout that inhabit Bell Lake are well fed, colorful, and provide excellent angling. However, note that these are Idaho waters and therefore require an Idaho license.

Option: Continuing west from Bell Lake might seem tempting, but the 4.6-mile segment of trail between the lake and Spruce Creek includes several hazardous fords and is anything but straightforward. Seasoned trail veterans have reported "nightmare" conditions and a formidable "maze of blowdowns" along these upper reaches of Paradise Creek Trail (522X). Trail crews have not maintained it anytime in recent memory and the USFS has no plans to do so in the future. So if you decide to venture this way, be forewarned.

Side trip: An unmaintained route leading into the Grizzly Lakes basin branches from the mainline trail atop the Bitterroot Divide. Following this unkempt but passable tread, you ascend timbered slopes before reaching the log-strewn outlet of Milepost Lake after 0.5 mile of forest travel. Milepost is a small subalpine tarn—partially rockbound and with marginal campsites—lying barely within Montana. After crossing the outlet, the trail proceeds to Little Grizzly Lake. The smallest and arguably most attractive of the three tarns, Little Grizzly offers scattered campsites and good angling. Several granite fingers extend into the lake, providing plenty of room for a backcast.

From Little Grizzly the trail continues to a set of campsites at the far northwest end of Big Grizzly Lake, where it promptly ends. Big Grizzly is a very deep, very cold mountain lake with a population of elusive rainbow and cutthroat trout. One could devote an entire weekend to exploring the Grizzly Lakes and surrounding country without seeing everything—all the more reason to return for a second or third visit.

ADDITIONAL TRAILS

North Lost Horse Creek (59X), 3.4 miles (5.5 km). This dim route begins as an old spur roadbed 100 yards east of the bridge over North Lost Horse Creek along the Lost Horse Road (429). It initially follows a poor, steep tread traversing bedrock ledges and shelves elevated well above the stream, then parallels the watercourse for another 3 miles. Brush, downed trees, and faint tread make for difficult hiking. There is an old outfitter camp near the terminus of the route.

South Lost Horse Creek (128W), 4 miles (6.4 km). Accessing the trail from its inception along the Lost Horse Road (429) requires fording Lost Horse Creek—usually unsafe for wading until midsummer. Once across, the trail closely follows South Lost Horse Creek upstream, offering access to its many pools and riffles. Before the wildfires of 1988, the trail was regarded as one of the most pleasant stream-bottom hikes in the Bitterroots, on par with such perennial favorites as Blodgett Canyon and Bear Creek. But so many fire-killed snags blocked the interior miles of the trail after 1988 that the USFS abandoned the route beyond its lowermost 4 miles. Try hiking its entire length and you will find many hundreds of downed fir and lodgepole trees across the trail—it takes hours and hours to pick your way through the maze.

North Fork Trapper Creek (505X), 0.9 mile (1.4 km). This originates as a spur trail in an old clearcut along Trapper Creek. At one time it was used to access the unpatented Rocci Mine in the lower reaches of the North Fork; prospecting activity ceased years ago and the route is apparently well on its way to oblivion. I found no evidence of its junction with the Trapper Creek Trail (598S) in late August 1998.

Stevensville Ranger District

16 Bear Creek Overlook

Highlights:	A spellbinding vantage of the Bear Creek drainage and Bitterroot Range.
Type of hike:	Out-and-back day hike.
Total distance:	2.8 miles or 4.5 kilometers (round trip).
Difficulty:	Moderate.
Best months:	July through September.
Elevation gain:	1,160 feet.
Map:	Gash Point USGS quad.

Trailhead access: Take U.S. Highway 93 to Tucker Crossing, 3 miles south of Victor, and follow Bear Creek Road west for 2.3 miles. Turn right at the marked intersection and continue north along Red Crow Road for another 2 miles. Next turn west on Pleasant View Drive, which makes several 90-degree turns as it approaches the Bitterroot foothills. The paved road switches to a good dirt surface before arriving at a marked junction with Forest Road 1325 after 3.9 miles. From here simply follow the twisting mountain road for the final 3.6 miles to reach the trailhead. Although it lacks a signpost denoting it as such, the trailhead is located just below the gated terminus of FR 1325. Parking space is sufficient for perhaps six vehicles.

Keypoints:
- 0.0   Inception of trail at the gated terminus of FR 1325.
- 1.4   Trail reaches the Bear Creek Overlook.

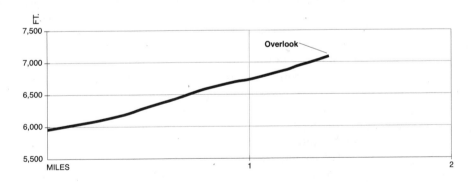

The hike: It takes no more than an hour to reach the Bear Creek Overlook via the route described below. Yet for the modest effort involved, no other Bitterroot trail quite equals the visual impact of this particular destination. From the stony balconies of the overlook unfolds a view of high scenic caliber—definitely a sight to behold!

From the upper end of an overgrown clearcut, the trail begins its ascent of the east-facing slope. With the trailhead road quickly receding from sight

Bear Creek Overlook • Sweathouse Falls
Glen Lake • Gash Point

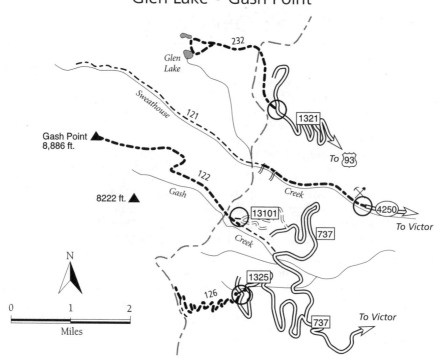

downhill, the first of nearly two dozen switchbacks takes the trail through a shady forest of Douglas-fir and lodgepole pine. At one point the terrain momentarily flattens out atop a timbered bench, but the respite is only temporary and a steeper pitch resumes as you follow the zigzags farther upslope. The unremarkable forest assumes a different character as the trail closes in on the canyon rim, with numerous fallen trees littering open woodland. One trail becomes two at the final switchback: The right-hand fork, not depicted on any map, continues for an indeterminate distance below the ridgeline to the northwest. The main trail follows an obvious tread southwest and soon emerges at the windswept canyon rim.

The overlook consists of lichen-covered mylonite faces whose westward view showcases the breadth of the Bear Creek drainage and its three principal forks. Wind-borne ice has gnarled and pruned the hardscrabble fir and pine into ghastly forms that adorn its windward faces. From this isolated point the pale gray granite, delicate snowfields, and bottomland forest merge in lines that are visually dramatic yet impart a subtle, almost timeless quality to the scene. Five miles to the northwest rises 8,792-foot Sky Pilot Peak, a pyramid-shaped mountain overshadowing Bear Lake, itself nestled unseen in the headwaters of the North Fork.

The South Fork Bear Creek drainage as seen from the Bear Creek Overlook.

17 Sweathouse Falls

See Map on Page 70

Highlights: A pair of small waterfalls plummeting over granite precipices.
Type of hike: Out-and-back day hike.
Total distance: 4 miles or 6.4 kilometers (round trip).
Difficulty: Easy.
Best months: July through September.
Elevation gain: 1,330 feet.
Maps: Gash Point and Victor USGS quads.

Trailhead access: From Victor, take Fifth Avenue west and turn north at the T intersection with Pleasant View Drive after 1 mile. Continue north for 0.5 mile before turning west once again on Sweathouse Creek Road. At this point simply follow the dusty rural road west for 3 miles—crossing through several private residences in the process—to reach the trailhead parking area along Sweathouse Creek. The available parking space can easily accommodate up to eight vehicles, provided mining equipment does not already occupy it. Note that the Sweathouse Falls Trailhead lies exclusively on private land; however, sportsmen access is available due to a block management agreement between the landowner and Montana Department of Fish, Wildlife, and Parks. Please respect the privilege.

Keypoints:

  0.0   Inception of trail at the Sweathouse Falls Trailhead.
  1.8   Trail passes lower Sweathouse Falls.
  2.0   Trail reaches upper Sweathouse Falls.

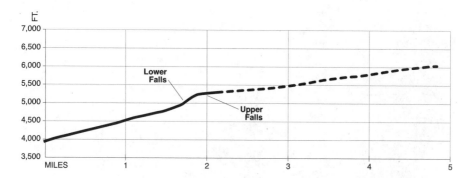

The hike: Relatively unknown and often overlooked, the Sweathouse Creek drainage affords an intriguing diversion for visitors to this lightly traveled expanse of the Selway-Bitterroot Wilderness. Although the drainage itself is not unduly scenic, the trail is short and its two waterfalls are pleasing in their own regard. Due to the deteriorated condition of the trail above the upper falls, travel beyond the wilderness boundary is neither straightforward nor particularly worthwhile.

From its inception alongside Sweathouse Creek, the trail follows a wide tread northwest into a dark bottomland forest. The route narrows to a single tread soon after entering the Bitterroot National Forest. A steady ascent takes you farther into the canyon while Sweathouse Creek remains close at hand but largely unseen as it flows down a log-choked, dropping course in the audible distance. Continuing upstream, trail and stream part company once more as the tread threads its way among the massive moss-covered granite blocks of a forested boulder field. Winter windstorms have decimated the surrounding woodland, particularly on the opposite side of the Sweathouse Creek, where wind-shorn trees have been strewn across the hillside like so many matchsticks.

Leaving the stream bottom, you follow switchbacks between boulders and under fallen trees, until lower Sweathouse Falls suddenly emerges from the forest below. An obvious footpath—use of which is strongly discouraged due of the steep grade and loose dirt surface—leads downslope to reach a good vista of the falls, which incur a total drop approaching 60 feet. The trail continues its climb, then traverses the fern-dotted hillside to reach a small granite pool at the crest of the falls. A small campsite is located nearby. After more listless forest travel you draw abreast of upper Sweathouse Falls. Lying well off the trail, its waters plummet over a 30-foot precipice on their way downstream.

Option: The trail continues upstream to its dead-end conclusion, dying out some 4.8 miles from the trailhead. The USFS reports the route is no longer maintained beyond the wilderness boundary. Beyond the upper falls the tread

Lower Sweathouse Falls plummets over a granite precipice.

gradually deteriorates and soon comes to a signpost prematurely announcing the wilderness boundary. Were it not for the scattered blaze marks, the route would be almost impossible to navigate due to encroaching brush and accumulating deadfall. All remaining vestiges of a trail disappear as the route fades to nothingness in the remote, silent bottomlands of Sweathouse Creek.

18 Little Saint Joseph Peak

Highlights: A lightly used trail with an unusual view of Saint Joseph Peak.
Type of hike: Out-and-back day hike.
Total distance: 5.2 miles or 8.4 kilometers (round trip).
Difficulty: Strenuous.
Best months: July through September.
Elevation gain: 3,030 feet.
Elevation loss: 70 feet.
Map: Saint Mary Peak USGS quad.

Special considerations: Well marked and generally easy to follow for the first mile, this scenic route becomes difficult to discern as it approaches timberline—and vanishes altogether upon reaching exposed scree above the 8,600-foot contour. Except for the single reliable source noted below, surface water is scarce.

Trailhead access: Follow U.S. Highway 93 to its junction with Bass Creek Road, 4 miles south of Florence. Turn here and continue west for 2.5 miles to the Charles Waters Memorial Campground, then take Forest Road 1136 for an additional 6.5 miles to reach the trailhead loop on the northern rim of the Bass Creek canyon. The trailhead can accommodate as many as eight vehicles, and a primitive campsite is available nearby. A shot-up sign denotes the trail's point of origin.

Keypoints:
 0.0 Inception of trail at the Bass Creek Overlook.
 2.5 Trail enters the Selway-Bitterroot Wilderness above timberline.
 2.6 Terminus of established trail atop Little Saint Joseph Peak.

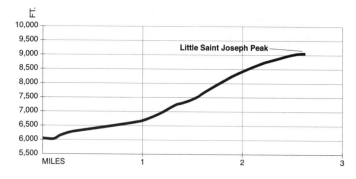

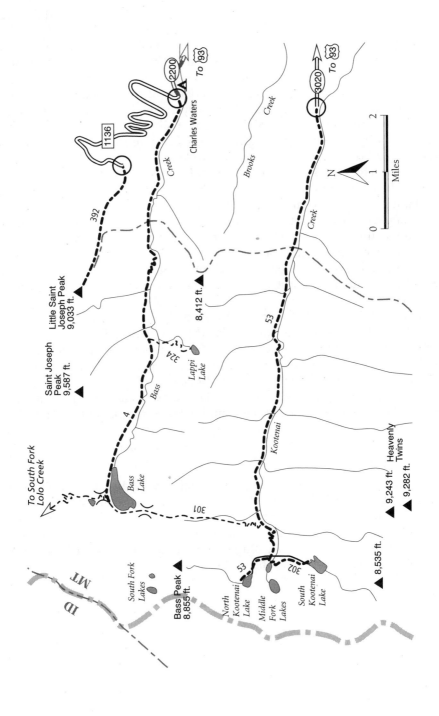

The hike: The overlook trail provides a challenging ascent along the rim of the Bass Creek canyon, culminating with an exceptional view of 9,586-foot Saint Joseph Peak from an unusual eastern perspective. The trail is steep, poorly defined, and difficult to decipher in its final mile. Although the route is rather difficult, the "sweat equity" makes a worthwhile hike.

From its beginnings at the canyon rim, the trail initially descends across the south-facing canyon slope, only to regain the lost elevation in a sudden uphill surge. A handful of worn footpaths depart the official trail at odd intervals, and most lead to impressive overlooks of the Bass Creek drainage and the anonymous peaks that rise to form seemingly unclimbable palisades along the opposite side of the canyon. Following a gradual ascent, you reach terrain gentle enough to afford a brief respite from an otherwise tedious uphill effort. But it does not last for long.

Among a forest of lodgepole pine and subalpine fir, the trail follows blazes and maneuvers on makeshift switchbacks in what amounts to the toughest sustained climb of the entire trail. There is little to see for some time before the route emerges in a lofty park situated alongside a shallow marshland in the mountainside at approximately the 7,800-foot contour. With its readily available water and lightly used campsites, this location makes an ideal base camp for mountaineers interested in climbing Saint Joseph Peak. The Heavenly Twins and other assorted peaks offer scenic diversions of their own to the southwest.

Beyond this point the route becomes a truly intermittent affair stitched together with the assistance of widely scattered cairns. Turning northwest within a stone's throw of the canyon rim, the route leaves alpine larch parkland and parlays its steep ascent into a gentler traverse of broken rock and low-growing flora. Although it is not particularly difficult, the final 0.25 mile to Little Saint Joseph Peak seems especially drawn out due to the telescoping effect of distance. Atop the stark summit landscape rises a large mylonite outcrop. A tapering ridgeline extends west to the massive, rust-colored crest of Saint Joseph Peak, whose eastern flanks are guarded by a series of snowfields and shredded escarpments.

Option: Saint Joseph Peak is the possible objective of an extended day hike. While not technically difficult, the ridge leading west to the summit is fully exposed and subject to gale-force winds; several large snowfields with potentially unstable snow cornices blanket the terrain well into summer. Prospective mountaineers should be prepared for adverse conditions and schedule an early start from the trailhead.

19 Glen Lake

See Map on Page 70

Highlights: A small mountain lake with good shoreline access and fine scenery.

Type of hike: Out-and-back day hike or overnighter.

Total distance: 5.4 miles or 8.7 kilometers (round trip).

Difficulty: Easy.

Best months: July through September.

Elevation gain: 1,080 feet.

Elevation loss: 300 feet.

Map: Gash Point USGS quad.

Trailhead access: Take U.S. Highway 93 to Bell Crossing, approximately 2 miles north of Victor. Turn here and follow the wide dirt road west for 0.3 mile, around two 90-degree turns, and continue an additional 1 mile to reach Forest Road 738. At this point the road proceeds northwest, crossing the reclaimed Curlew Mines, and soon arrives at the turnoff to the Big Creek Trailhead. Keep left and follow the winding FR 1321 until you reach the Glen Lake Trailhead at a reasonably spacious but unimproved switchback. The elapsed road distance from U.S. Highway 93 is 10.9 miles.

Keypoints:

- 0.0 Inception of trail at the Glen Lake Trailhead.
- 1.3 Trail enters the Selway-Bitterroot Wilderness.
- 2.7 Trail peters out at the head of Glen Lake.

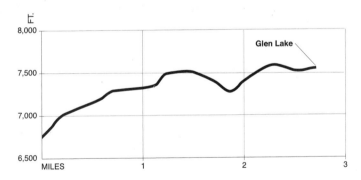

The hike: This trail provides a short-length day hike to an attractive mountain lake overlooking a portion of the Bitterroot Valley near Victor. Due to heavy use and the relatively short distances involved, Glen Lake is a poor choice for backpacking and offers little satisfaction for those seeking true wilderness solitude. As an indication of just how popular this trail is, more than a dozen vehicles occupied the trailhead at the time of my June 28, 1998, visit.

A well-defined tread leaves the parking area to begin a modest climb of lodgepole-covered slopes to the northwest. After a short time the trail reaches level ground before crossing a waterless gully and resuming its ascent. From a mountain flank timbered with various fir and pine, you soon emerge at a site of eerie devastation in which acres of silver trees stand as victims of a low-intensity wildfire.

With the snowy face of 8,886-foot Gash Point prominently visible some 3 miles to the southwest, the trail approaches its apex at the wilderness boundary. Upon returning to unburned forest, a descent ensues—gentle at first but becoming progressively steeper with each additional step. Upon reaching the sagging swale to the west, you have only a moderate final ascent into the lake basin. (At one point, the trail branches. Do not take the right-hand fork, which leads to an unnamed pond described elsewhere in this narrative, but instead continue left along a southwest bearing.) Straddling the 7,560-foot contour, the trail rounds a timbered hillside and quietly dies out above Glen Lake.

With a surface area of about eight acres, Glen Lake is a deep blue-green body set among subalpine forest and gleaming talus fields. A low boulder dam crouches at the outlet, just a stone's throw from several of the overused campsites located along the lake perimeter. (Your fishing gear will add only weight to your pack—the lake is devoid of fish.) An informal footpath continues into the draw north of Glen Lake and later arrives at an even smaller lake after a climb of several hundred feet. Late-season snowfields and a whitebark pine forest encompass these infertile, fishless waters.

Option: Hidden Lake is a choice objective for visitors frustrated by Glen Lake's apparent overpopularity. Reaching this isolated pool requires tracing an unmaintained trail northwest from Glen Lake, along the high Sweathouse–Big Creek divide, and into the cirque below. Hidden Lake lives up to its billing and occupies a forested and talus-strewn basin high above the Big Creek drainage. Rainbow trout comprise the bulk of the catch.

20 Saint Mary Peak

See Map on Page 81

Highlights: An inactive fire lookout with a phenomenal view.
Type of hike: Out-and-back day hike.
Total distance: 6.4 miles or 10.3 kilometers (round trip).
Difficulty: Moderate.
Best months: July through September.
Elevation gain: 2,490 feet.
Map: Saint Mary Peak USGS quad.

Special considerations: Beware of inclement weather and anticipate the possibility of a high-altitude storm by stowing foul-weather gear in your backpack. You should definitely filter any drinking water obtained from the trailside spring, since it is so heavily used (by people and stock alike).

Trailhead access: Take U.S. Highway 93 to the trailhead signs at Indian Prairie Loop, 3.6 miles south of the Stevensville turnoff. Follow the road west for

1.3 miles, then turn right on Saint Mary's Road and continue to the next road junction 0.5 mile beyond. Hang a left and follow the winding dirt road for 10.8 miles to the trailhead. There are several forks along the way, but these are clearly marked to avoid any confusion. The end-of-the-road trailhead is sufficient for at least 10 vehicles. A hitchrail and outhouse are located nearby.

Keypoints:
   0.0   Inception of trail at the Saint Mary Peak Trailhead.
   1.0   Trail reaches a fenced spring.
   2.0   Trail enters the Selway-Bitterroot Wilderness.
   3.2   Terminus of trail atop Saint Mary Peak.

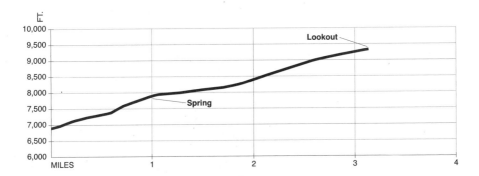

The hike: Saint Mary Peak rises dramatically from timbered foothills west of Stevensville, where Father Pierre Jean DeSmet and his followers founded Montana's oldest settlement at the Saint Mary's Mission in 1841. A moderately difficult climb to the crest draws hundreds of visitors each summer to a timeless scene first enjoyed by Catholic missionaries more than 150 years ago.

The trail begins its ascent without delay, following switchbacks up a forested ridge northwest of the parking area. An old sign located immediately above the trailhead indicates a one-way trail distance of 4.5 miles. The actual distance is slightly more than 3 miles, so don't let this inaccuracy discourage you. As you continue upslope, you are awarded with first glimpses of the heretofore hidden Bitterroot Valley. After a mile of insistent climbing the trail passes a fenced spring and then makes a high traverse just below the divide standing between the McCalla and Sharott drainages. A forest of whitebark pine surrounds you as the route edges west through sparse alpine parks to reach the wilderness signpost in a small clearing below timberline. You intercept timberline shortly thereafter, leaving the few remaining trees behind.

Just as the altitude reduces the whitebark forest to a mantle of shrubbery, so also do the high flanks of Saint Mary Peak disclose the presence of the mighty Bitterroot Range. With the Saint Mary Lookout in view for the first time, the grade completes a lengthy switchbacked run to reach a high landing 0.25 mile shy of the peak. A classic view of the Bitterroot Valley and

79

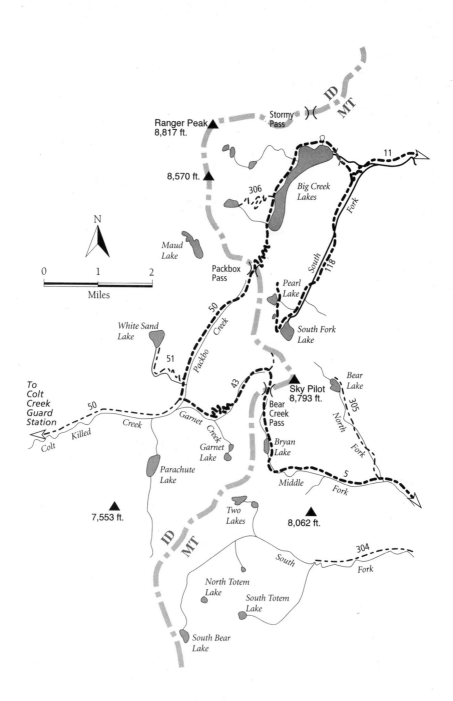

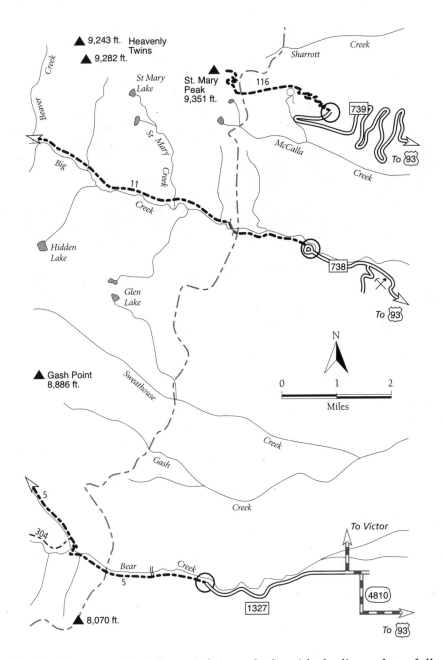

Sapphire Range greets visitors at this overlook, with the lines of carefully surveyed tracts and townships in the valley juxtaposed against the unrefined angles of the mountains. Cairns then lead the trail to its terminus at the summit of Saint Mary Peak.

Retired from active service in 1971 and renovated in 1998, the 14-by-14-foot structure houses a summit register along with a cast-iron stove and other miscellaneous lookout gear. Directly west of the summit loom the Heavenly Twins, two great granite prominences dressed in delicate snowslips that

Near timberline on Saint Mary Peak.

together rise to altitudes nearly the equal of Saint Mary itself. An armada of mountain peaks guards untold secrets in the miles beyond, where terra firma merges imperceptibly with the heavens.

Side trip: Nameless lakes at the headwaters of McCalla Creek provide a side trip possibility if you're willing to follow a faint, unmaintained footpath south from the main trail to reach them. A single stone cairn denotes the take-off point about 200 yards beyond the wilderness boundary signpost. The primitive route descends through whitebark pine forest to reach the northern-most lake, then peters away enroute to its southern counterpart. Both of these fishless lakes hover in separate subalpine pockets just below the 8,000-foot contour. A selection of tent spaces is available at each.

21 Gash Point

See Map on Page 70

Highlights: A challenging and seldom-traveled wilderness route.
Type of hike: Out-and-back day hike.
Total distance: 7 miles or 11.3 kilometers (round trip).
Difficulty: Strenuous.
Best months: July through September.
Elevation gain: 3,170 feet.
Map: Gash Point USGS quad.

Special considerations: This little-known route is often faint and difficult to follow, particularly as it draws closer to the equally indistinct timberline. It's included in this guidebook *only* for those with considerable wilderness savvy, including faint trail skills and competence with map and compass. (Don't even consider Gash Point if you're unsure of your route-finding capabilities, because losing the trail is all too easy—and reacquiring it is next to impossible at times.)

Trailhead access: Take U.S. Highway 93 to Tucker Crossing, 3 miles south of Victor, and follow Bear Creek Road west for 2.3 miles. Turn right at the marked intersection and continue north along Red Crow Road for another 2 miles. Next, turn west on Pleasant View Drive, which makes several 90-degree turns on its approach to the Bitterroot foothills. The pavement quickly grades into a good dirt tread and comes to a marked junction with Forest Road 1325 after 3.9 miles. Continue north on FR 737 for another 5 miles, then take FR 13101 west for a rough 1.5 miles to reach the trailhead. The trailhead consists of an unmarked switchback with parking space for only two vehicles, and the trail, whose beginnings are unmarked, takes off to the west.

Keypoints:
    0.0   Inception of trail along FR 13101.
    0.2   Trail enters the Selway-Bitterroot Wilderness.
    3.5   Trail reaches the crest of Gash Point.

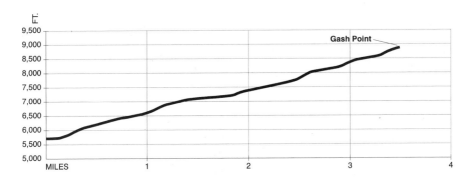

The hike: Gash Point overlooks the Bitterroot Valley from the apex of a windswept ridge nine miles northwest of Victor. With its outstanding perspective of the valley and of the Bear Creek drainage to the west, this taxing climb handsomely rewards those who visit each summer. And unlike some of the other Bitterroot peaks visible from the summit, you're almost guaranteed to have this mountain to yourself.

From the trailhead along FR 13101, the trail undertakes a sidehill ascent while Gash Creek rushes unseen through the canyon below. A forest of fir and lodgepole pine provides a shaded passage as you venture into the wilderness and swing north. The uphill effort seems to resemble tiers in a series as the grade alternates between robust rises and level segments. Gash Creek's din soon fades, replaced by the lonely hush of thin mountain air issuing through the trees. The tread grows increasingly indistinct as it crosses two sparkling brooklets in rapid succession. With all the deliberation of a wilderness route in no particular hurry, you continue north to reach the southern rim of the Sweathouse Creek canyon, where a granite monolith rises from the forest floor.

The tread becomes entirely incoherent beyond this point. The only reliable indicators of the approximate route, which more or less adheres to the ridgeline within 100 yards of the canyon rim, consist of sawn logs and hatchet-hewn blazes. If the blazes disappear, the proper route may be picked up by faithfully sticking to the ridgeline and continuing west until the next turns up. The ridge advances west, and scattered cairns guide the way once blazed trees grow scarce. With Gash Point looming large on the horizon ahead, views of other Bitterroot peaks thrust into prominence as well—the Heavenly Twins being foremost among them. Pink snowfields blanket the mountain's flanks as the ridge merges with another building in from the southeast.

A hiker pauses on the ridgeline southeast of Gash Point.

84

The ascent becomes a scramble as you make your way among a miniature forest of tenacious alpine larch and snowfield-covered talus.

After reaching a high saddle, the route turns northwest and follows the exposed ridgeline for 0.25 mile to reach the lonely heights of 8,886-foot Gash Point. To the southeast unfolds the Bitterroot Valley and its rectangular patchwork of sections and property lines centered on the town of Victor, while the rugged forms of ridge after superimposed ridge extend west, penetrating deep into Idaho. Most alluring is the view of Bear Lake and Sky Pilot Peak, poised together at the headwaters of the North Fork Bear Creek.

22 Fred Burr Reservoir

See Map on Page 90

Highlights: An easy-to-follow stream-bottom trail best suited for a casual, unhurried day hike.
Type of hike: Out-and-back day hike or overnighter.
Total distance: 9.2 miles or 14.8 kilometers (round trip).
Difficulty: Easy.
Best months: May through October.
Elevation gain: 1,020 feet.
Elevation loss: 200 feet.
Maps: Hamilton North and Printz Ridge USGS quads.

Special considerations: You must remain on the designated trail and refrain from camping and fishing along Fred Burr Creek until reaching the locked gate at the Bitterroot National Forest boundary, 1.7 miles from the trailhead. The trail is open to all nonmotorized modes of travel as far as the foot of Fred Burr Reservoir, but only stock and foot traffic may continue beyond that point. You may encounter motor vehicles used by Fred Burr landowners, USFS employees, and irrigation district "ditch riders." The road is not open to motorized use by the general public, however.

Trailhead access: Take U.S. Highway 93 to Bear Creek Road, 3.5 miles south of Victor, and continue west for 2.3 miles to the T intersection with Red Crow Road. Turn left and follow the road as it completes a 90-degree turn and continues west, leaving pavement to reach an open gate after 2.5 more miles. Follow the road through a 0.5-mile private parcel and an additional 0.2 mile to the wooded trailhead loop. A spacious parking area with room for 10 or more vehicles marks the trail's inception.

Keypoints:
0.0   Inception of trail at the Fred Burr Creek Trailhead.
0.2   Trail merges with jeep road below the canyon entrance.
1.2   Trail reaches signed bypass of private cabins; bear left.
1.5   Trail returns to the old jeep road.
1.7   Locked gate at the Bitterroot National Forest boundary.
4.4   Trail crosses bridge over Fred Burr Creek.
4.6   Inception of Fred Burr Trail (38S) at Fred Burr Reservoir.

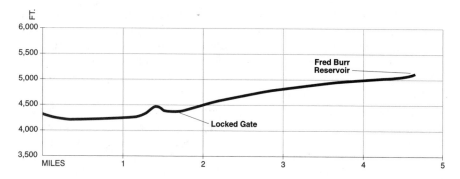

The hike: This trail follows an old jeep road to its terminus at the Fred Burr Reservoir. Its gentle profile and low elevation offer a very pleasant hike that is passable earlier than many other Bitterroot trails. Hikers are not the only outdoor enthusiasts to find their way to Fred Burr Reservoir; ever since public access was restored in 1995, Fred Burr has grown increasingly popular with mountain bikers and equestrians as well.

The trail wanders west through heavy foothill forest, passing through privately owned land posted against trespassing. After a short descent the trail merges with the Fred Burr Road (733), rounds a hillock, and continues toward the approaching canyon portal. The route passes south of a private bridge and cabin before reaching a marked junction with a route bypassing several other buildings along the road. A locked gate announces the national forest boundary at 1.7 miles.

A streamside ascent ensues as the trail meanders through the timber on its way upstream; occasional views of high granite prows enliven the proceedings. The trail momentarily traverses forest burned in the 1988 fires, then sidesteps a nice expanse of riffles, pools, and shallow gravel bars along the stream channel. You reenter unburned forest and return streamside to cross Fred Burr Creek atop a heavy wooden bridge situated just downstream of a low concrete weir. The road reaches its terminus at a hitchrail northeast of the reservoir a short time later.

Granite peaks and burned-over forest interspersed with green timber provide a backdrop for Fred Burr Reservoir. The waters are impounded behind a large earthen dam with riprap on the upstream face and a narrow spillway along its far abutment. By late summer the reservoir begins to show the unattractive effects of irrigation drawdown, with an apron of mud around the receding shoreline. The route continues along a narrow, rocky tread above the northern shoreline to reach a group of nice campsites at the head of the reservoir.

23 Larry Creek Complex

<table>
<tr><td align="right">Highlights:</td><td>A low-elevation trail complex offering lots of choices for easy three-season hiking.</td></tr>
<tr><td align="right">Type of hike:</td><td>Multiple loops (network).</td></tr>
<tr><td align="right">Total distance:</td><td>0.4 to 6.5 miles or 0.8 to 10.5 kilometers. (All distances cited are based on USFS trail wheel measurements. Your actual mileage may vary.)</td></tr>
<tr><td align="right">Difficulty:</td><td>Easy.</td></tr>
<tr><td align="right">Best months:</td><td>April through November.</td></tr>
<tr><td align="right">Maps:</td><td>Saint Mary Peak and Stevensville USGS quads.</td></tr>
</table>

Special considerations: The USFS marked the Larry Creek Complex and installed a new trailhead sign in 2000, so finding your way around the trail network and its many junctions and road crossings is no longer the problem it once was. The entire Larry Creek Complex falls within the Bass Creek Recreation Area. Except for the Charles Waters and Larry Creek campgrounds (available for use by reservation only), overnight camping is prohibited.

Trailhead access: Take U.S. Highway 93 to Bass Creek Road, 4 miles south of Florence, and follow signs for the Charles Waters Campground. The road forks shortly after crossing a narrow bridge over Bass Creek; stay right and continue north to the day use parking area (0.3 mile) or to the Larry Creek Campground (1 mile). Stock amenities and plentiful parking are available at both. Drinking water and an outhouse are provided at the Larry Creek facility.

The complex: The Larry Creek Complex offers more than 10 miles of hiking and horseback riding trails in the rolling Bitterroot foothills southwest of Florence. It was developed primarily for the benefit of equestrians but is also open to other nonmotorized use, including day hikers and mountain bikes. With loops ranging in length from 0.4 to 6.5 miles, the trail network provides a selection of hikes in a reasonably compact area. And due to its accessibility and low elevation, the complex is a good place to put in a few miles before snow vacates the backcountry in spring and after it returns in the fall.

Fitness Trail (390ML), 0.4 mile (0.6 km). Beginning at the wooden sign along Forest Road 1316, this trail makes a very short loop through the foothills just east of the Bass Creek Picnic Area. The brush-free tread is wide and suitable for trail running, with a blanket of soft pine needles underfoot. Along the way are fitness stations that include pull-up bars and short hurdles, among others. It passes through open pine forest that is perhaps more reminiscent of a suburban park than a wilderness setting, but it is worth a look all the same.

Nature Trail (391ML), 0.5 mile (0.8 km). Although only slightly longer than the nearby Fitness Trail, this loop is the more attractive of the two and passes through low-elevation forest and riparian habitat along Bass Creek.

Larry Creek Complex

Footbridges provide dry crossings over a small rivulet along the way, and the trail itself offers plenty of shade. A USFS brochure describes vegetation and other points of ecological significance identified at a series of waypoints along the route, offering a self-guided tour as you walk.

Fire Ecology Trail (129ML), 2.5 miles (4 km). This short loop offers a pleasant stroll through the rolling foothills south of Larry Creek, traversing portions of a 1994 prescribed burn. The trail provides occasional views of the Bitterroot Valley, and there are a number of cutoff trails (not shown) over which you may either shorten or lengthen your walk. The USFS has prepared an excellent interpretive brochure—entitled "Larry Creek Fire Ecology Trail," describing the role that wildfires play in forest ecology at 19 marked stopover points along the route. Each stopover illustrates natural processes or various beneficial aspects of wildfires, discussing such topics as fire-adapted species, the effects of fire exclusion on wildlife habitat, and the value of prescribed burns in restoring forest diversity. The brochure makes for interesting reading and is available at the trailhead information board or at any Bitterroot National Forest office.

Bass Creek Day Use Trail (129ML), 6.5 miles (10.5 km). This route is really just an extension of the Fire Ecology Trail and offers the longest loop possibilities of the Larry Creek Complex. It passes through low-elevation forest similar to that found along elsewhere in the area, traversing open stands of ponderosa as well as heavier riparian forest along Larry Creek and its tributaries. For the most part the route maintains an easy contour and reaches a maximum elevation of 4,200 feet at its northwest end. Several cutoff trails (see map) allow shorter variations from the main trial, as does the intersecting Forest Road 1316. Until recently portions of the route strayed onto private property adjacent to the national forest boundary. To correct this problem, the USFS completed 2.2 miles of relocation work in 1999 and marked the new route, along with the adjoining Fire Ecology Trail, the following year.

24 Sheafman Creek

Highlights:	Three high mountain lakes with splendid scenery and their own individual allure.
Type of hike:	Out-and-back day hike or overnighter.
Total distance:	12.8 miles or 20.6 kilometers (round trip).
Difficulty:	Moderate.
Best months:	July through September.
Elevation gain:	2,240 feet.
Elevation loss:	200 feet.
Maps:	Hamilton North and Printz Ridge USGS quads.

Special considerations: Although the best time to visit Sheafman Creek begins in July, I recommend waiting until after July 15 to make the trip. Earlier attempts are an unpredictable proposition because you are likely to encounter flooded trail segments, swift stream fords, and melting snow above and below Garrard Lake.

Trailhead access: Take U.S. Highway 93 to the Woodside interchange, 2 miles north of Hamilton, and follow Dutch Hill Road west from the flashing yellow caution light. Dutch Hill Road reaches a T intersection 3 miles from the highway; turn right and follow the paved road as it completes two 90-degree turns. Continue to West Cow Creek Road, turn left, and follow this dusty mountain road through a residential neighborhood and heavy forest for an additional 4.9 miles. A wide but otherwise unmarked pullout for six vehicles denotes the Sheafman Creek Trailhead. Views of the Bitterroot Valley and Saint Mary Peak are especially nice from this location.

Fred Burr Reservoir • Sheafman Creek • Mill Creek
Fred Burr Creek to Mill Creek

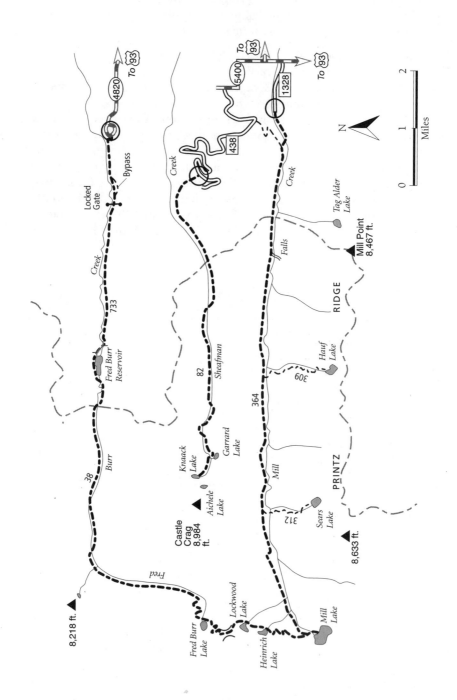

Keypoints:

- 0.0   Inception of trail at the Sheafman Creek Trailhead.
- 2.1   Trail enters the Selway-Bitterroot Wilderness.
- 2.6   Trail fords Sheafman Creek to reach its north bank.
- 4.7   Trail fords Sheafman Creek.
- 5.2   Trail fords Sheafman Creek once more.
- 5.5   Fourth and final ford of Sheafman Creek.
- 5.9   Trail reaches the foot of Garrard Lake.
- 6.4   Terminus of trail at Knaack Lake.

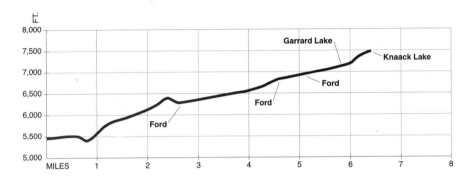

The hike: Berthed in the evening shade of 8,984-foot Castle Crag, the lakes of Sheafman Creek reside in relative anonymity 10 miles northwest of Hamilton. The entire trail is pack-animal accessible and well suited for either a full day excursion or an easy overnight trip. In fact, the only real hazards are four wet crossings of Sheafman Creek; these fords remain negotiable during spells of high water, although in late June the current is swift and frigid enough to discourage any misstep.

The trail begins by following an abandoned logging spur above the site of an old clearcut. Upon entering timber you contour through lupine-lit forest prior to reaching the canyon rim, where a sketchy footpath veers right for a good overlook of the lower Sheafman drainage. The main route turns with the topography and bears west as it undulates in steep pitches and modest drops. Gradually the trail draws near Sheafman Creek and reaches its first crossing, where a knee-deep ford awaits. A short but steep climb brings you abreast of the first of four incoming boulder fields overlooked by ashen escarpments crowning the canyon heights. After crossing the toe of a final talus spread the trail returns to Sheafman Creek for an ankle-deep ford of its icy waters.

The route then assumes the guise of a rivulet and stays waterlogged for another mile prior to reaching a second shallow ford of Sheafman Creek. A third and final encounter with the rushing watercourse follows a short time later. West of the uppermost ford, a soggy tread ushers you through dark bottomland in which large examples of living fir and spruce stand amid an equal number of the dead. Heavy winter snows have exacted a brutal toll: Many trees stand shattered 20 or more feet above the forest floor, shorn clean from the weight of excess snow. As it draws to within 0.25 mile of Garrard Lake, the trail turns south and meets a shallow woodland pond in full view of Castle Crag.

Garrard Lake is a small blue-green tarn nestled between dark green forest and high granite slopes. Scree islets rise from the cold waters, which harbor pan-sized cutthroat trout and reflect the distant but nonetheless impressive eastern face of Castle Crag. With its campsites and plentiful firewood, Garrard Lake is a prime candidate for an overnight stay. (Garrard Lake is still identified on some outdated maps as Sheafman Lake.)

Continue just below the old irrigation works at the outlet and then cut north to follow a cairn-marked route. After crossing an especially swift early-season streamlet, the route turns west and follows the rushing waters to their source at Knaack Lake. The excellent campsites available here are seldom free of snow until late July. The bare slopes west of the lake are an excellent example of granite exfoliation, an important geologic process in which crystalline igneous rocks fracture in large concentric sheets of varying thickness. Over time the exposed granite slabs break free at random, producing an unevenly terraced surface reminiscent of a peeling onion.

Option: Although the trail peters out alongside Knaack Lake, you may elect to visit the loftiest lake in the Sheafman group—tiny Aichele Lake. The route of choice involves a steep ascent of the ridge northwest of Knaack Lake. Attractive vantages of the upper Sheafman basin are its redeeming qualities. Castle Crag looms west of Aichele Lake, its fractured flank standing slightly askew like a tombstone in some forsaken graveyard.

25 Sweeney Ridge

Highlights:	A series of four subalpine lakes with good angling opportunities.
Type of hike:	Out-and-back day hike or overnighter.
Total distance:	15 miles or 24.1 kilometers (round trip).
Difficulty:	Difficult.
Best months:	July through September.
Elevation gain:	3,580 feet.
Elevation loss:	1,580 feet.
Maps:	Carlton Lake, Dick Creek, Saint Joseph Peak, and Saint Mary Peak USGS quads.

Trailhead access: Take U.S. Highway 93 to the junction with Sweeney Creek Road, 1.5 miles south of Florence, and follow signs west for 0.9 mile toward the approaching mountain front. Forest Road 1315 leaves the pavement at a marked intersection just below the canyon entrance and veers right to follow the narrow mountain road for another 6.1 miles. Although the final mile is especially steep and rough, the road is passable to low-clearance vehicles. The final mile below the trailhead is steep, narrow, and unsuitable for horse trailers or other large vehicles, as noted on a USFS sign posted along the road. Use the wide turnout available here. No facilities are present at the trailhead, and parking is limited to seven available spaces.

Sweeney Ridge

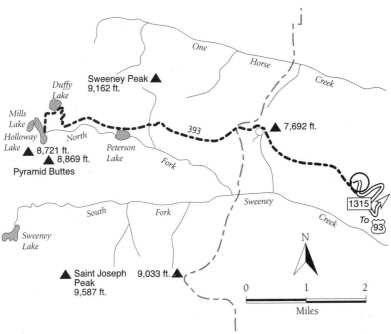

Keypoints:

- 0.0 Inception of trail at the Sweeney Ridge Trailhead.
- 1.6 Overlook of the Sweeney Creek drainage.
- 2.2 Trail reaches a spring near its initial apex.
- 2.7 Trail enters the Selway-Bitterroot Wilderness.
- 4.9 Trail draws abreast of Peterson Lake.
- 6.5 Trail shuffles past a nameless pond.
- 6.6 Abandoned irrigation dam at Duffy Lake.
- 7.2 Terminus of trail near Holloway Lake.
- 7.5 Bedrock isthmus below Mills Lake.

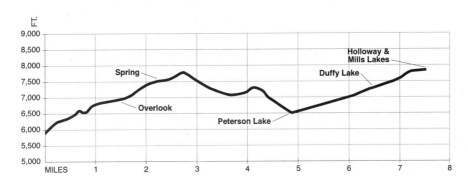

The hike: There is perhaps no more scenic a destination within an hour's travel of Missoula than this splendid canyon. As an approach route to

9,162-foot Sweeney Peak, the trail offers access to four high lakes nestled within sight of the Bitterroots' crest and sees heavy recreational use throughout the summer.

The trail begins with a steep climb on switchbacks before entering Douglas-fir parklands spread across the shady canyon slopes beyond. At one point the route wanders within sight of a fissured stone balcony from which you may gauge the scale of the Sweeney drainage and the size of Saint Joseph Peak on the southwest horizon. The trail resumes its climb beyond this overlook and reaches an unprotected spring after a time. A signpost denoting the wilderness boundary follows shortly. In the next 2 miles the trail fails to maintain its elevation, and Saint Joseph Peak sinks slowly out of sight behind an intervening ridgeline. As the descent continues, a pair of tumbling tributaries and interspersed clearings herald the approach of Peterson Lake.

Rotten driftwood booms and weedy channels choke the outlet of Peterson Lake, whose depths harbor large numbers of rainbow trout. The only legitimate campsites lie scattered in vicinity of the inlet bar—steep shorelines and heavy timber preclude camping elsewhere. Expect shattered solitude at this popular weekend spot.

The trail reenters timber above Peterson Lake and bears west through damp bottomlands. After vaulting an icy perennial stream the trail doubles back and closes the remaining distance to Duffy Lake in 1 mile of steep climbing. Once atop a wooded bench, the trail files past a mudbottomed pond before sauntering through level forest for an additional hundred yards to reach its larger neighbor.

Duffy Lake rests atop a wooded shelf in full view of the Pyramid Buttes, so named for a host of high battlements and miters that loom across the canyon. A ruptured earthen dam still molders in the woods below the lake, serving to remind the visitor of its former status as an irrigation reservoir. Finding a good campsite should not be a problem. Most tree cover is left behind as the trail parts with Duffy Lake and heads for higher ground to the southwest. The sketchy route soon fades into oblivion, leaving you to undertake a cross-country scramble amid granite boulders and bleached snags to complete the journey into the uppermost lake basin.

Holloway Lake occupies an elongate tract overlooking Peterson Lake and the Bitterroot Valley. Nice trout have been reported in these waters. However, persistent wind and the scarcity of level ground suggest no obvious campsites. Holloway shares the basin and its eerie qualities with Mills Lake, a smaller tarn to the immediate west. A small irrigation dam at Mills Lake still augments downstream demand, but unlike the outlet works at Duffy, this has not yet been abandoned to the ravages of time and harsh Bitterroot winters.

94

The Pyramid Buttes rise beyond Peterson Lake.

26 Bear Creek

See Map on Page 80

Highlights: A pleasant streamside trail leading to a mountain lake with good fishing and high scenic value.

Type of hike: Out-and-back day hike or overnighter.

Total distance: 15.4 miles or 24.8 kilometers (round trip).

Difficulty: Moderate.

Best months: July through September.

Elevation gain: 2,730 feet.

Elevation loss: 60 feet.

Maps: Gash Point and White Sand Lake USGS quads.

Trailhead access: Take U.S. Highway 93 to Tucker Crossing, 3 miles south of Victor, and follow Bear Creek Road west for 2.3 miles. Turn right at a marked intersection with Red Crow Road, proceed north for 0.8 mile, and veer left for the final 3 miles. The Bear Creek Trailhead offers generous parking and packstock facilities. Primitive overnight campsites are available on the wooded flat just below the lot.

Keypoints:

0.0	Inception of trail at the Bear Creek Trailhead.
1.5	Falls along Bear Creek.
1.9	Trail enters the Selway-Bitterroot Wilderness.
2.6	Trail completes a wide ford of Bear Creek.
2.8	Unmarked junction with the South Fork Bear Creek Trail (304S).
5.0	Trail crosses the North Fork.
5.1	Unmarked junction with the abandoned North Fork Bear Creek Trail (305X).
7.4	Trail crosses the Middle Fork.
7.5	Trail returns to the east bank of the Middle Fork.
7.7	End of trail description at Bryan Lake.

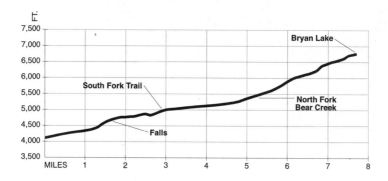

The hike: With its whitewater cascades, towering granite battlements, and ancient larch forests, the trail along Bear Creek easily qualifies as one of the most enjoyable stream-bottom hikes in the Bitterroots. It is also, unsurprisingly, one of the most popular. Bryan Lake attracts the most interest from hikers, and two unmaintained spur trails offer prime alternatives for wilderness challenge and solitude.

The trail saunters west through green woodland and soon crosses the toe of an extensive talus field. A pleasant stream-bottom hike ensues beyond the talus as the trail edges upstream within earshot of Bear Creek. At one point, you happen upon an unusual cascade in which the booming waters of Bear Creek tumble headlong through a narrow, mortised channel before vanishing around a bend downstream. With looming granite faces frequently visible along the northern canyon wall, the route continues through the forest. Only when the trail reaches a second talus spread does the drainage begin to disclose its true extent, with deeply glaciated canyons unfolding to the west and northwest. Sky Pilot Peak—a tall, triangular summit 6 miles to the northwest—makes its initial appearance as well. After crossing the wilderness boundary, the trail comes to its first crossing of Bear Creek. You can easily avoid this wide, swift ford by taking advantage of a convenient log crossing just upstream.

Once across Bear Creek, the trail passes an unmarked junction with the South Fork Bear Creek Trail (304S) before continuing northwest through an ancient forest of larch and Douglas-fir. Except for glimpses of the nearby mountainsides and the meandering North Fork, there is little in the way of scenic hiking over the next 2 miles. The route turns west as it approaches its only ford of the boulder-strewn North Fork. Even at high water this stream may be crossed minus wet feet; several slippery log footbridges are available for this purpose. There are several nice waterfalls just upstream of the crossing, where the North Fork drops over a series of bedrock terraces.

In a forest of blowdowns and ancient evergreens, you soon arrive at an obscure trail junction 150 yards beyond the crossing. This is the North Fork Bear Creek Trail (305X), an abandoned USFS route that once followed the North Fork to its source at Bear Lake. For its part the mainline trail continues along a westerly bearing and maintains a healthy distance with the Middle Fork, following switchbacks across an increasingly rocky tread. Attractive glimpses of the nearby mountainsides furnish the first direct views of the approaching Bitterroot Divide. Low waterfalls and wide granite aprons appear alongside stream and trail.

As you draw to within 1 mile of the Montana-Idaho border, the route swings north for two simple crossings of the Middle Fork. Another series of switchbacks tackles the final grade to Bryan Lake, passing several overtaxed campsites beside the slow-moving stream. Ahead unfolds the majestic breadth of the canyon headwaters, with Bryan Lake nestled like a rare jewel in its midst. Sheer igneous faces, bright snowfields, and sparse forest provide the basic scenic elements. The lake is home to a thriving population of cutthroat trout.

The trail continues above Bryan Lake and undertakes a steep ascent to Bear Creek Pass—itself not completely visible from the lake outlet. Reaching this high pass into Idaho entails a sustained effort well worth the southerly views toward the receding lake and overshadowing peaks that produce a remarkably picturesque composition.

Bryan Lake.

Side trips: Spur trails along the North and South forks of Bear Creek offer a higher degree of seclusion and route-finding challenge than does the mainline trail to Bryan Lake. Brief descriptions of each follow below.

▲ The **South Fork Bear Creek Trail (304S)** diverges from the mainline route at an unmarked junction 2.8 miles west of the Bear Creek Trailhead. From the junction, the trail descends to a scary high-water crossing of the Middle Fork, then climbs through forested terrain on the opposite side. The route gets sketchy as it ventures onto open, moss-covered bedrock just ahead, but by looking carefully you should be able to pick up the correct route and follow it upstream.

This is a rather rough trail and the tread, which alternates between rocky stretches and a carpet of soft pine needles, is poorly defined in places. It requires a steady climb with frequent short descents and a few large-diameter blowdowns to cross (two minor reroutes direct the trail around the worst of the obstructions). You can follow the path upstream for a total of 3.1 miles from the junction, where it abruptly ends. Various maps show the trail continuing west to a dead end near Two Lakes, but there is nothing that even closely resembles a trail on the ground.

▲ The **North Fork Bear Creek Trail (305X)** splits from the mainline trail at an unsigned junction 5.1 miles from the trailhead. At first the route follows a fairly obvious tread to a crossing of the North Fork. From there it deteriorates significantly until *virtually no trace* of the original route remains. The few surviving remnants of the trail do generally conform to the location shown on the 1989 Selway-Bitterroot Wilderness map; however, hundreds of blowdowns and a serious lack of blaze marks make for lots of head scratching. If you get discouraged but still want to visit the lake, just scramble through talus along the western side of the drainage or follow the North Fork upstream to its source.

Bear Lake sits in a high glacial bowl at the intersection of three huge avalanche zones roughly 7 miles from the trailhead. The immediate lakeshore consists of heavy timber, wet meadows, and talus; above, the impressive eastern face of 8,792-foot Sky Pilot casts a sheet of darkness across the lake and its surroundings by early evening. Campsite selection ranges from several lightly used sites around the inlet to a single tent space very close to the lake's long-abandoned irrigation dam. There is something spooky about this place: It had a palatable eeriness about it when I first visited on the afternoon of September 24, 1999.

27 Bass Lake

Highlights:	Attractive canyon scenery and a large mountain reservoir.	See Map on Page 75

Highlights: Attractive canyon scenery and a large mountain reservoir.
Type of hike: Out-and-back day hike or overnighter.
Total distance: 16.8 miles or 27 kilometers (round trip).
Difficulty: Moderate.
Best months: July through September.
Elevation gain: 3,240 feet.
Elevation loss: 180 feet.
Maps: Saint Joseph Peak and Saint Mary Peak USGS quads.

Trailhead access: Take Bass Creek Road from its intersection with U.S. Highway 93, 4 miles south of Florence. This paved road continues west and crosses a narrow bridge over Bass Creek to reach the Charles Waters Memorial Campground after 2.5 miles. Parking is available at the upper end of the recreation area.

Keypoints:
0.0 Charles Waters Memorial Campground.
1.8 Abandoned dam and reservoir on Bass Creek.
2.4 Trail enters the Selway-Bitterroot Wilderness.
2.8 Junction with an obsolete southern route; bear right.
4.0 Trail reconnects with its southern counterpart.
4.8 Unmarked junction with the Lappi Lake Trail (324W).
6.1 Trail passes through wide avalanche meadows.
7.3 Trail reaches the irrigation dam at Bass Lake.
7.8 Signed junction with the abandoned Bass Pass Trail (301X). End of maintained trail.
8.4 End of description at the head of Bass Lake.

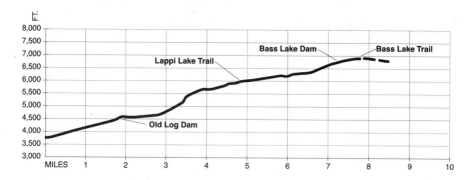

The hike: This trail follows an old dozer grade from the foothills of the Bitterroot Range to a sprawling reservoir berthed at the headwaters of Bass Creek. The trail has a good deal to offer in terms of scenic interest, even though an earthen dam at Bass Lake slightly tempers its overall attractiveness. Connections with routes leading into the adjacent Kootenai Creek and South Fork drainages provide for extended trip possibilities via their respective passes.

From its inception at the canyon portal, the trail retreats upstream in heavy forest. Bass Creek remains close at hand as the trail gradually tapers into a gentle gradient and wanders within sight of several deep pools nestled between moss-covered boulders. After crossing the toe of a minor ridge, you arrive at a shallow pond impounded with the wreckage of an abandoned damsite. The shallows of this log-strewn waterway mirror the spectacular vertical rise of the northern canyon wall, which towers ominously in the distance.

A level grade takes you through dark bottomlands to reach the boundary of the Selway-Bitterroot Wilderness. After a time the trail ventures upon an unmarked but obvious junction whose obsolete southern fork once forded Bass Creek. The main trail cuts upslope and soon enters a brushy talus spread drained by a single rivulet. On the horizon southwest of this clearing looms a stunning assemblage of battlements and turrets, whose fluted forms rise like the ruins of a long-forgotten castle to ice-hewn points on the canyon rim. As the canyon narrows ahead, the trail traverses Douglas-fir forest and passes a series of low waterfalls on Bass Creek before returning to the old road grade. Here the route reconnects with its abandoned southern counterpart and continues west.

Upon meeting a wide aspen grove, the trail clears a rushing brooklet and contours around the foot of an incoming ridge to reach an unmarked junction with the Lappi Lake Trail (324W) at 4.8 miles. Streamside meadows are rather uncommon through the Bitterroot Range, but in the glaciated upper reaches of Bass Creek the trail happens upon several such clearings. Views from the vicinity of these subalpine meadows are of a broad subalpine basin enclosed between imposing mountain flanks. After a final segment of forest travel the trail reaches the low slopes of Saint Joseph Peak and then makes a beeline for the outlet dam at Bass Lake, completing its traverse atop a rocky tread.

Bass Lake occupies a deep and sparsely wooded canyon overlooked from the southwest by 8,855-foot Bass Peak. Impounded behind an unsightly earthen dam and subject to heavy irrigation drawdown, Bass Lake showcases the late-season "reservoir look" all too common in the Bitterroots. A narrow tread follows above the shoreline from the damsite to a marked junction with the unmaintained Bass Pass Trail (301X) before reaching well-used campsites near the lake's southwest embayment. This vague route, primitive and unmaintained, continues over the pass south of Bass Lake and later ties in with the Kootenai Creek Trail (53ML). Owing to its great depth, the lake provides consistently good angling for cutthroat and rainbow trout.

Options: Connecting trails leading into the South Fork and Kootenai Creek drainages offer the possibility of longer point-to-point hikes. Specific details regarding those drainages and their trails are discussed elsewhere in this book.

Side trip: Lappi Lake, a little-known tarn lodged in the southern wall of the Bass Creek canyon, lies at the end of a very poor foot trail (324W) originating from the Bass Creek thoroughfare (its junction remains unmarked as this book goes to print). This difficult and often hard-to-follow route traces cairns downslope from its junction with the mainline trail to a low-clearance log that crosses Bass Creek. Sawn-out logs and faint ax blazes define the trail as it runs south through ancient Douglas-fir and Engelmann spruce for an ensuing 1,100-foot ascent.

Once the trail reaches open terrain, cairns guide you upslope and toward a shallow ravine leading to the foot of Lappi Lake. Several lightly used campsites are available near the outlet, where dual stone-and-mortar dams still stand. Slabs of salmon-colored bedrock rise from the blue-green depths of the lake, lending an evanescent beauty to the waters. What better setting exists to reflect the rugged splendor of Saint Joseph Peak?

28 Kootenai Creek

See Map on Page 75

Highlights: A long streamside retreat to four spectacular lakes, among the Bitterroots' most popular.
Type of hike: Out-and-back day hike or overnighter.
Total distance: 19 miles or 30.6 kilometers (round trip).
Difficulty: Moderate.
Best months: July through September.
Elevation gain: 2,680 feet.
Maps: Saint Joseph Peak and Saint Mary Peak USGS quads.

Trailhead access: Take U.S. Highway 93 to its marked junction with the North Kootenai Road, 8 miles south of Florence. Turn here and follow this potholed county road west for 2 miles to a wide parking lot below the canyon entrance. This otherwise undeveloped parking area can accommodate as many as two dozen vehicles.

Keypoints:
0.0 Inception of trail at the Kootenai Creek Trailhead.
2.4 Trail enters the Selway-Bitterroot Wilderness.
7.7 Unmarked junction with the Bass Pass Trail (301X).
8.5 Trail fords the northern fork of Kootenai Creek.
8.6 Junction with the Kootenai Lakes Trail (302ML); stay left.
8.7 Trail fords outlet stream below the Middle Fork Lakes.
9.5 Terminus of trail at South Kootenai Lake.

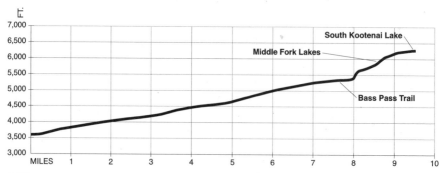

The hike: A longtime favorite of local equestrians, backpackers, and rock climbing enthusiasts, the Kootenai Creek Trail sustains as much use in one summer weekend as some trails receive all year. Overuse is especially prevalent along its lower 4 miles. The final ascent to the lakes heralds a dramatic improvement in otherwise average scenery; indeed, the lakes themselves are blazing blue jewels set in some of the most sublime country the Bitterroot Mountains have to offer.

Starting west from the parking lot, you follow a gentle grade into a deep, shaded defile whose moss-covered cliffs amplify the din of rushing water. The trail—which tends to gain elevation in short but steep increments—remains in close quarters with Kootenai Creek as it passes a concrete headgate and continues upstream. Old cottonwoods crowd the watercourse, leaning over the frigid waters in a perilous bid for sunlight. The trail ventures into designated wilderness at 2.5 miles. A suite of large side canyons enters the Kootenai Creek drainage from north and south over the next four miles, including no fewer than 4 major rivulets.

After nearly 7 miles of uneventful travel, the trail returns streamside once more and soon reaches a hillside clearing. Snow-draped heights towering over the Kootenai Lakes first become apparent at this location, even though the lakes themselves are still several miles distant. In another 0.5 mile, the trail vaults a wide perennial tributary and meets an incognito junction with the abandoned Bass Pass Trail (301X). As you climb on switchbacks, the trail passes several open landings with fine views of the surrounding glaciated terrain. With the Heavenly Twins now partially visible to the southeast, the trail completes its remaining switchbacks and contours west for a knee-deep ford of Kootenai Creek's northern fork. No sooner does this stream disappear behind you than the trail converges at an obvious junction with the Kootenai Lakes Trail (302ML) just below the Middle Fork Lakes.

From this junction the trail forges straight ahead for a waist-deep ford before pausing at the foot of the Middle Fork Lakes. Situated at the lower end of an attractive glacial bowl, the breadth of this cirque alludes to the presence of a second lake farther west. This upper lake, which requires a cross-country bushwhack to reach, is surrounded by a spectacular granite headwall and early-season waterfalls. California golden trout were introduced here nearly 50 years ago; however, no trace of trout—goldens or otherwise—survives.

The route climbs several switchbacks above the Middle Fork Lakes and runs south across rock ledges long ago blasted out to accommodate stock use. Bass Peak recedes from view to the north as the final segment to South Kootenai Lake traverses level forest and boggy terrain. The trail then makes a wide ford of the slow-moving south fork to reach a heavily used set of campsites on the opposite side. (Since these sites are occupied on a more-or-less continuous basis, please take care to practice low-impact techniques.) South Kootenai Lake is a stunning azure jewel surrounded by exfoliated rock walls, angular talus slides, and a deep green forest. The excellent angling here makes for an enjoyable afternoon, and an intriguing basin above the lake invites off-trail exploration.

Side trip: North Kootenai Lake is definitely worth a look if you are out for more than a day hike. From the junction below the Middle Fork Lakes, an obvious trail veers north and sets out within earshot of a rushing stream hidden in the trees below. The unseen watercourse appears as the route ventures streamside, crosses the ankle-deep channel, and turns west to complete its journey to North Kootenai Lake. Surrounded by heavy forest and snow-mantled rock faces, this deep tarn supports a population of rainbow trout. There is a good selection of campsites available, with those near the outlet being the most frequently occupied. Sites near the inlet were obliterated by avalanche debris during the winter of 1998–99.

29 South Fork Big Creek

See Map on Page 80

Highlights:	Exceptional scenery and fishing; an excellent alternative to the Big Creek Lakes.
Type of hike:	Out-and-back overnighter.
Total distance:	20 miles or 32.2 kilometers.
Difficulty:	Moderate.
Best months:	July through September.
Elevation gain:	2,830 feet.
Elevation loss:	50 feet.
Maps:	Gash Point and Victor USGS quads.

Special considerations: The USFS strongly discourages stock use on the South Fork Big Creek Trail (118S) due to numerous large-diameter blowdowns and extended segments of boggy tread.

Trailhead access: To find the Big Creek Trailhead, take U.S. Highway 93 to the flashing yellow caution light at Bell Crossing, 1.8 miles north of Victor. Turn here and follow the wide dirt road west for 0.3 mile, around two 90-degree turns, and continue an additional mile to reach Forest Road 738. At this point you proceed northwest, passing through the reclaimed Curlew Mine, and soon arrive at the marked turnoff to the Big Creek Trailhead. Veer right and follow the road to its terminus—4.6 miles from US 93. The trailhead includes an outhouse, picnic tables, and parking for more than a dozen vehicles. Stock unloading ramps and hitchrails are also present.

Keypoints:
- 0.0 Inception of trail at the Big Creek Trailhead.
- 1.3 Trail enters the Selway-Bitterroot Wilderness.
- 1.4 Pack bridge over Big Creek.
- 2.7 Trail crosses Saint Mary Creek.
- 4.9 Trail reaches the Teepee Rock area.
- 5.7 Log footbridge over Beaver Creek.
- 6.8 Log footbridge over Big Creek.

7.3 Junction with the South Fork Big Creek Trail (118S); stock use not recommended.

8.2 Trail crosses the South Fork Big Creek.

9.1 Trail returns to the western side of the South Fork.

10.0 End of description at South Fork Lake

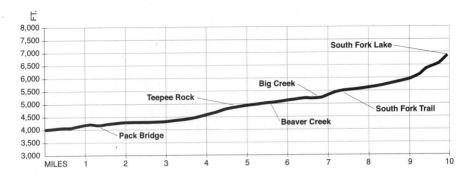

The hike: With the likes of the Big Creek Lakes less than 2 miles away, it is hardly surprising that South Fork Lake is seldom treated as a destination in its own right. Most folks are apparently discouraged by the poor condition of the South Fork Big Creek Trail (118S); those who venture into the area generally do so from base camps at the Big Creek Lakes. Why not give the South Fork a try, and see what everyone else is missing!

The trail begins as a pleasant yet uneventful streamside retreat and quickly passes several side paths leading down the rushing creek. There is little to see as you proceed northwest into the wilderness and reach a pack bridge spanning Big Creek's boulder-covered channel. Upon reaching the far streambank, the trail ambles along within earshot of the watercourse for the next several miles. You encounter Saint Mary Creek and scattered pockets of grand fir and cedar over the next 2 miles, but progress is difficult to gauge without the benefit of any prominent landmark.

After a time you arrive at Teepee Rock, a boxcar-sized granite block situated on the flat at 4.9 miles. A granite overhang protruding from this massive 1,000-ton boulder provides temporary shelter from summer rainstorms and gives the site its name. Rain or shine, Teepee Rock is a fine spot for a quick snack break before heading farther up the trail. Old larch and evergreens surround the trail as you continue upstream to the footbridge over Beaver Creek. Another footbridge—this time over Big Creek itself—spans the stream at a slow-moving meander 6.8 miles from the trailhead. The route soon comes to a marked junction with the South Fork Big Creek Trail (118S); taking the left-hand fork puts you on the trail to South Fork Lake.

The South Fork Trail follows a deteriorated tread southwest from the main Big Creek Trail for 2.7 miles, crossing the South Fork Big Creek via fallen logs on two occasions. Good canyon vistas are available at a few select points, but the trail is primarily routed in the trees. Blowdowns are a frequent obstacle, and the trail grows indistinct as it crosses several avalanche openings interspersed throughout otherwise densely forested stream bottom.

Boggy terrain sometimes makes for difficult footing. You reach South Fork Lake after a total ascent of 1,280 feet from the junction.

South Fork Lake greets few visitors. It is a large, scenic body nestled directly below the Bitterroot Divide and Sky Pilot Peak, both beautifully rendered in a dozen shades of gray. Excessive leakage and water level fluctuation are not the problems some other guidebooks have made them out to be: The old stone irrigation dam was dismantled and removed years ago. South Fork Lake sees little fishing pressure but supports a large population of cutthroat trout that provides consistently excellent fishing. Any number of campsites are available, so have a look around before you stake your tent. And if you must have a campfire, keep it small and scatter the ashes before you leave.

Options: A combination loop of roughly 24 miles is possible if you hike into South Fork and Pearl lakes, cross over to Packbox Pass the following day, follow the trail northeast past Big Creek Lakes, and retrace your steps downstream to the Big Creek Trailhead. *Be advised that no trail ever existed between Pearl Lake and Packbox Pass.* This rugged traverse offers an outstanding view of the Big Creek Lakes but is steep and extremely treacherous when wet. There is no easy route across the rock, so be careful!

Side trip: Pearl Lake lies within easy walking distance of a base camp at South Fork Lake. An ascent of roughly 500 feet ensues as you trace remnants of an unmaintained tread from the western end of South Fork Lake, past a pair of shallow frog ponds, and downhill to the small subalpine jewel. This is a truly gorgeous setting, definitely one of the more spectacular high Bitterroot lakes. Campsite selection is limited to a few nondescript sites near the outlet (no campfires please). Cutthroat trout reportedly fin these waters, but the lack of spawning grounds means that no natural reproduction takes place. The few surviving fish are old-timers to be sure.

30 Blodgett Canyon

Highlights:	Majestic canyon scenery with good opportunities for wildlife viewing.
Type of hike:	Out-and-back overnighter.
Total distance:	23 miles or 37 kilometers (round trip).
Difficulty:	Moderate.
Best months:	July through September.
Elevation gain:	2,660 feet.
Elevation loss:	120 feet.
Maps:	Blodgett Mountain, Hamilton North, and Printz Ridge USGS quads.

Special considerations: Many tent sites in the lower 4 miles of the canyon show signs of chronic overuse; to minimize your impact in this popular area, I strongly recommend limiting your activities to day hiking rather than an overnight stay. Stock users should also note that the popular campsite at

Blodgett Canyon

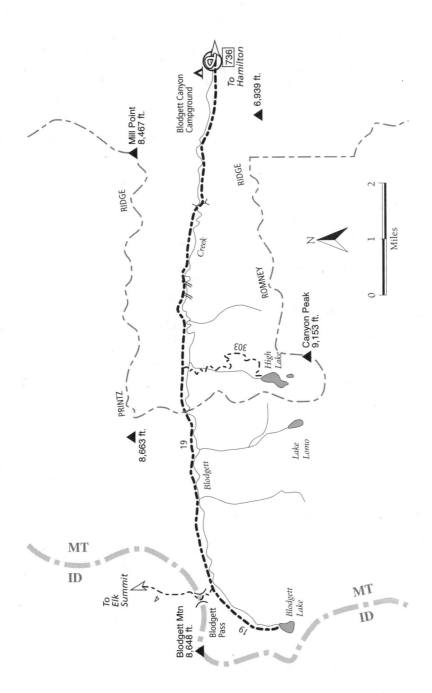

Ninemile Meadow is closed to stock use. USFS signs clearly mark the closure, both at the trailhead and at the campsite in question.

Trailhead access: Take U.S. Highway 93 to its junction with Bowman Road at the Donaldson Brothers cement plant 2 miles north of Hamilton. Turn here and follow hiking signs (located at most intersections) along Bowman Road for 0.6 mile, then turn and follow Ricketts Road south for 2 more miles to reach a four-way intersection. Continue straight on Blodgett Camp Road and stay right at the marked intersection with Forest Road 735 after 2.4 miles. From there drive the remaining 1.5 miles to the combined Blodgett Canyon campground and trailhead. Among the amenities provided are stock unloading ramps, hitchrails, an outhouse, and a large parking lot sufficient for two dozen vehicles or more. The six campsites at the campground include picnic tables and fire rings; a five-day occupancy limit currently applies.

Keypoints:

0.0	Inception of trail at the Blodgett Canyon campground.
0.1	Trailside monument to the late Don Mackey.
2.9	Pack bridge over Blodgett Creek.
4.4	Chasm waterfall on Blodgett Creek.
4.8	Stairstep waterfall on Blodgett Creek.
5.9	Junction with the High Lake Trail (303S).
6.7	Trail enters the Selway-Bitterroot Wilderness.
6.9	Trail passes through the Sevenmile Meadow.
9.2	Trail reaches the Ninemile Meadow.
10.0	Junction with the Blodgett Pass Trail (310ML).
11.5	Terminus of trail at the foot of Blodgett Lake.

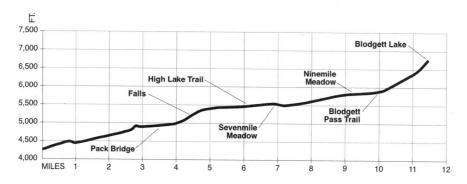

The hike: This trail showcases the majestic length of Blodgett Canyon, centerpiece of the many east-west canyons found in the Montana portion of the Selway-Bitterroot Wilderness. It offers an exceptionally pleasant and scenic passage culminating in a high mountain lake whose beauty nicely complements the Bitterroots' most spectacular canyon. Additionally, the trail offers two potential side trips; the short diversion to Blodgett Pass in particular is not to be missed.

The trail wanders upstream and merges with the stock driveway after 250 yards, then continues through heavy forest for the first mile. Occasional side trails lead to riffles and pools along Blodgett Creek; sheer granite faces loom in the distance. These tantalizing glimpses hint of things to come, but not until the trail emerges from the forest in a series of talus fields and forest that was razed in the early 1980s wildfires does the full extent of the canyon become apparent. As the rocky tread passes underfoot, you are treated to many fine views of Blodgett Canyon, including the impressive array of granite spurs protruding from the flanks of Printz Ridge to the north. Of equal interest on the southern rim of the canyon is a natural rock arch whose narrow silhouette first appears as you approach the pack bridge over Blodgett Creek at 2.9 miles. From the bridge and surrounding area you can watch the play of light and shadow unfold across the canyon walls from passing clouds or simply the changing angle of the sun alone.

The trail passes a beaver dam and accompanying pond, saunters through another talus field, and then proceeds to a charming waterfall in which Blodgett Creek spills through a narrow, moss-draped defile. A second stairstep falls follows after another 0.4 mile. You continue through heavy forest on a very gentle grade to reach a junction with the High Lake Trail (303S) at 5.9 miles (a sign clearly marks the once elusive take-off point). The route remains in the trees as you officially enter the wilderness and emerge at the toe of a large avalanche chute known informally as Sevenmile Meadow. This is a popular camping area for hunters in fall, when wall tents and stock typically occupy the best sites. Another heavily used camping area shows up just before the trail enters the boulder-studded expanse of Ninemile Meadow. More heavy forest ensues above this clearing as you close in on the signed junction with the Blodgett Pass Trail (310ML) at 10 miles. As the sign indicates, keep left for Blodgett Lake.

The main trail bends southwest and steepens noticeably as it runs along the toe of several brushy avalanche slopes, crosses pockets of stunted fir, and traverses stands of taller spruce. Rushing rivulets and a few downed trees provide the only serious obstacles to your headway—and they are minor ones at that. Initially 920 feet above you at the junction, Blodgett Pass soon draws to eye level as the trail ambles ever closer to its destination. An easy final stretch takes the route past a sprawling talus field before circling over to the foot of Blodgett Lake.

Blodgett Lake is a small tarn cradled in a rockbound amphitheater at the headwaters of Blodgett Creek. Two unnamed pyramid-shaped peaks overlook the lake from the south while the granite fin of Blodgett Mountain provides a rugged backdrop to the north; all around, exfoliated granite glistens with meltwater into midsummer. The lake offers several campsites—little used though they are—along with a resident cutthroat fishery that provides good angling.

Options: Adventurous hikers may treat Blodgett Canyon as the first segment of a longer out-and-back hike to Big Sand Lake (16.6 miles) or shuttle to the USFS guard station and campground complex at Elk Summit (23.8 miles). The entire route to Elk Summit receives annual maintenance; however, winter avalanche activity below Blodgett Pass and along the upper reaches of Big Sand Creek often leaves downed trees and other debris across the trail.

Looking north toward Blodgett Pass from the Blodgett Canyon Trail.

Equestrians should keep this in mind before attempting the trail on horse-back—be sure to check with the Lochsa Ranger District if in doubt (see Appendix A for contact information).

Side trips: There are two good side trip opportunities for backpackers headed into Blodgett Lake. These include the High Lake (303S) and Blodgett Pass (310ML) trails, as discussed below.

▲ Whenever a conversation turns to the **High Lake Trail (303S)**, a blank expression is never far behind. Some folks merely shrug their shoulders when asked about the lake, having never seen High Lake themselves. Others liken the task of setting foot on its shore as an exercise of almost deranged conviction. You might be inclined to agree after making the attempt.

From its marked junction, the trail first runs south through wet fir bottomlands and crosses the two shallow channels of Blodgett Creek—with the assistance of fallen timber—before a final log crossing over High Lake's outlet stream. From here the trail climbs sharply uphill through a jungle of downfall to reach level ground in a false cirque 1 mile north of the lake. The trail becomes especially difficult to follow as it next tackles the granite slopes to the east, where rockslides long ago obliterated most of the original route. *Do not be fooled into making the dangerous straight-line ascent along the lake's outlet stream, as inaccurately shown on the Printz Ridge quadrangle.* Careful observation is necessary to detect the trail as it traverses the high slopes above and contours through windblown fir just north of the as-yet-unseen lake. You reach High Lake some 2.2 miles after leaving the mainline trail on Blodgett Creek.

High Lake occupies a deep cirque in full view of 9,153-foot Canyon Peak and offers good angling for emaciated rainbow trout. Scattered about the lake's spillway are the rusting relics of a narrow-gauge rail system once used to transport riprap from its quarry west of the dam; a rustic log cabin seemingly on the verge of collapse molders amid the whitebark pine on a nearby hillside. Widely scattered campsites are available.

▲ The **Blodgett Pass Trail (310ML)** cuts from the main route at a marked junction and ascends the mostly open slopes above, following a fair tread through pockets of subalpine fir and spruce. The terrain appears highly avalanche-prone, so much so that when I hiked to the pass on October 13, 1999, dozens of fir and pine had been shorn by slides, and the debris still lay across the trail from the previous spring. Sheer granite faces confine the trail to a fairly narrow swath of the hillside, which it climbs in a series of steep switchbacks. A spectacular vantage greets you after the 920-foot climb to the pass, with views of Blodgett Mountain and Blodgett Lake, as well as the delightful scene extending down the glaciated length of Blodgett Canyon and into the Bitterroot Valley beyond.

31 Mill Creek

See Map on Page 90

Highlights:	A long, glaciated canyon with several high lakes below the Bitterroot Divide.
Type of hike:	Out-and-back overnighter.
Total distance:	23 miles or 37 kilometers (round trip).
Difficulty:	Moderate.
Best months:	July through September.
Elevation gain:	3,710 feet.
Elevation loss:	400 feet.
Maps:	Blodgett Mountain, Hamilton North, and Printz Ridge USGS quads.

Trailhead access: Follow U.S. Highway 93 to the Woodside interchange, located 7 miles south of Victor and 4 miles north of Hamilton. Take Dutch Hill Road west from the highway for 2.2 miles and turn left onto Bowman Road at the T intersection. After leaving the pavement and crossing a narrow bridge over Mill Creek, turn right on Forest Road 1328, then continue west for 0.8 mile to the unimproved trailhead loop. Stock unloading ramps, hitchrails, and generous parking space for up to 15 vehicles are available at this trailhead, a designated day-use–only site.

Keypoints:
    0.0   Inception of trail at the Mill Creek Trailhead.
    0.6   Footbridge over Mill Creek.
    2.0   Trail enters the Selway-Bitterroot Wilderness.

2.9 Trail draws abreast of falls on Mill Creek.
4.7 Unmarked junction with Hauf Lake Trail (309W).
7.6 Junction with Sears Lake Trail (312W).
10.3 Junction with Fred Burr Trail (38S) below Mill Lake.
10.5 Trail reaches the foot of Mill Lake.
11.1 Abandoned dam at the outlet of Heinrich Lake.
11.5 End of description at Lockwood Lake.

The hike: Mill Creek is just one of the deeply glaciated canyons penetrating the Bitterroots' eastern ramparts. The drainage offers a selection of possible destinations, including several secluded mountain lakes accessible only via unkempt foot trails. Scenery tends to improve the farther upstream you travel, with Heinrich and Lockwood lakes being prime examples of the trend.

From its forested beginnings, the trail retreats upstream and crosses several irrigation ditches before entering the canyon mouth beyond. A log footbridge with handrail spans the watercourse at 0.6 mile. As it continues west, the trail files through heavy timber and saunters below soaring cliffs. The trail rises and falls but gains elevation overall as it travels upstream and passes the wilderness boundary.

As it approaches the 3-mile mark, the route completes a short climb to reach a boulder-strewn clearing just above a nice set of falls on Mill Creek. The falls drop perhaps 30 feet as they empty into a deep swimming hole whose cold, green waters sparkle invitingly on a hot summer afternoon. Campsites are available just upstream of the falls, but these are quite close to the trail and offer little privacy. Mill Creek itself is visible from time to time as the trail resumes its western course and follows a good tread farther into the drainage. After several uneventful miles, the route comes to an inconspicuous junction with the Hauf Lake Trail (309W), about 100 yards east of an obvious trailside campsite.

In the miles beyond this junction the trail traverses virgin timber and brushfields that make the most of rather limited scenery in the area. Uneventful forest travel encourages a rapid pace as you enter the first of several brushy clearings. An inconspicuous sign fastened to an old Douglas-fir denotes the junction with the Sears Lake Trail (312W), which veers left from the trail upon entering a wide meadow.

The trail encounters no fewer than six bridges—each spanning an intermittent brooklet—in varying stages of decay in the 2 miles following the Sears Lake junction. After crossing the outlet streams flowing from Lockwood and Heinrich lakes, you make a steep streamside ascent to reach a marked junction with the Fred Burr Trail (38S) (an enameled metal sign once noted this junction with lettering for "Heinrick" Lake). Shortly thereafter, the trail crosses Mill Creek by means of another collapsed log footbridge and takes you to Mill Lake.

Given the long miles required to reach this high mountain basin, Mill Lake is something of an anticlimax. A massive earthen dam rises above the outlet, its facade of fitted stones approximating the appearance of a medieval castle wall; below, debris from a narrow-gauge railway rusts incongruously amid the native granite. The lake itself is subject to acute surface level fluctuation as water is withdrawn for irrigation each summer, exposing unsightly mud flats and silver-gray stumps along the shoreline. Campsites at the lake are widespread and spacious.

From the previously mentioned junction below Mill Lake, the Fred Burr Trail veers right and follows an unkempt tread north through heavy bottomland forest for 0.5 mile. Crossing several streamlets, the trail traverses sloping rock faces and continues its ascent on switchbacks. The surrounding forest soon gives way to granite outcrops and boulder-strewn beargrass spreads, providing an excellent vantage of Mill Lake and its attendant peaks. With these scenic elements receding to the south, you follow cairns upslope and around a sparsely timbered hillside to reach Heinrich Lake.

Situated in the very shadows of the Bitterroot Divide, Heinrich Lake is a sensational blue-green jewel whose waters support a population of elusive rainbow trout. Campsites consist of only a few choice spots near the abandoned outlet dam—please do without the campfire if you decide to stay. An eastward glance from this point showcases the influence of Pleistocene glaciers on the Mill Creek drainage, with the view extending down a graceful U-shaped canyon corridor and into the Bitterroot Valley beyond.

Upon leaving Heinrich Lake, scattered cairns guide you to the outlet arm of Lockwood Lake. This mud-bottomed tarn is impounded behind an overgrown embankment of cobbles and soil that illustrates the transitory nature of man's crude refinements. With a surface elevation of 7,445 feet, Lockwood Lake is of questionable value as a fishery. From Lockwood Lake it is possible to continue north and enter the remote upper reaches of Fred Burr Creek. Careful routefinding is essential, particularly if you encounter melting snowfields and slippery granite. And keep in mind that this traverse is not usually free of snow until the middle of July.

Option: If you are out for a longer hike, continue north from Lockwood Lake and follow cairns to a high pass leading into the Fred Burr drainage, then continue downstream to the Fred Burr Trailhead. Interestingly enough, a few industrious souls have reported hiking the entire 24.6 miles in a single day—but at least four days are needed to fully appreciate the country.

Pocket meadows along the Mill Creek Trail.

Side trips: If you are interested in side trips, Mill Creek has two intriguing possibilities in Hauf and Sears lakes.

▲ Unless you watch carefully for the Hauf Lake junction, located about 5 miles upstream of the trailhead, you will likely miss it. A number of blazed lodgepole pines occur near the junction, but the tree of interest bears a 6-inch carved arrow filled with sap. From here the **Hauf Lake Trail (309W)** heads south on a horse-furrowed tread to reach a knee-deep ford of Mill Creek. Beyond the crossing, the trail traverses level terrain before encountering a pile of rotting debris strewn across the forest floor. A short detour is all that you need to reacquire the tread, which continues south at a very steep pitch. Frequent cross-canyon views provide a needed diversion from the business at hand. The staggering 2,100-foot ascent is relentless and exhausting, consuming the elevation via switchbacks over a distance of only 1.4 miles.

At last the trail emerges below the irrigation impoundment at Hauf Lake, an earthen structure with fitted stones on its downstream face. This small subalpine lake is cradled in an isolated basin very close to the crest of Printz Ridge. Hauf Lake's record as a fishery dates back until at least the early 1950s, but I was unable to verify reports of a few large cutthroat during my September 30, 1998, reconnaissance. An old bunkhouse still stands northeast of the lake, along with several dated outbuildings and other rusting relics.

▲ The junction to Sears Lake occurs as the mainline trail enters a stream-bottom clearing—one of several in the area—7.6 miles from the trailhead.

Watch carefully for a primitive sign that appears immediately before the trail emerges from the trees. From its junction the **Sears Lake Trail (312W)** goes south to a simple boulder crossing over Mill Creek and passes several excellent campsites in the process. Beyond the far streambank, the trail becomes a steep, rough route that runs upslope for almost 1,000 vertical feet.

Sears Lake occupies a lonely hanging cirque just below the imposing buttress of Printz Ridge, whose granite heights gaze dispassionately down. Far removed from the Mill Creek thoroughfare, Sears Lake's remote location provided little protection from development by Bitterroot Valley irrigators—bare earthworks, piled up logs, and flooded stumps are the unattractive result. Several lightly used campsites are located at the northeast quarter of the lake, along with rusting implements of the dam builders' craft.

32 Fred Burr Creek to Mill Creek

See Map on Page 90

Highlights: A lightly used series of lakes and magnificent views of two major watersheds and the Bitterroot Divide.
Type of hike: Four-day backpacking shuttle or base camp.
Total distance: 24.6 miles or 39.6 kilometers.
Difficulty: Difficult.
Best months: July through September.
Elevation gain: 4,140 feet.
Elevation loss: 4,320 feet.
Maps: Blodgett Mountain, Hamilton North, and Printz Ridge USGS quads.

Special considerations: Please stay on the designated trail and refrain from camping and fishing along Fred Burr Creek until you reach public lands beyond a locked gate at the Bitterroot National Forest boundary. The trail along the upper reaches of Fred Burr Creek is fairly primitive, with four major fords (wet feet likely) and several faint and overgrown segments. Blowdowns from the 1988 fire are a frequent obstacle as well, so take along a crosscut if you are traveling on horseback.

Trailhead access: To reach the Fred Burr Trailhead, take U.S. Highway 93 to Bear Creek Road, 3.5 miles south of Victor and continue west for 2.3 miles to the T intersection with Red Crow Road. Turn left and follow the road as it completes a 90-degree turn and continues west, leaving pavement to reach an open gate after 2.5 more miles. Follow the road through a 0.5 mile private parcel and an additional 0.2 mile to the wooded trailhead loop. A spacious parking area with room for 10 or more vehicles greets you.

For the Mill Creek Trailhead, follow U.S. Highway 93 to the Woodside interchange, located 7 miles south of Victor and 4 miles north of Hamilton.

Take Dutch Hill Road west from the highway for 2.2 miles and turn left onto Bowman Road at the T intersection. After crossing a narrow bridge over Mill Creek, turn right on Forest Road 1328 and continue west for 0.8 mile to the unimproved trailhead loop. Stock unloading ramps, hitchrails, and generous parking space for up to 15 vehicles are available at this trailhead, a designated day-use–only site.

Keypoints:

0.0	Inception of trail at the Fred Burr Trailhead.
0.2	Trail merges with jeep road below the canyon entrance.
1.2	Trail reaches signed bypass of private cabins; bear left.
1.5	Trail returns to the old jeep road.
1.7	Locked gate at the Bitterroot National Forest boundary.
4.4	Trail crosses bridge over Fred Burr Creek.
4.6	Inception of Fred Burr Trail (38S) at Fred Burr Reservoir.
5.2	Trail fords Fred Burr Creek to reach its south bank.
5.5	Trail enters the Selway-Bitterroot Wilderness.
5.6	Trail returns to north side of Fred Burr Creek.
7.5	Third ford of Fred Burr Creek.
8.5	Fourth and final ford of Fred Burr Creek.
11.9	Trail crosses the irrigation dam at Fred Burr Lake.
12.9	High pass into the Mill Creek drainage.
13.1	Outlet arm of Lockwood Lake.
13.5	Trail passes below Heinrich Lake.
14.3	Junction with the Mill Creek Trail (364ML) north of Mill Lake.
17.0	Junction with the Sears Lake Trail (312W).
19.7	Unmarked junction with the Hauf Lake Trail (309W).
21.7	Trail passes above Mill Creek Falls.
22.6	Trail leaves the Selway-Bitterroot Wilderness.
24.0	Footbridge over Mill Creek.
24.6	Terminus of trail at the Mill Creek Trailhead.

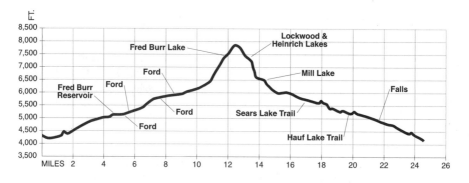

Suggested itinerary: Well-conditioned backpackers can hike the entire route described below in a marathon day, but to fully appreciate this wild country you should plan on staying at least three days. The arrangement outlined below allows you an entire day to take in the splendid scenery between Fred Burr and Heinrich lakes but leaves a long hike out to the Mill Creek

116

Trailhead for the final afternoon. (The Mill Creek Trail is shaded and down-hill most of the way, however.) Add an additional day or two to your schedule if you are interested in side trips to either Hauf or Sears lakes.

First day	—	Fred Burr Trailhead to Fred Burr Reservoir, 4.6 miles.
Second day	—	Fred Burr Reservoir to Fred Burr Lake, 7.3 miles.
Third day	—	Fred Burr Lake to Mill Lake, 1.6 miles.
Fourth day	—	Mill Lake to Mill Creek Trailhead, 10.1 miles.

The hike: The Fred Burr to Mill Creek circuit offers one of the few opportunities for a shuttle hike entirely on the Montana side of the Bitterroots. Among its many attractions are five trail-accessible lakes, good wildlife viewing opportunities, and generous campsite selection. Shutterbugs take note: Between Fred Burr and Heinrich lakes lies some of the Bitterroots' most picturesque country.

The trail wanders west through heavy foothill forest, passing through privately owned land posted against trespassing. After a short descent the trail merges with the Fred Burr Road (733), rounds a hillock, and continues toward the approaching canyon portal. The route passes a privately owned bridge and cabin before reaching a marked junction with a route bypassing several other buildings along the road. There is a locked gate at the Bitterroot National Forest boundary, 1.7 miles from the trailhead.

A streamside ascent ensues as the trail meanders through the timber on its way upstream. Occasional views of high granite prows enliven the proceedings as the trail momentarily traverses forest burned in the 1988 fires, then sidesteps a nice expanse of riffles, pools, and shallow gravel bars along the stream channel. You reenter unburned forest and return streamside to cross Fred Burr Creek atop a heavy wooden bridge; the road reaches the reservoir a short time later.

Granite peaks and burned-over forest interspersed with green timber provide a backdrop for Fred Burr Reservoir. Impounded behind a large earthen dam, the reservoir is drawn so very low for irrigation that by early October only Fred Burr Creek meanders across the emergent lakebed. The route continues along a narrow, rocky tread above the northern shoreline to reach a group of nice campsites at the head of the reservoir. (These sites are sheltered in heavy forest and thus are more desirable for camping than those near the dam.) Shortly thereafter the trail crosses Fred Burr Creek at the first of four stream crossings in as many miles.

The trail returns to the north side of the stream just beyond the Selway-Bitterroot Wilderness sign and continues through heavy stream-bottom forest, soon entering an expanse of timber razed in a 1988 wildfire. Views from the burn take in rugged country on either side of the canyon in addition to 8,984-foot Castle Crag. There is a good campsite in a clearing just past the third ford of Fred Burr Creek at 7.5 miles, but the usual urge is to press on to better sites located just past the fourth and final crossing of the stream. Among the stream-bottom meadows you will find a few lightly used sites well away from the main trail.

Beyond the fourth stream crossing the drainage doglegs south and returns to heavy spruce-fir forest with the sound of Fred Burr Creek flowing through the trees close by. Although you pass through a number of avalanche clearings, the route is mostly through wooded country with few scenic views. Drawing to within 1 mile of Fred Burr Lake, the trail begins an aggressive ascent on switchbacks, climbing the east-facing slopes continuously toward the unseen tarn.

Fred Burr is a high mountain lake set directly below the Bitterroot Divide. The presence of glacial silt in the water column gives the waters their special refractive properties and the lake its unusual emerald color. The water is so cold that large ice floes still drift about in late July. A few nice campsites are found near the outlet, where an unsightly irrigation dam remains in use.

The trail crosses the irrigation dam at Fred Burr Lake and continues its insistent climb along the ridge to the south. Venturing into increasingly attractive alpine country, you reach several nice overlooks of the lake before turning south for the high traverse into Mill Creek. Late lingering snowfields blanket much of the surrounding terrain, but cairns guide the way as you contour across the slopes ahead. This is an exceptionally scenic area: To the north unfolds the remote upper reaches of the Fred Burr drainage, and Canyon Peak and a host of other summits tower in the distance on the southern skyline.

Some 12.9 miles after leaving the trailhead you reach the windswept pass into Mill Creek, elevation 7,700 feet. With the Mill Creek watershed now visible for the first time, the route follows cairns to the foot of Lockwood Lake, where a low stone dam crouches beneath the trees. The cairn-marked

The high pass into Mill Creek consists of graceful snowfields and open granite slopes.

Lockwood Lake and the Bitterroot Divide.

route next descends to beautiful Heinrich Lake before reaching a marked junction with the Mill Creek Trail (364ML) north of Mill Lake. From there the route follows a good tread to your waiting vehicle some 10.3 miles downstream. For further details concerning Mill Creek and its lakes, refer to the Mill Creek description.

Option: You can try this hike in reverse with no additional difficulty.

Side trips: If you are interested in side trips, try scrambling to the crest of the Bitterroot Divide west of Lockwood Lake. Trails to Hauf and Sears lakes provide two other side trip possibilities.

33 Big Creek to Bear Creek

See Map on Page 80

Highlights: Impressive panoramas from the Bitterroot Divide and good fishing in many of the trail-accessible lakes.

Type of hike: Four-day backpacking shuttle or base camp.

Total distance: 26.3 miles or 42.3 kilometers.

Difficulty: Strenuous.

Best months: July through September.

Elevation gain: 5,700 feet.

Elevation loss: 5,600 feet.

Maps: Gash Point, Victor, and White Sand Lake USGS quads.

Special considerations: The Big Creek Lakes draw heavy recreational use throughout the summer months, and the onslaught of visitors routinely exceeds the available space during holiday weekends. Packstock use is especially prevalent, although the lakes attract a large number of backpackers as well. Keep in mind that campsites scattered around the lakeshore are dreadfully overused and subject to occasional closure to permit their recovery.

Trailhead access: To reach the Big Creek Trailhead, take U.S. Highway 93 to the flashing yellow light at Bell Crossing, 1.8 miles north of Victor. Turn here and follow the wide dirt road west for 0.3 mile, around two 90-degree turns, and continue an additional mile to reach Forest Road 738. At this point you proceed northwest, crossing the old Curlew Mine, and soon arrive at marked turnoff to the Big Creek Trailhead. Veer right and follow the road to its terminus 4.6 miles from the highway. The trailhead includes an outhouse, picnic tables, and parking for more than a dozen vehicles. Stock unloading ramps and hitchrails are also available.

For the Bear Creek Trailhead, follow U.S. Highway 93 to Tucker Crossing, 3 miles south of Victor, and take the Bear Creek Road west for 2.3 miles. Turn right at a marked intersection with Red Crow Road, proceed north for 0.8 mile, and veer left for the final 3 miles. This trailhead offers generous parking space and packstock facilities. Primitive overnight campsites are available on the wooded flat just below the lot.

Keypoints:

0.0	Inception of trail at the Big Creek Trailhead.
1.3	Trail enters the Selway-Bitterroot Wilderness.
1.4	Pack bridge over Big Creek.
2.7	Trail crosses Saint Mary Creek.
4.9	Trail reaches the Teepee Rock area.
5.7	Log footbridge over Beaver Creek.
6.8	Log footbridge over Big Creek.
7.3	Junction with the South Fork Big Creek Trail (118S).
8.0	Pack bridge and dam at the Big Creek Lakes.
8.4	Flowing spring above Big Creek Lakes.
8.5	Unmarked junction with the abandoned Big Storm Trail (307X).
9.6	Unmarked junction with the Big Creek Divide Trail (306W).
10.3	Trail leaves the head of Big Creek Lakes.
11.5	Trail reaches the Montana-Idaho line at Packbox Pass.
14.1	Junction with the White Sand Lake Trail (51S).
14.5	Junction with the abandoned Garnet Creek Trail (43X); bear left.
17.1	Trail reenters Montana atop Bear Creek Pass.
18.5	Trail leaves the foot of Bryan Lake.
18.7	Trail crosses the Middle Fork.
18.8	Trail returns to east bank of the Middle Fork.
21.2	Unmarked junction with the abandoned North Fork Bear Creek Trail (305X).
21.3	Trail crosses the North Fork.
23.5	Unmarked junction with the South Fork Bear Creek Trail (304S).
23.7	Trail makes a wide ford of Bear Creek.

24.4   Trail leaves the Selway-Bitterroot Wilderness.
24.8   Falls along Bear Creek.
26.3   End of description at the Bear Creek Trailhead.

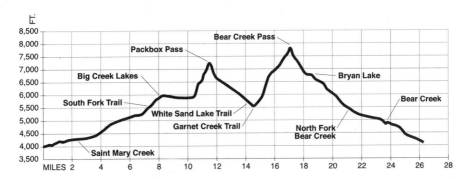

Suggested itinerary: This hike is best suited for a four-day backpacking trip. Perhaps the best way to divvy up the miles is to integrate White Sand Lake (technically a side trip) into your schedule, adding a mere 3.2 miles to the total distance cited above. The four-day arrangement outlined below allows plenty of passing time between campsites and for the two strenuous climbs over Packbox and Bear Creek passes, and leaves an easy downhill hike to the Bear Creek Trailhead for the final day. Tailor your travel plans and add extra days according to the number of side trips that you wish to make—on this trail alone there are more than enough possibilities to keep you occupied for a week or longer!

First day	—	Big Creek Trailhead to Big Creek Lakes, 9.6 miles; or to nameless lake, 11.2 miles.
Second day	—	Big Creek Lakes to White Sand Lake, 6.1 miles.
Third day	—	White Sand Lake to Bryan Lake, 6 miles.
Fourth day	—	Bryan Lake to Bear Creek Trailhead, 7.8 miles.

The hike: Without a doubt, the Big Creek Lakes are one of the Bitterroots' most scenic waterways, lying in a long glaciated valley just below the Bitterroot Divide. But as popular as they are, the lakes represent only the first leg of an exceptional point-to-point hike over two mountain passes to the Bear Creek Trailhead. Along the circuit you will find a variety of wildlife and some exceptionally scenic country. Views from the Bitterroot Divide are especially striking. With the very important *exception* of the Colt Killed Creek–Bear Creek Pass segment, the entire route follows mainline trails that present no route-finding difficulty.

The trail begins as a pleasant yet uneventful streamside retreat and quickly passes several side paths leading down the rushing stream. There is little to see as you proceed northwest into the wilderness and reach a pack bridge spanning Big Creek's boulder-covered channel. Upon reaching the far streambank, the trail ambles along within earshot of the waters, wandering past several campsites and gravel bars along the creek. (These are located quite close to the trail, however, and offer little privacy.) You encounter Saint Mary Creek and scattered pockets of grand fir and cedar over the next 2 miles, but progress is difficult to gauge without the benefit of any salient landmark.

After almost 5 miles of forest travel the trail arrives at Teepee Rock, where a boxcar-sized granite block is situated in a flat expanse of widely spaced fir and pine. A granite overhang protruding from this massive boulder provides temporary shelter from rainstorms. Just beyond this wooded flat, the trail enters a narrow defile with moss-covered boulders on the opposite hillside. Old larches and evergreens surround the trail as you continue to the footbridge over Beaver Creek. Another footbridge—this time over Big Creek itself—spans the stream at a slow-moving meander 6.8 miles from the trailhead. The route soon comes to a marked junction with the South Fork Big Creek Trail (118S); staying with the right-hand fork keeps you on the trail to Big Creek Lakes. Numerous earthen steps take the trail northwest through the trees to reach a buttressed concrete irrigation dam at the outlet of Big Creek Lakes. Pack bridges span Big Creek below the dam as well as the emergency spillway just beyond. From the dam area the well-traveled trail conveys you to an initial vantage of the deep blue waters.

Overlooked by treeless peaks of the Bitterroot Divide and adjoined by several thousand acre-feet of water stored for irrigation, the Big Creek Lakes are indeed a sight to behold. Several exceptionally picturesque views of the lakes and surrounding peaks are available as you traverse ledges south of Stormy Pass, where you may notice an unmarked junction with the long-abandoned trail (307X) that once led north to its crest. Campsites scattered at odd intervals along the entire lake perimeter offer a range of choices, with

A balmy autumn afternoon at the Big Creek Lakes.

those sites near the head of the lakes receiving the lightest use. Some of the sites more closely resemble scenes from a suburban park than a rugged wilderness camp; all, however, offer good access to the lake for anglers in pursuit of the resident rainbow and cutthroat trout. Big Creek Lakes is an extremely popular weekend spot, especially with stock users, and it shows.

A faint junction with the Big Creek Divide Trail (306W) turns up at the foot of a brush-filled clearing located just beyond the narrowest segment of the lakes. (If you find conditions at the Big Creek Lakes a bit too crowded and don't mind the extra effort, it may be worthwhile to give this trail a try.) The main trail begins a long switchbacked ascent to Packbox Pass soon after leaving the far southern end of the lakes and ties in with the Colt Killed Creek Trail (50ML) at the Bitterroots' crest. A small sign and exceptional view of the Big Creek Lakes greet visitors from this windswept point of entry into Idaho.

The trail descends into the headwaters of Packbox Creek and enters a landscape decidedly different from that east of the Bitterroot Divide. Unlike the high peaks found elsewhere in the Selway-Bitterroot, the summits west of the divide are significantly lower and lack the austere qualities of their Montana counterparts. The route passes through alternating timber and avalanche clearings in the upper reaches of the drainage, staying away from Packbox Creek itself but encountering a handful of puncheon walkways in varying stages of collapse. High grass and occasional blowdowns complicate matters as the descent continues; some stretches are deeply furrowed from years of erosion. A large horse camp and blazed tree marks the junction with the White Sand Lake Trail (51S) at 14.1 miles. White Sand Lake is a steep but worthwhile 1.6-mile departure from the main route—and its good fishing and campsites more than justify the added effort. Its location, roughly midway between the Big Creek and Bryan lakes, makes it a convenient stopover.

Beyond the White Sand Lake turnoff you continue downstream through heavy forest to a signed junction with the Garnet Creek Trail (43X). (Keep your eyes peeled for the junction, because the sign faces downhill and is easily overlooked!) Here you leave the mainline trail, cross Colt Killed Creek, and begin the long uphill pull toward Bear Creek Pass. This segment of the trail is unmaintained and in very poor condition, following a dim route with brush and lots of downed timber to slow your progress. There is little to see until you reach a talus field and begin switchbacking through the subalpine forest above. Views take in the upper length of the Colt Killed Creek drainage as well as Grave Peak on the western horizon and the basin containing Garnet Lake to the south. Cairns and cutout logs define the route as you swing northeast along a tributary of Garnet Creek.

The trail crosses and recrosses this small rivulet to reach an obscure junction at approximately the 7,600-foot contour. There is no easy way to recognize it unless you have been there before. The more distinctive left-hand fork follows a very old USFS trail through a patchwork of subalpine meadows and to a series of bluffs overlooking South Fork Lake on the Montana side of the Bitterroots. It makes a pleasant aside to the hike but will get you no closer to your destination; instead, follow the poorly defined right-hand fork south toward 7,800-foot Bear Creek Pass. Cairns mark the route and you will find a few gurgling springs that provide an unexpected source of water after the last snowfields have melted away.

Reentering Montana at Bear Creek Pass, the trail descends a rubble-strewn landscape at the headwaters of the Middle Fork Bear Creek drainage. Evidence of an old wildfire is fairly obvious in the haunting beauty of fire-killed snags. Bryan Lake grows larger in the basin ahead as you approach its rather narrow expanse and then draw alongside the shore at 18.3 miles. From the foot of Bryan Lake the route continues downstream to reach the Bear Creek Trailhead, 7.8 miles away. For further details regarding this drainage and its lakes, refer to the Bear Creek description.

Side trips: To escape the shoreline crowds and general clamor of the Big Creek Lakes, spur trails offer two possible avenues of investigation. Relatively few backpackers attempt either of them. These include the South Fork Big Creek (118S) and Big Creek Divide (306W) trails.

▲ The **South Fork Big Creek Trail (118S)** follows a deteriorated tread southwest from the main Big Creek Trail for 3.7 miles, twice crossing the South Fork Big Creek via downed logs. Good canyon vistas are available at a few select points, but the trail is primarily routed in the trees. Boggy terrain will cause problems for those traveling on horseback. Downed trees are a frequent obstacle, and the trail grows indistinct as it crosses several avalanche openings interspersed throughout otherwise densely forested stream bottom. You reach South Fork Lake after a total ascent of 1,300 feet from the junction. This deep lake harbors a healthy population of cutthroat trout and sparkles like a sapphire in the shadows of Sky Pilot Peak, beautifully rendered in a dozen shades of gray to the south.

▲ The trickiest part of hiking the **Big Creek Divide Trail (306W)** lies in simply finding its takeoff point. The unmarked junction is located by following the mainline trail southwest around the Big Creek Lakes for approximately 1.6 miles. It shows up at a small campsite immediately south of where you cross two narrow, brushy clearings in close succession. (A bit of poking around in the forest may be necessary, but the trail, once found, is unmistakable.)

The trail climbs steeply on switchbacks, angling southwest up the wall of the canyon for 1.4 miles to the nameless lake. The route is mostly through stands of Engelmann spruce and Douglas-fir, with a few brushy areas in between. Fresh blazes and saw works defined the route during my October 3, 1999, visit. You reach the remote lakeshore following a steep, 1,000-foot ascent. There are some good campsites around the foot of the lake and near its outlet, and for the most part they seem little used. Subalpine forest provides a natural windbreak and sheer granite faces rising abruptly from the head of the lake to the very crest of the Bitterroot Range. A cutthroat fishery thrives in these deep, cold waters. At one time the trail actually continued southwest over the Bitterroot Divide to merge with the Maud Creek Trail (64X) above Maud Lake; today, only fleeting remnants of the original route remain.

Looking south into the Middle Fork headwaters from Bear Creek Pass.

Three other side trips along the Big Creek to Bear Creek circuit are also available. These include spur trails along the North and South forks of Bear Creek and to White Sand Lake on the Idaho side of the Bitterroots. All three are discussed in greater detail elsewhere in this book.

ADDITIONAL TRAILS

Bass Pass (301X), 3.8 miles (6.1 km). This trail connects Bass Lake with the Kootenai Creek Trail (53ML) via a low pass between their respective drainages. It is a fairly rough trail and was abandoned by USFS trail crews years ago. South of Bass Pass the trail is reportedly steep and difficult to follow among the beargrass and pockets of aspen. Its junction with the Kootenai Creek Trail is unmarked; nevertheless, an experienced backcountry traveler can successfully follow the route. Plan to take your time if you want to give it a try.

Big Storm (307X), 1.3 miles (2.1 km). This hike leads north to Stormy Pass from an unmarked junction above the Big Creek Lakes, just west of the spring shown on USGS maps. It offers a very steep route into Idaho, climbing 1,320 feet through subalpine forest and heavy brushfields to the 7,340-foot pass. The descent into the South Fork Storm Creek headwaters on the Idaho side is extremely steep and difficult. The trail was originally constructed during the 1920s but has been abandoned by the USFS for decades, as have the upper 5.4 miles of the Storm Creek Trail (99ML) on the adjoining Clearwater National Forest.

125

West Fork Ranger District

34 Baker Lake

Highlights:	A collection of lakes with excellent angling and spectacular scenery.
Type of hike:	Out-and-back day hike.
Total distance:	2.4 miles or 3.9 kilometers (round trip).
Difficulty:	Easy.
Best months:	July through September.
Elevation gain:	880 feet.
Maps:	Burnt Ridge and Trapper Peak USGS quads.

Trailhead access: From the settlement of Conner, follow Montana Highway 473 south for 3 miles. Shortly after passing the Trapper Creek Job Corps, USFS signs announce turnoffs to the Trapper Creek and Baker Lake trailheads in rapid succession. Take the Baker Lake turnoff and follow the rough and frequently rutted Pierce Creek Road (5634) for 10 additional miles to its terminus. The undeveloped trailhead can accommodate as many as seven vehicles, but there is scant room even to turn around.

Keypoints:
- 0.0 Inception of trail at the Baker Lake Trailhead.
- 0.2 Trail passes west of Baker Point.
- 1.2 Terminus of maintained trail at Baker Lake.

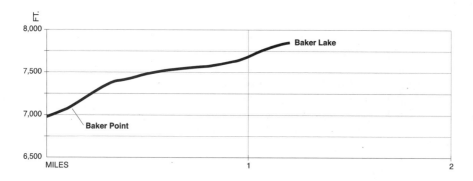

The hike: This short and easy-to-follow route offers access to three small lakes lodged within the granite flank of Trapper Peak. The lakes themselves are enchanted jewels encountered in order of increasing allure. Baker Lake in particular is an excellent choice for older folks or families with small children, making it quite popular.

The trail leads south from the parking area before running uphill at the edge of a bald talus shoulder. Frequently coarse and rocky underfoot, the route gains elevation steadily but is never steep for prolonged periods. A bit more climbing leads you to the shattered caricatures of Baker Point, whose

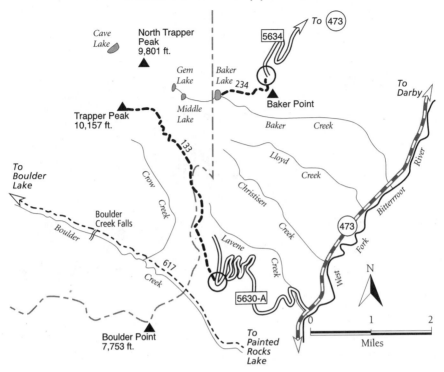

Baker Lake • Trapper Peak

eastern vista encompasses a variety of peaks ranging from those in the Anaconda Range to equally mysterious summits in the Sapphire Mountains. Upon leaving Baker Point, the trail retreats west and completes a brief traverse to reach Baker Lake. Guarded by the imposing eastern ridge of 10,157-foot Trapper Peak, Baker Lake draws anglers with its excellent cutthroat fishing. Campsites are scattered in the forest at either end of the lake, but most have been badly degraded from years of high-impact camping. Please adhere to zero-impact camp ethics if you decide to spend the night.

Option: From the inlet at Baker Lake, an obvious but unmaintained route continues upstream and soon passes a weedy marshland where Baker Creek meanders in sinuous oxbows. The tread quickly disappears as it enters designated wilderness; downed timber requires you to make several "detours" enroute to Middle Lake. The lake itself is a small, stone-studded pool nestled in a wooded pocket. Although a few small trout manage to survive in these waters, fishing is of secondary importance given its scenic qualities.

All traces of a trail vanish as the route ascends exposed bedrock above Middle Lake. With shredded battlements towering overhead, you soon arrive at Gem Lake. Salmon-colored slabs decorate the depths of this unusually attractive lake, whose waters glow in sea green phosphorescence. The surrounding cirque walls—harboring perpetual snowfields within their

Baker Lake.

fluted fortifications—shelter the location from prevailing winds and cast the lake in early evening shadow. In the interest of preserving the delicate surroundings, visitors are encouraged to refrain from building campfires.

35 Boulder Point

Highlights: A historic L-4 fire lookout with a spectacular panorama.
Type of hike: Out-and-back day hike or overnighter.
Total distance: 4.2 miles (round trip).
Difficulty: Difficult.
Best months: July through September.
Elevation gain: 2,550 feet.
Map: Boulder Peak USGS quad.

Special considerations: This ridgeline trail offers no practical access to water, so top off your canteens before setting out. Don't count on finding water in Barn Draw—its upper reaches are usually waterless by August.

Trailhead access: From Darby follow U.S. Highway 93 south for 4.4 miles to the junction with Montana Highway 473. Continue south for 13.2 miles to Barn Draw Road (373). Turn right and proceed for 1.9 miles, passing various side roads in the meantime, to reach a marked forest road junction for the Boulder Point Trailhead. Turn right once more and follow the good dirt

Boulder Point • Nelson Lake • Boulder Creek

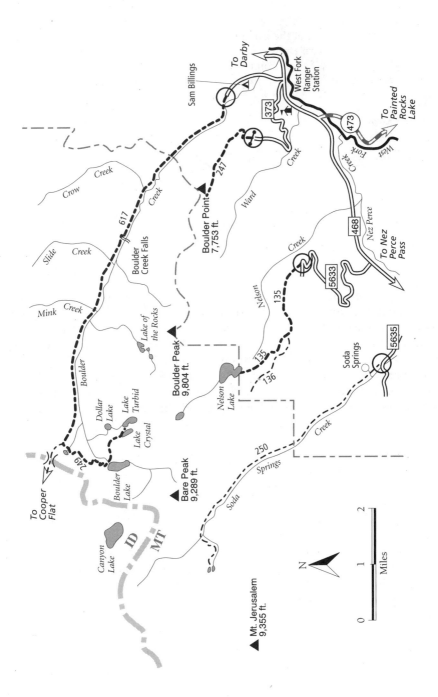

road for another 1.1 miles to the signed trailhead. The amenities are rather sparse—parking for 10 vehicles, a sign with inaccurate trail distances, and a barricaded road are all you will find.

Keypoints:
- 0.0 Inception of trail at the gated terminus of FR 373.
- 0.2 Trail crosses Barn Draw.
- 0.7 Trail runs atop School Point.
- 2.1 Boulder Point Lookout.

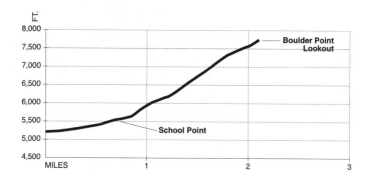

The hike: The lookout atop Boulder Point ranks as one of the Bitterroots' most underrated and least known destinations. This steep route remains in generally good repair, with only a few downed trees and a poorly defined segment atop School Point to confuse the issue. Use is light—decidedly less than many other trail-accessible Bitterroot peaks.

From the barricaded terminus of Barn Draw Road, the trail sets out with the former roadbed underfoot, contours across Barn Draw, and turns southeast below 5,559-foot School Point. The misdirection is only temporary, however, and soon a steep ascent ensues as you double back to follow an abandoned jeep trail northwest across the bald shoulder and gain the ridgeline atop School Point. This open expanse furnishes sights of early scenic interest, including northwest views to Trapper Peak as well as an overlook of the valley cut by the West Fork Bitterroot River. The route then resumes its ascent with renewed focus and forges upslope at a very steep pitch.

There is little to see for some time due to heavy forest cover, but the trail generally remains within 150 yards of the main ridge and tackles the slope with interspersed switchbacks. Approaching the 7,200-foot contour, the trail swings west to avoid a steep expanse of loose talus on its way across the slopes high above Ward Creek. Additional switchbacks escort you until the lookout at last emerges from the broken rocks and whitebark pine forest to the northeast.

The rustic outpost, a classic L-4 structure, was originally constructed in 1937. As of 1998 the lookout was unmanned but open to public use. Relics left from bygone days include two castiron stoves and the original bronze alidade once use to plot forest fire coordinates. An informal logbook contains entries ranging from weather observations to high praise for Boulder

Boulder Peak rises beyond the Boulder Point Lookout.

Point as "the Bitterroots' finest trail." An impressive vantage greets the odd traveler from the lookout's creaking catwalk—views of 10,157-foot Trapper Peak and Boulder Peak are especially memorable.

Options: Boulder Point Lookout is the traditional staging point for year-round mountaineering expeditions to 9,804-foot Boulder Peak. There is no established trail. The summit ascent entails a 2,100-foot climb over a distance of about 3 miles, depending on the route you take. The USFS welcomes public use of the lookout on a first-come basis. Please respect the privilege. (And be sure to latch the shutters and secure the door before you leave!)

36 Bad Luck Mountain

Highlights:	Scenic views of the Selway River canyon, the White Cap drainage, and numerous peaks and points.
Type of hike:	Out-and-back day hike.
Total distance:	5.2 miles or 8.4 kilometers (round trip).
Difficulty:	Difficult.
Best months:	May through September.
Elevation gain:	2,360 feet.
Elevation loss:	100 feet.
Maps:	Burnt Strip Mountain and Mount George USGS quads.

Bad Luck Mountain

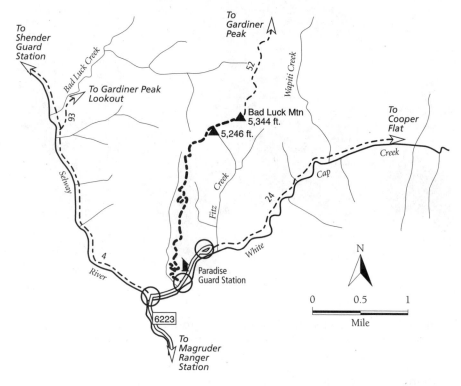

Special considerations: This steep, hot trail offers no convenient access to drinking water for the final 2 miles. Carry extra water in your pack and be sure to stay alert for rattlesnakes as well.

Trailhead access: Take U.S. Highway 93 to its junction with Montana Highway 473, 4.4 miles south of Darby. Continue southwest for 14.3 miles to Nez Perce Road (468), and veer right. Follow this high-standard gravel road across the Bitterroot Divide at Nez Perce Pass and downstream to Paradise Guard Station, 46 miles from MT 473. Plentiful parking is available at the trailhead, but take care not to block the road or other vehicles in this popular staging area. The take-off point is located along the road 100 yards west of Paradise Guard Station; it was unmarked but obvious at the time of my June 2, 1999, visit.

Keypoints:
- 0.0   Inception of trail at Paradise Guard Station.
- 2.4   False west summit of Bad Luck Mountain.
- 2.6   End of description atop Bad Luck Mountain.

The hike: At first glance, the trail to Bad Luck Mountain appears so short and insignificant that you might guess it to be boring. Not so. This ridgeline route is surprisingly deep in scenic value, traversing mostly open terrain with

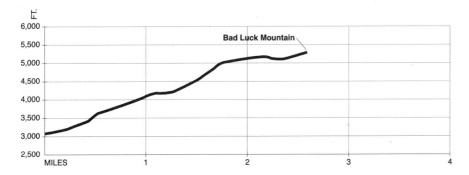

generous views of the Selway-Bitterroot backcountry. Bad Luck was a very pleasant surprise the first time I hiked it.

The trail ventures into the brush and trees above the road, initially making its way through green undergrowth but soon emerging onto open slopes that characterize so much of the route to Bad Luck Mountain. Steep switchbacks guide the trail sharply uphill through clearings filled with arrowleaf balsamroot. Views of the surrounding country improve in dramatic fashion as the trail gains the ridgeline and continues north. The mountain flanks directly southeast across the canyon are especially striking, razed years ago in a wildfire that reduced conifer forest to deciduous brushfields but spared stringers of timber along some of the minor ridges and draws.

Passing through stately stands of ponderosa and Douglas-fir, the trail eases into a more moderate grade before resuming its steep ascent. As the elevation continues to build, multiple peaks thrust into view while a succession of high mountainsides dive precipitously toward the Selway River, which remains unseen in the canyon to the south. The route then angles northeast along the crest of the ridge to reach a false peak—not to be confused with Bad Luck Mountain—0.5 mile west of the actual lookout site. High above the head of Fitz Creek the well-defined path intersects numerous crisscrossing game trails, some so distinctive as to rival the main trail in appearance. Distractions aside, you reach the former lookout site atop Bad Luck Mountain 2.6 miles after leaving the trailhead.

Bad Luck Mountain is little more than an unimposing knob protruding above the rest of the ridge. But even without its long-gone lookout, the quality of the view belies its modest elevation. According to one popular legend, Bad Luck takes its name from a den of rattlesnakes uncovered during construction of the lookout in 1939. A convenient story or the truth—I'll let you decide.

Option: The trail continues northeast beyond Bad Luck Mountain, straddling the divide between the Wapiti and Bad Luck drainages. Simply follow this undulating ridge, which offers excellent opportunities for wildlife viewing, as far as you like before retracing your steps to the trailhead.

37 Castle Rock

Highlights:	An unobstructed view of the Bitterroot Mountains and Blue Joint Wilderness Study Area (WSA) from atop Castle Rock.
Type of hike:	Out-and-back day hike.
Total distance:	5.4 miles or 8.7 kilometers (round trip).
Difficulty:	Moderate.
Best months:	June through September.
Elevation gain:	1,400 feet.
Elevation loss:	260 feet.
Maps:	Bare Cone and Nez Perce Peak USGS quads.

Special considerations: This is strictly a ridgeline trail, offering no convenient access to springs or streams for drinking water. Note also that the final 0.2 mile is cross-country and may entail some scrambling on all fours. Those who visit Castle Rock in early June should expect some minor difficulties because snowpack will likely conceal the most obvious routes to the top.

Trailhead access: Take U.S. Highway 93 to its junction with Montana Highway 473, 4.4 miles south of Darby. Follow the pavement southwest for 14.3 miles to Nez Perce Road (468), keep right, and continue on the good gravel road to Nez Perce Pass in another 16 miles. A large parking area greets you atop the pass; outhouse and stock facilities are available. (Please avoid parking on the USFS helicopter landing site located here.) The trail to Castle Rock starts into the trees south of the pass.

Keypoints:
- 0.0 Inception of trail at Nez Perce Pass.
- 0.4 Junction with the Castle Rock Trail (627ML).
- 2.7 End of description atop Castle Rock.

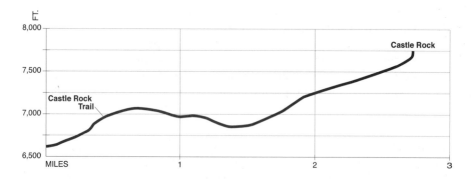

The hike: This route follows a segment of the old southern Nez Perce Trail east from Nez Perce Pass to the crest of 7,722-foot Castle Rock. Located within the 65,000-acre Blue Joint roadless area, this peak stands on the threshold of two vast wildernesses—the Frank Church–River of No Return and the

Castle Rock • Nez Perce Peak • Sheephead Creek Loop

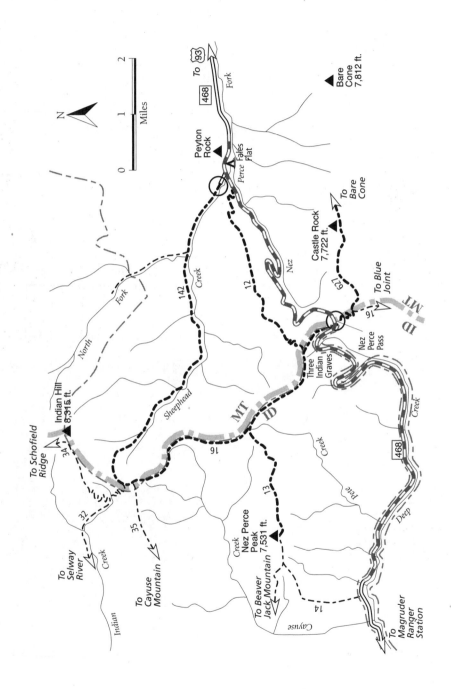

Selway-Bitterroot—but is currently part of neither. The summit view puts abstract acreage into perspective: From its summit you see only a fraction of the combined wilderness, which, at over 4 million acres, is large enough to encompass the state of Delaware three times over.

The trail starts south into timber just beyond the horse-loading ramp and snow course marker, straddling the ridge defining the boundary between Montana and Idaho. There is little to see at first as the trail ascends steeply to reach the junction with the Castle Rock Trail (627ML) in less than 0.5 mile. A weathered sign inscribed "Castle Rock" marks this branch point for posterity.

The steep grade soon levels upon entering a subalpine pocket meadow with northwest views extending toward Nez Perce Peak. A sharp northeast bend forces the ridgeline route downhill, where you reenter lodgepole and fir forest as the trail makes its way deeper into Montana. Reaching a wooded saddle 1 mile short of Castle Rock, the trail begins its ascent anew and, with its quarry occasionally visible above the terrain ahead, follows an easterly bearing toward the looming landmark. The well-defined route traverses areas that are mostly forested, but not impenetrably so.

Some 2.5 miles after leaving Nez Perce Pass you arrive at the foot of Castle Rock, its ramparts flanked with scree and snowfields. True to its name, the peak is fairly well fortified; the most viable routes to the summit originate on its southern slopes. Castle Rock owes its topographic prominence to the durable porphyritic andesite exposed throughout—actually the eroded core of a long-inactive volcano. A large cairn and multiple bronze benchmarks guard the highest point. Literally dozens of high Bitterroot peaks crowd the horizon as you stand atop the windswept heights of Castle Rock, but those to the north seem more spectacular than the rest. Mount Jerusalem, at 9,355

Castle Rock is the erosion-resistant core of an ancient volcano.

feet, looks especially impressive as it towers head and shoulders above its lesser neighbors some 7 miles away.

Option: You can follow the Castle Rock Trail as far east as Bare Cone, site of an active USFS fire lookout. The lookout is vehicle accessible, so arranging a shuttle between pass and peak is not out of the question.

38 Nelson Lake

Highlights:	A lightly used trail to a rockslide-impounded lake.
Type of hike:	Out-and-back day hike or overnighter.
Total distance:	5.4 miles or 8.7 kilometers (round trip).
Difficulty:	Difficult.
Best months:	July through September.
Elevation gain:	1,700 feet.
Elevation loss:	600 feet.
Map:	Boulder Peak USGS quad.

See Map on Page 129

Trailhead access: Take Montana Highway 473 from its junction with U.S. Highway 93, 4.4 miles south of Darby. Follow the paved route for 14.3 miles to its junction with the Nez Perce Road (468) and veer right. Continue to the Nelson-Gemmel Road (13402) after another 2.8 miles. (The mountain roads in this area are poorly marked and a bit confusing for first-time visitors, so don't forget to bring along the Bitterroot National Forest map for reference.) Turn right and follow this good dirt road into the foothills, taking the right-hand fork at an unmarked junction with Forest Road 5633 after 2.6 miles. From here continue 2.4 more miles to reach the trailhead pullout, where a broken signpost denotes the trail's point of origin. Parking in the immediate area is limited to room for eight vehicles, and no other amenities are available. The open hillside offers a nice southeast view of Piquett Mountain.

Keypoints:
- 0.0　Inception of trail along FR 5633.
- 1.6　Junction with the Nelson Lake Overlook (136X).
- 2.7　Trail enters the Selway-Bitterroot Wilderness at Nelson Lake.

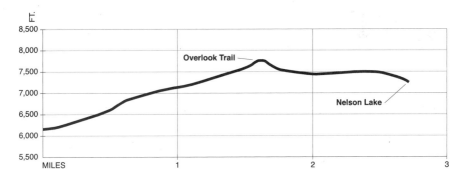

The hike: Here is a lightly used and delightfully primitive trail. Located less than 3 miles from the trailhead, Nelson Lake is something of an anomaly, receiving far fewer visitors than the short round-trip distance would seemingly imply. And unlike the irrigation dams so common throughout the Bitterroots, Nelson Lake's outlet conforms to no standard architecture and is instead backed up behind an enormous rockslide—an impressive illustration of the processes driving the evolution of mountain landscapes.

Beginning from its no-frills trailhead, the route follows an old skid road along a generally northwest bearing for a short distance. Traversing forested country high above the Gemmel and Halford drainages, the trail continues uphill until it gains the ridgeline and reaches the first partial views of Boulder Peak, a broad gray summit that rises 2 miles to the north. A second ascent follows close on the heels of the first, and the ridgeline route soon converges on an unmarked trail junction. The left fork leads to a delightful overlook of Nelson Lake and the surrounding wilderness, but the route to Nelson Lake follows the right-hand fork and soon begins a brief descent into the Nelson Creek drainage. (Both routes are blazed beyond the junction, so be careful to follow the appropriate fork.)

The route alternately gains and loses elevation beyond the unsigned junction as the surrounding views continue to change. After another 0.5 mile, the forest gives way to an unobstructed view of Boulder Peak and the canyon below, while the route carefully contours above a wide talus apron nestled directly beneath a series of overhanging cliffs. Cairns and blazes guide the trail, whose tread rapidly deteriorates, farther along the hillside. These navigational cues approximate the correct course as it undulates with changing topography straddling the 7,400-foot contour. Often the route is difficult to follow across the broken rock. Pleasant downstream views extend along the lower reaches of the Nelson Creek drainage as it descends through a roadless canyon and makes a wide turn out of sight to reach the West Fork of the Bitterroot River.

Approaching Nelson Lake, the canyon scene grows increasingly eerie—dead snags and enormous gray boulders attest to the devastation wrought in a rockslide that forever impounded Nelson Lake some centuries ago. The slide and its origins high in the southern flanks of Boulder Peak remain obvious to this day and allow you to gauge the scale of movement that took place. Passing above the incoming rubble-filled basin, the route charges to the crest of the boulders, then drops into the craterlike depression to reach the shoreline.

This deep body of water is surrounded by massive boulders and is overlooked from three directions by peaks both named and nameless. Having long ago been impounded by debris, the shoreline lacks any discernible outlet, and its surface elevation is subject to a 20-foot seasonal drawdown cycle as water leaks through the boulders and re-forms Nelson Creek nearly 1 mile downstream. Anglers have reported good cutthroat fishing at Nelson Lake, but I found the trout temperamental and entirely unwilling to take a hook during my September 12, 1998 visit. Available campsites largely occur above

Looking northwest across Nelson Lake.

the inlet and offer fine base camp opportunities for mountaineers interested in climbing 9,804-foot Boulder Peak or other summits in the area.

Side trips: As already noted, the Nelson Lake Overlook (136X) provides a sensational ridgeline ascent culminating with an excellent vantage of the Nelson Creek drainage and surrounding high peaks. This 1.3-mile diversion entails a sustained climb yet provides no practical access to water. Try this side trip in late September, when the many alpine larches show their fall colors and the rarified mountain air is at its clearest. Take along extra drinking water, and do not forget your camera.

39 Trapper Peak

See Map on Page 127

Highlights:	Outstanding high-altitude scenery atop the Bitterroots' mightiest summit.
Type of hike:	Out-and-back day hike.
Total distance:	8 miles or 12.9 kilometers (round trip).
Difficulty:	Strenuous.
Best months:	July through September.
Elevation gain:	3,820 feet.
Maps:	Boulder Peak and Trapper Peak USGS quads.

Special considerations: Although the route described below is nontechnical, certain segments near timberline are poorly defined and tricky to follow, particularly on the return trip. (This is especially true early in the summer, when extensive snowfields still blanket much of the high mountain flanks.) Be sure to take plenty of water because rivulets are scarce after the major snowfields disappear. An early start is also advisable, as is an accurate weather forecast.

Trailhead access: Take U.S. Highway 93 to its junction with Montana Highway 473, 4.4 miles south of Darby. Follow the pavement south for 11.4 miles to a marked turnoff for Trapper Peak. Climb the Lavene Creek Road 5630-A for 6.5 miles to reach the trailhead, an informal affair denoted by two wooden signs and a handful of parking spaces. Vehicles with two-wheel drive should have no problems.

Keypoints:
   0.0   Inception of trail at the Trapper Peak Trailhead.
   1.6   Trail enters the Selway-Bitterroot Wilderness.
   4.0   Trail reaches the summit of Trapper Peak.

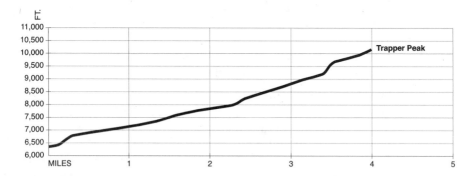

The hike: Trapper Peak and its northern counterpart rise together as a splendid granite massif 10 miles southwest of Darby. Those in search of serious Bitterroot altitude need look no further than this majestic peak, where the Selway-Bitterroot Wilderness reaches its zenith and a scene of dramatic allure surpassing that of any other summit in the range.

From its humble beginnings the trail climbs steeply through a mixture of Douglas-fir and lodgepole pine. After a brisk ascent of several hundred yards, the course tapers into a less visceral pitch on the leeward side of a boulder-strewn ridge. Narrow footpaths cut left to overlooks of the Boulder drainage and its namesake cataracts. Visible to the southwest is Boulder Point, site of one of the few remaining L-4 lookouts that have not lapsed into obsolescence and disrepair over the years. The main trail continues north into steep and generally featureless terrain before entering the tenuous realm of whitebark pine.

The trail bends northwest and soon gains its long-awaited liberation from the forest, emerging from windswept alpine larch at approximately the

140

Trapper Peak–the final ridge.

9,000-foot contour. A massive detachment of Trapper Peak is the most striking landmark on the western horizon while a dozen or more clearcuts in the southern breaks of the Bitterroot River provide the only objectionable note. The trail then fades into a mountaineer's route interrupted with late-season snowfields and marked only by cairns leading to a high saddle just east of the true summit. From here a brief talus scramble places you squarely atop the 10,157-foot peak. A metal summit register is available to record your accomplishment.

Harbored in a cirque below the peak is an exquisitely developed rock glacier, its lobes of ice and granite drawn by time and gravity toward azure Cave Lake. Beyond this foreground interest extends an undulating sequence of granite fins anchored by El Capitan, whose distinct silhouette looms several miles west of the mountain front but still well inside Montana. Almost lost to the curvature of earth and refraction of its atmosphere is 11,147-foot Torrey Mountain, which rises like a specter from the East Pioneer Mountains some 70 miles to the southeast.

40 Nez Perce Peak

See Map on Page 135

Highlights: A lightly traveled and exceptionally scenic ridgeline retreat.
Type of hike: Out-and-back day hike or overnighter.
Total distance: 10.8 miles or 17.4 kilometers (round trip).
Difficulty: Moderate.
Best months: July through September.
Elevation gain: 1,750 feet.
Elevation loss: 800 feet.
Map: Nez Perce Peak USGS quad.

Special considerations: The hike to Nez Perce Peak is high and waterless, lacking any convenient opportunity to replenish emptied water bottles. Fill a few extra bottles before you leave.

Trailhead access: Take U.S. Highway 93 to its junction with Montana Highway 473, 4.4 miles south of Darby. Follow the pavement southwest for 14.3 miles to the Nez Perce Road (468), keep right, and continue on the good gravel road to Nez Perce Pass in another 16 miles. A large parking area greets you atop the pass; outhouse and stock facilities are both available. The trailhead is quite spacious, so please avoid parking on the helicopter landing zone located here. The trail to Nez Perce Peak, marked here as the "Divide Trail 16," starts into the trees north of the pass.

Keypoints:
0.0   Inception of trail at Nez Perce Pass.
0.8   Marked junction with the Fales Flat Trail (12W); stay left.
1.0   Trail passes marked Indian graves.
2.9   Signed junction with the Southern Nez Perce Trail (13W); bear left.
5.4   End of trail description atop Nez Perce Peak.

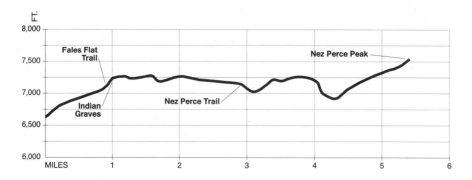

The hike: This is an unusually scenic out-and-back hike into some very interesting country. The trail receives light use throughout the summer months and will appeal to hikers with a preference for routes with lots of ups and downs. A considerable variety of wildlife inhabits the high country along the divide; the stateline area is thoroughly stalked by Montana and Idaho sportsmen each fall.

From its take-off point along the Montana-Idaho line, the trail climbs steadily through the timber northwest of Nez Perce Pass. The going is somewhat tedious for the first 0.5 mile, but the grade lessens significantly as you reach the first of an intermittent succession of subalpine meadows along the windward face of the Bitterroot Divide. A backward glance from here reveals the blocky mass of 7,722-foot Castle Rock rising well inside Montana 2 miles to the southeast.

One mile into the hike you meet an obscure junction with the Fales Flat Trail (12W) and pass the grave of Francis Adams, a Salish Indian interred a mere three paces from the trail and a stone's throw from the crest of the Bitterroot Range. A simple marble headstone marks his final resting place. Farther along, the route contours gently across the mostly open, south-facing mountainside. Access to the ridgeline above requires only a short jaunt to its crest. Here, too, high on the slopes above MacGregor Creek, Nez Perce Peak emerges from behind the topography, still some miles distant but appearing deceptively close at hand.

The trail bends northwest along the ridge and continues through more open parkland for a time, then reenters lodgepole forest above the headwaters of Pete Creek. A brief descent takes you to the marked junction to Nez Perce Peak at mile 2.9. (Three-foot-deep snowpack concealed much of the tread when I first hiked this trail on June 12, 1999.) From here the route continues west over a small humpback in the ridge and into a tree-covered saddle beyond. A crude hunter's camp is located here. A sharp ascent takes the trail into yet another expansive park; once more, there are numerous peaks and canyons to divert your gaze as you traverse this clearing. Fir and pine again surround the trail as it heads straight to the top of 7,531-foot Nez Perce Peak in a fairly steep final pitch.

From the metasedimentary bedrock exposed atop the peak unfolds a scene of primeval splendor—not so much as a single clearcut mars the view. From Salmon Mountain to Bare Cone and from Indian Hill to Three Prong Ridge, distant peaks and seemingly impenetrable terrain extend in every compass direction. A rectangle constructed from the native bedrock marks the outline of a USFS cabin that stood here for two decades. In its absence, rusty nails and shards of glass still litter the crevices among the stones.

Option: In addition to the out-and-back route to Nez Perce Peak, the Schumaker Ridge Trail (14X) leaves open the possibility of an 8.1-mile shuttle from Nez Perce Pass to a point 0.2 mile west of the Kit Carson outfitter camp on the corridor road. Before attempting such a hike, note that the terrain west of Nez Perce Peak is quite steep and the trail, which incurs a drop of 2,590 feet between Nez Perce Peak and Deep Creek, has been abandoned and dropped from the USFS trail inventory.

41 Spot Mountain Lookout

Highlights:	Dramatic scenery and a lightly used trail to one of the Bitterroots' least visited lookouts.
Type of hike:	Out-and-back day hike or overnighter.
Total distance:	11.8 miles or 19 kilometers (round trip).
Difficulty:	Strenuous.
Best months:	July through September.
Elevation gain:	4,750 feet.
Elevation loss:	140 feet.
Map:	Spot Mountain USGS quad.

Special considerations: This is an arduous hike, steep and strenuous throughout. Bring plenty of water. Even well-conditioned hikers will have trouble reaching the lookout in less than four hours, so get an early start and plan to take your time.

Trailhead access: Take U.S. Highway 93 to its junction with Montana Highway 473, 4.4 miles south of Darby. Continue southwest for 14.2 miles to Nez Perce Road (468), veer right, and follow this high-standard gravel road over Nez Perce Pass and downstream to the Spot Mountain Trailhead, 38.9 miles from MT 473. A sign and steel pack bridge over the Selway denote the beginnings of the trail to Spot Mountain. Facilities include a stock unloading ramp and parking space for up to five vehicles in the pullout beside the road.

Keypoints:
- 0.0 Trail crosses the Selway River via pack bridge.
- 5.0 Marked junction with the Mount Aura Trail (40S).
- 5.2 Trail runs past a mountainside spring.
- 5.9 End of description at the Spot Mountain Lookout.

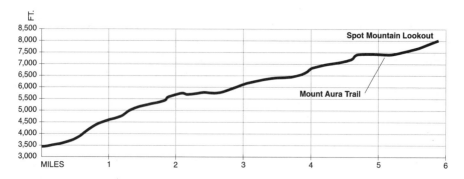

The hike: This well-defined trail provides a strenuous day hike to the crest of Spot Mountain, site of a USFS fire lookout still manned during the summer months. The peak is a long way from anywhere and sees very few visitors; recreational use is virtually nonexistent outside of hunting season. Originally excluded when Congress designated the Selway-Bitterroot

Spot Mountain Lookout

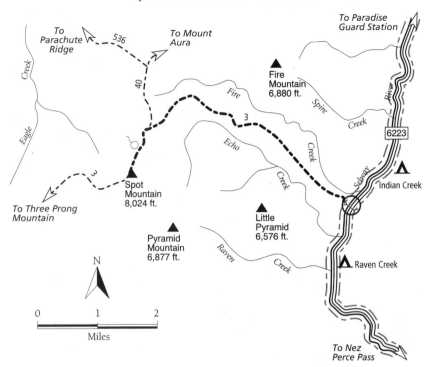

Wilderness in 1964, full federal protection for Spot Mountain and much of the upper Selway country was restored with passage of the Central Idaho Wilderness Act of 1980.

The trail first crosses the steel bridge over the Selway River and then immediately starts up the steep, forested hillside on switchbacks. A blistering ascent ensues as you climb without pause for the next 2 miles opposite 5,750-foot Nick Wynn Mountain. Upon gaining the ridgeline the trail traverses ponderosa stands offering views to the south of Little Pyramid and the forested lower reaches of Echo Creek. The route straddles the divide with Fire Creek and drops into a timbered saddle, only to later reemerge in open lodgepole forest from which Spot Mountain is visible to the southwest for the first time. The peak appears almost perfectly symmetric from this vantage, with the lonely summit house standing atop a pyramid of its own.

Intervening terrain abruptly terminates this view of this peak as you venture into terrain razed in a 1996 wildfire. The trail gains elevation at a steady rate and circles above a burned-over bowl at the head of Fire Creek. From here you may look northwest beyond 6,880-foot Fire Mountain to some of the mightiest Bitterroot summits, including the likes of El Capitan and the Como Peaks. The few lightly used campsites found nearby offer no convenient access to water.

The tread continues southwest and, following another very steep uphill pitch, reaches somewhat level terrain cloaked in green subalpine forest. Among the fir and pine you soon arrive at a junction with the Mount Aura Trail (40S), marked with a metal sign. The trail to Spot Mountain stays left and next converges on a spacious trailside campsite at 5.2 miles. An excellent spring issues from the ground in this area and provides a reliable, easy-to-find source of water throughout the year. Farther along, the tread makes its way into the burn again and pauses at the foot of a steep final rise still blanketed with snowdrifts in early July. A rough footpath lunges straight up the ridge to the lookout (visible above) while an easier grade continues around the peak's western flank to reach the same.

Spot Mountain is the site of a third-generation USFS lookout still manned each summer. The summit boasts a commanding view of much of the upper Selway country, and views extend to the higher peaks in virtually every corner of the Selway-Bitterroot Wilderness. There are the usual suspects, such as El Capitan and Trapper Peak, along with the less recognizable Wylies Peak and Mount Paloma. With such a sweeping panorama it is little wonder why Spot Mountain Lookout survives as an active lookout into the 1990s when so many others in the Selway were decommissioned and destroyed in the decades before.

Option: If you're out for more than a day hike, consider extending your itinerary to include 8,182-foot Three Prong Mountain. The trail between Spot Mountain and Three Prong Ridge is no better than marginal and is recommended only for those with excellent navigation and faint-trail skills.

Looking north toward Green Ridge and Mount Aura from the Spot Mountain Lookout.

42 Flat Creek

Highlights:	Solitude of a degree unmatched elsewhere on the West Fork District.
Type of hike:	Out-and-back day hike or overnighter.
Total distance:	14.2 miles or 22.8 kilometers (round trip).
Difficulty:	Moderate.
Best months:	July through September.
Elevation gain:	330 feet.
Elevation loss:	2,330 feet.
Map:	Magruder Mountain USGS quad.

Special considerations: This unusual trail requires a steep, steady descent with few convenient campsites and limited water availability. Other than Flat Creek and the Little Clearwater River, a spring-fed perennial stream midway along the trail is the only water close at hand: Top off your bottles and be prepared for a slow ascent on the return trip.

Trailhead access: Take U.S. Highway 93 to its junction with Montana Highway 473, 4.4 miles south of Darby. Continue southwest for 14.2 miles to Nez Perce Road (468), veer right, and follow this high-standard gravel road over Nez Perce Pass and downstream to the Selway River Bridge, 34.9 miles from MT 473. The well-maintained road leading west from the Selway River is especially steep and narrow, so drive slowly and stay alert for oncoming vehicles. You reach the Flat Creek Trailhead after another 8.7 miles. Reflecting its light use, there are only two or three vehicle spaces here, along with a hitchrail and USFS sign describing the Magruder Massacre for which the corridor was named. This is no place for a flat tire: Trailheads between Burnt Knob and the Selway River are among the most remote in the lower 48.

Keypoints:
- 0.0   Inception of trail at the Flat Creek Trailhead.
- 1.2   Unmarked junction with an abandoned inlead trail (15X); stay right.
- 1.3   Trail traverses Magruder Saddle.
- 1.4   Unsigned junction with the Southern Nez Perce Trail (13W); bear left.
- 3.4   Trailside spring.
- 6.8   Trail crosses Flat Creek.
- 7.1   Trail fords the Little Clearwater River to reach an outfitter's camp.

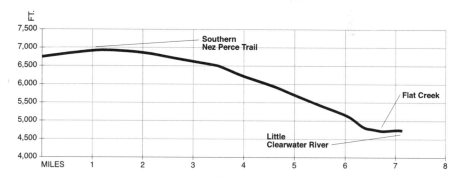

Flat Creek

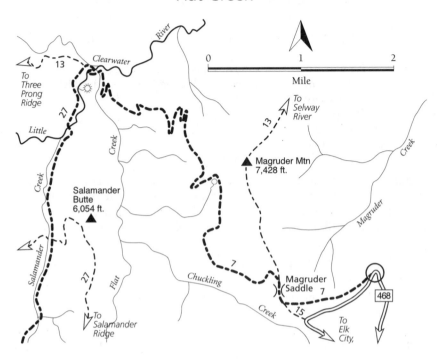

The hike: To many hikers familiar with other parts of the Selway-Bitterroot, the obscure country west of the Selway River remains terra incognita. Trails in this remote region are typically steep and difficult to follow, but the Flat Creek Trail, with its excellent tread and wide, sweeping switchbacks, is a welcome departure from the norm. In the aftermath of the Lonely/Wilderness Complex Fires of 2000 you can observe the natural succession of vegetation as new shrubs and trees take root and the forest is born anew.

The trail initially contours away the corridor road, passing through fir and pine on its way west through the trees. After a brief hike you arrive at a junction with an unsigned but obvious side trail (15X) dropping in from the south; this nonsystem route receives no USFS maintenance. Here the route turns north and straddles a forested swale known as Magruder Saddle. There are occasional glimpses of the surrounding country, but for most part the trail remains concealed in the timber over the next mile. Another trail, indistinct and easy to miss, peels away from the mainline route at 1.4 miles. This is the Southern Nez Perce Trail (13W) leading north over Magruder Mountain, and its unassuming, cairn-marked junction belies its historical significance.

Beyond this junction the route edges west and gently descends the hillside high above Chuckling Creek. Views of the wooded flanks of 7,783-foot Deadtop Mountain are available as you continue through the trees, passing through several intermittent burns before reaching a spring-fed rivulet at 3.4 miles. An obvious spur descends to a fall hunting camp in the trees below the trail at this point, roughly halfway between the trailhead and the Little

Clearwater River. The tread remains in excellent shape as it rounds a burned knob and traverses more burned-over forest in wide-sweeping switchbacks that reveal the extent of the Little Clearwater drainage and its many attendant peaks including, among others, the likes of Lonely Mountain, Sabe Mountain, and Three Prong Ridge.

At times the switchbacks grow steep and jarring, but the grade lessens noticeably as you reach a bench above Flat Creek. Drawn by a natural mineral lick less than 0.25 mile to the west, deer and elk have created an intricate network of game trails that crisscross the forest floor; however, the whereabouts of the Flat Creek Trail never grows doubtful. Several more switchbacks bring the trail to a campsite beside Flat Creek at 6.8 miles. Take your pick: Crossing the stream requires either a calf-deep ford or tricky footwork across downed trees.

The trail crosses the toe of Salamander Ridge, then doubles back and drops through marshy bottomlands to reach a broad ford of the Little Clearwater River. Although intimidating at high water, this crossing, like Flat Creek before it, is perfectly manageable by midsummer. Excellent campsites are available on the opposite side, but prospective campers should note these sites are reserved for outfitter use during the fall hunting season.

---

43 Sheephead Creek Loop

See Map on Page 135

Highlights:	Wildlife-rich stream bottom and ridgeline country with good scenery and campsite selection. One of the few true loop hikes on the Montana side of the Bitterroots.
Type of hike:	Day hike or overnight loop.
Total distance:	16.2 miles or 26.1 kilometers (complete loop).
Difficulty:	Difficult.
Best months:	July through September.
Elevation gain:	3,410 feet.
Elevation loss:	3,410 feet.
Maps:	Bare Cone, Mount Jerusalem, Nez Perce Peak, and Watchtower Peak USGS quads.

Special considerations: You can hike this loop in either direction, but the counterclockwise route is more practical because the Southern Nez Perce Trail (12W) is extremely steep and difficult to follow from its inception along the Nez Perce Road near Fales Flat. First-time visitors should note that two key junctions—with the Stateline (16ML) and Old Nez Perce (12W) trails—are badly misplaced on forest maps and corresponding quadrangles. Experienced backpackers might prefer to tackle the loop as a long day hike, but an overnight trip allows a more leisurely pace and the opportunity of a side trip to 8,315-foot Indian Hill.

Trailhead access: Take U.S. Highway 93 to its junction with Montana Highway 473, 4.4 miles south of Darby. Follow this paved road southwest for 14.2

miles to the Nez Perce Road (468) and veer right. Continue for another 10.6 miles to reach the signed turnoff for Sheephead Creek. The informal trailhead includes several primitive campsites as well limited parking space and a few pullouts for horse trailers. If you find this trailhead crowded—as it is likely to be during the fall hunting season—try the Fales Flat Campground across the road. There you will find stock unloading ramps, outhouses, and plenty of additional room for parking.

Keypoints:
   0.0   Inception of trail at the Sheephead Creek Trailhead.
   1.6   Trail crosses the North Fork Sheephead Creek.
   6.8   Junction with the Stateline Trail (16ML); veer left.
   7.0   Junction with the Cayuse Mountain Trail (35S).
   9.9   Junction with the Southern Nez Perce Trail (13W).
   11.9 Trail passes marked Indian graves.
   12.1 Junction with the Fales Flat Trail (12W).
   16.2 Completion of loop upon returning to Fales Flat.

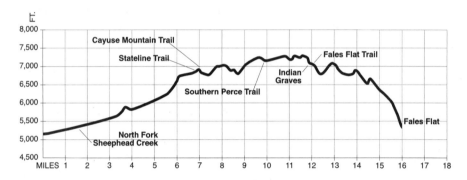

The hike: The Sheephead Creek Loop provides one of the most unusual and underrated hikes on the Montana side of the Bitterroots. If offers scenery quite different from the standard glaciated fare found elsewhere in the eastern reaches of the Selway-Bitterroot Wilderness and affords the discriminating hiker an opportunity to see lots of interesting country without retracing a single step along the way. I have spent some enjoyable time hiking this loop, which sees very few visitors outside of hunting season.

   The trail traces an old jeep road beside Sheephead Creek for a short distance, then rises along the mostly open hillside above. Following the drainage as it bends northwest, the route continues upstream while 7,822-foot Bare Cone recedes beyond the canyon entrance to the southeast. At 1.6 miles the trail descends to a lodgepole flat on its way to the North Fork Sheephead Creek. (A hunter's trail cuts right from an unmarked junction near the North Fork and continues to a deadend at several outfitter camps a mile or so upstream.) This sizable tributary presents a difficult crossing at high water unless some protruding boulders or downed trees are available. There are a few nice campsites west of the crossing.

150

More of the same follows for the next 2 miles as the route alternately ascends open terrain and drops into timbered draws to cross several small rivulets. The forest on the south-facing slopes above the trail tends to include open fir and pine parks, whereas the opposite side of the drainage is cloaked in vast, even-aged lodgepole cover. Nothing about the Sheephead Creek is visually spectacular, traversing mostly open lodgepole forest as it does, but the tread itself is in good shape and is easy enough to follow.

The drainage swings northwest some 4 miles from the trailhead and begins climbing at a progressively steeper pitch. At times the route runs right beside Sheephead Creek itself, but for the most part it remains well above the rushing stream. Campsites show up along the trail from time to time; private hunting parties have apparently staked out the prime locations. Continuing its ascent, the trail bends around the westernmost fork of Sheephead Creek to reach a marked junction with the Stateline Trail (16ML) at 6.8 miles. This trail descends to an outfitter camp at the headwaters of Indian Creek; the left-hand fork follows the Montana-Idaho line in the opposite direction. Stay left to complete the loop.

The well-blazed trail follows the Bitterroot Divide southeast past a marked junction to Cayuse Mountain (35S) and a series of wooded knobs and saddles. There is little to see as the route meanders through heavy lodgepole forest draped across this segment of the divide, and at times the going gets a bit tedious. After nearly 10 miles of hiking you reach a signed junction with the trail out to Nez Perce Peak (13W). Scenic fortunes improve dramatically beyond this junction as the trail ventures into the open once again and contours through large grassy clearings spread across the windward face of the divide. Views from these open slopes are among the best the loop has to offer, taking in a swath of heavily forested country extending deep into the Frank Church–River of No Return Wilderness to the southwest.

Just as the trail returns to timbered surroundings you come upon a solemn sight: A simple marble headstone beside the trail marks the grave of Francis Adams, a Salish Indian buried here in 1900. Shortly thereafter the main route intersects the Fales Flat Trail (12W) at a signed junction (once again, stay left to complete the loop). The rough route goes east from the junction, crosses the Bitterroot Divide, and then drops to a timbered saddle on the Montana side of the Bitterroots. The trail leads northeast from the saddle, straddling the ridge at first before settling into a more casual sidehill from which views of Castle Rock and Bare Cone are available. It is obvious that the USFS never maintained this trail to a high standard—if at all—but a few helpful blazes and cutout trees denote the trail's location as it begins the steep final descent toward Fales Flat. In certain areas switchbacks appear superimposed on the original Indian trail, which makes an extremely rugged straight-line descent along the spine of the ridge. The trail rapidly loses definition as you draw closer to your destination; its location grows increasingly speculative among the outcropping rocks. When the route at last emerges at the foot of the slope you will find yourself on the Nez Perce Road some 200 yards west of Fales Flat.

Indian Hill (right-center) and peaks of the Bitterroot Divide as seen from the Fales Flat Trail.

Side trips: Those who hike the Sheephead Creek Loop without making a short side trip to Indian Hill are cheating themselves of some of the finest scenery in the southern reaches of the Selway-Bitterroot Wilderness. The most direct route to the summit follows the Stateline Trail (16ML) northeast along the Bitterroot Divide and entails modest off-trail routefinding through subalpine fir and pine forest. All told, the hike to Indian Hill makes a 4.4-mile round trip. Between the junction and peak lies an enormous open hillside that is one of most idyllic settings in the entire wilderness.

Option: The ancestral Fales Flat Trail (12W) is extremely steep and difficult to find and follow when hiked from east to west. So unless your patience and route-finding skills are of above-average caliber, hiking the Sheephead loop in a clockwise fashion is inadvisable.

44 Boulder Creek

See Map on Page 129

Highlights: A charming waterfall, scenic mountain lakes, and good fishing. Popular with backcountry horsemen.
Type of hike: Out-and-back overnighter.
Total distance: 19 miles or 30.6 kilometers (round trip).
Difficulty: Moderate.
Best months: July through September.
Elevation gain: 2,810 feet.
Elevation loss: 220 feet.
Maps: Boulder Peak, Mount Jerusalem, and Tin Cup Lake USGS quads.

Special considerations: Equestrians should note that packstock is forbidden in the Lake Crystal area, where years of carelessness and heavy use have damaged the delicate surroundings. Regardless of your mode of travel, take care to practice zero-impact camping and leave no trace of your presence.

Trailhead access: Follow U.S. Highway 93 to its junction with Montana Highway 473, 4.4 miles south of Darby. Continue south along the West Fork of the Bitterroot River for 13.5 miles to reach the marked turnoff for the Boulder Creek Trailhead. Turn here and follow Forest Road 5731 past the Sam Billings Campground for the remaining 1.4 miles to its terminus at the trailhead. Essentially an undeveloped parking lot with few amenities other than basic packstock accommodations, the jumping-off spot offers parking for perhaps a dozen vehicles, including horse trailers.

Keypoints:
0.0   Inception of trail at the Boulder Creek Trailhead.
1.6   Trail enters the Selway-Bitterroot Wilderness.
2.5   Trail makes an easy crossing over Crow Creek.
3.4   Rendezvous with Boulder Creek Falls.
3.9   Trail shuffles across Slide Creek.
5.0   Trail meets and crosses Mink Creek.
8.4   Junction with the Boulder Lake Trail (249ML).
8.5   Trail reaches the foot of Pickle's Puddle.
9.5   Terminus of maintained trail at Boulder Lake.

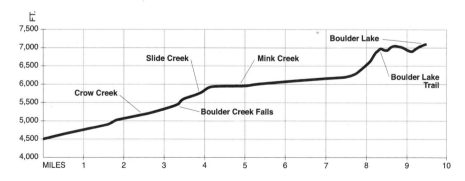

The hike: Boulder Creek is the southernmost of the major Bitterroot River tributaries originating within the Selway-Bitterroot Wilderness. Its beautiful lakes, colorful pocket meadows, tumbling waterfalls, and good angling attract backpackers by the dozen each summer. That the drainage is one of the Bitterroots' most popular should come as no surprise.

The trail starts west at a lackadaisical grade, wandering at first along an old roadbed in stream-bottom forest. As you enter the canyon, the route rises and falls with four incoming talus fans and continues upstream. Except for limited southwest views of Boulder Point, there is little to see from the trail itself, which enters the Selway-Bitterroot Wilderness at 1.7 miles. The trail continues its climb—crossing Crow Creek at one point—before traversing open hillsides with parting vistas downstream toward the rapidly receding canyon portal. After crossing an aspen-filled talus slide, switchbacks take you sharply upslope to a rendezvous with Boulder Creek Falls. Here, outlet waters from six high-mountain lakes tumble in unison down a wide granite sluice, spill into a deep emerald pool, and then vanish out of sight downstream. Campsites available above the falls are overused and of marginal quality.

Encroaching canyon walls force stream and trail together for a time, until the canyon broadens once again into a deeply glaciated trough. You negotiate crossings of Slide Creek and Mink Creek in the next several miles while openings in the forest permit cursory views of a primeval canyon landscape. At least one such clearing provides a glimpse of the high shelf concealing Lake of the Rocks, whose almost inaccessible waters rank among the Bitterroots' least visited. As the miles ahead pass underfoot, the trail encounters no fewer than six colorful subalpine meadows, each enclosed by dark spruce-fir forest.

The slope steadily increases as the trail draws to within 1 mile of the Bitterroot Divide. In doing so, a variety of new and interesting mountains—including 9,289-foot Bare Peak—rise in dramatic fashion to the southwest. Following a workmanlike ascent, the trail reaches an unmarked junction with the Boulder Lake Trail (249ML). The left-hand fork takes you to a stony brook and then ventures to a shallow, fishless tarn known as Pickle's Puddle. Beyond this point the route maintains an uneven keel, rising and falling without purpose, and reaches the logstrewn outlet of Boulder Lake after another mile.

With an outline in the vague shape of a footprint, Boulder Lake is a deep green body of water bordered by high boulder fields and dense forest. Burned timber surrounds its far southern embayment. The lake occupies a wide glacial amphitheater whose ancient walls are held in tasteful check by elongate snowy crescents. Campsite selection at first might appear limited to the heavily used sites below the lake; however, the distant southwest shore, with its flat timbered terrain, has possibilities.

Option: Lakes Crystal and Turbid are an obvious extension of the Boulder Lake Trail (249ML). From the foot of Boulder Lake, a good footpath saunters across an old stonework dam, pauses at the foot of an upcoming rise, and then tackles the timbered slope beyond. After a series of switchbacks, the route makes a tough straight-line ascent and enters a dry wash 200 yards below Lake Crystal. Although of rather modest size and shallow depth, reports of nice cutthroat in these waters have continued to surface in recent years. Limited tree cover in the area includes the tenacious alpine larch, whose feathery copses appoint an otherwise austere scene above the lake. Excellent campsites are well distributed throughout the area, but please practice zero-impact camping if you stay.

Nearby Lake Turbid is a placid mountain pool with an irregular shoreline, single wooded island, and wet weedy inlet. Pan-sized trout are the rule rather than the exception here. From a base camp at either of these lakes it is possible to continue north via bushwhack to reach Dollar Lake, cradled within its own secretive forested pocket well below its two larger neighbors.

45 Watchtower Creek to Sheephead Creek

Highlights:	An extremely rugged route showcasing the Bitterroot Mountains at their most sublime. Strictly for well-conditioned hikers with considerable off-trail expertise.
Type of hike:	Three-day backpacking shuttle.
Total distance:	20 miles or 32.2 kilometers.
Difficulty:	Strenuous.
Best months:	July through September.
Elevation gain:	4,090 feet.
Elevation loss:	3,990 feet.
Maps:	Bare Cone, Mount Jerusalem, and Watchtower Peak USGS quads.

Special considerations: Unlike most of the other trails featured in this guide, this hike is one of the few requiring significant cross-country travel. Be forewarned—the off-trail segment traverses very rough country and involves several hours of difficult and time-consuming scrambling along the Montana-Idaho line. In the steeper areas you may encounter slow-melting snowfields or shifting talus; some scrambling on all fours may be necessary, all the better if you have any mountain goat genes encoded in your DNA.

Trailhead access: To reach the Watchtower Creek Trailhead, take U.S. Highway 93 to its junction with Montana Highway 473, 4.4 miles south of Darby. Follow the pavement southwest for 14.2 miles to Nez Perce Road (468), veer right, and drive another 8.9 miles to the signed turnoff for Watchtower Creek. Forest Road 5638 continues 0.4 mile to the trailhead loop. The trailhead is located in a spacious clearing and includes an outhouse, stock unloading ramp, and plentiful parking. A rail fence enclosure prevents motorized use beyond the trailhead.

For the Sheephead Creek Trailhead, follow Nez Perce Road (468) west from Montana Highway 473 to reach the marked turnoff for Sheephead Creek after 10.6 miles. The informal trailhead lies at the end of a 0.2-mile spur

Watchtower Creek to Sheephead Creek

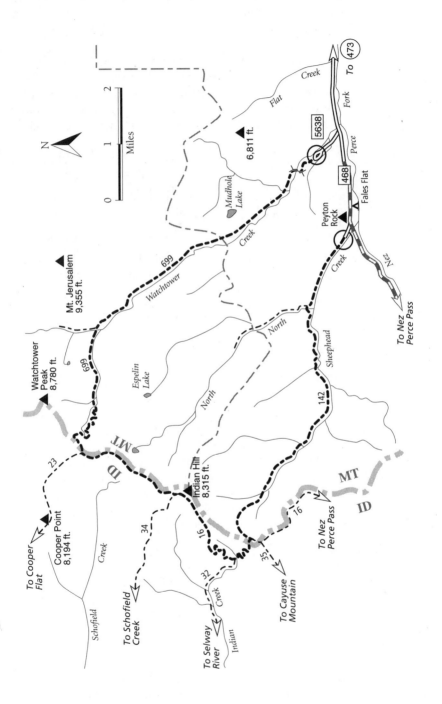

road and includes several undeveloped campsites, as well limited parking space and a few pullouts for horse trailers. If you find the trailhead too crowded, try the Fales Flat Campground, located just across the road. There you will find stock unloading ramps, outhouses, and plenty of additional room for parking.

Keypoints:

0.0	Inception of trail at the Watchtower Creek Trailhead.
0.7	Trail crosses Watchtower Creek.
2.7	Trail enters the Selway-Bitterroot Wilderness.
5.6	Northern fork of Watchtower Creek.
8.8	Trail reaches the Montana-Idaho line atop the Bitterroot Divide.
10.8	Route rejoins the Schofield Ridge Trail (34S) northwest of Indian Hill.
13.2	Trail leaves the Selway-Bitterroot Wilderness. Marked junction with the Sheephead Creek Trail (142ML); bear left.
18.4	Trail crosses North Fork Sheephead Creek.
20.0	Trail reaches the Sheephead Creek Trailhead near Fales Flat.

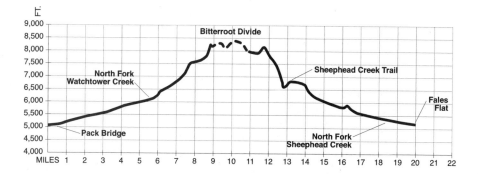

Suggested itinerary: Because of this hike's above-average scenic value and difficulty, I recommend a three-day backpack for experienced hikers only. Camping near the heads of Watchtower and Indian creeks on the first and second nights out, respectively, is a logical way to divvy up the 20 miles into segments of roughly equal length. Alternately, the nameless lake at the head of North Fork Sheephead Creek makes an excellent choice for those wanting to spend only one night in the woods.

The hike: Here is the gold standard of the West Fork District. Very few trails so powerfully convey the essence of hiking the Bitterroot Mountains as this delightful route. The reason? Watchtower-Sheephead offers outstanding scenic value along the Bitterroot Divide and is unusually rich in wildlife throughout. While hiking this route I have encountered elk, deer, mountain lions, and a rare gray wolf—all on the same afternoon. It remains one of the Bitterroots' more underrated hikes, seeing relatively light use during the summer months.

The route starts along an old jeep road going northwest through a few aspen-lined clearings and into the timber. At first the hiking is decidedly low-key, and the trail, well maintained as far as the Montana-Idaho line, gains little elevation. A good pack bridge provides dry passage over Watchtower Creek at 0.7 mile. From here you follow a course parallel with the stream for the next 2 miles, crossing several small tributaries in the process.

Towering canyon walls soon arise from timbered foothills on either side of the Watchtower Creek to form a dramatic, deeply glaciated landscape through which the trail passes. Encroaching scree and avalanche chutes force the forest aside for the first good look at 8,780-foot Watchtower Peak, which looks over the canyon headwaters from the Bitterroot Divide. Keep your eyes peeled for mountain goats and bighorn sheep that roam the canyon walls above.

Resurgent spruce and fir soon rescind these scenes, and the drainage slowly bends west, crossing three tributaries in close succession: The third and largest of these is the north fork of Watchtower Creek (here a primitive trail, intermittent and unmaintained, branches away from the main route and continues north toward Watchtower Lake). Roughly 100 yards beyond the north fork you pass the decaying remnants of a partially collapsed trapper cabin in the trees below the trail. From here the trail climbs at a noticeably steeper grade on its way to the headwaters of Watchtower Creek. Several pocket clearings enliven the otherwise forested ascent until the route ventures above timberline.

With the hulking mass of Mount Jerusalem fully visible for the first time, the trail follows a very steep series of switchbacks to a high landing overlooking the head of Watchtower Creek. There are some attractive campsites in this area. Rather than aiming for either of the two obvious passes at the head of the canyon, the switchbacks instead run to the crest of the point in between. A commanding view of the Bitterroots greets you atop the divide. Especially prominent is Watchtower Peak, which rises to a steep pyramid only 1 mile away. The trail continues west over 8,194-foot Cooper Point and eventually reaches Cooper Flat, but to return to civilization via Sheephead Creek you must leave the trail and begin hiking southwest along the divide.

The 2-mile-long traverse along the Bitterroot Divide is no leisurely walk in the woods. Nothing bearing any resemblance to a maintained trail exists along the divide, and careful routefinding is essential. (I found the Idaho sideslopes blanketed with shifting talus but nevertheless preferable to the even steeper Montana side of the divide.) You first traverse burned-over country above Schofield Creek and then descend into a saddle from which views of a remote lake at the headwaters of the North Fork Sheephead Creek are available. From there the route ventures into increasingly difficult terrain near Peak 8,450 and later ties in with the Schofield Ridge Trail (34S) about 0.5 mile northwest of Indian Hill.

The well-defined trail contours southwest, goes over a wooded point straddling the state boundary, and descends through an enormous sloping meadow on the Idaho side of the divide. Note that forest maps show a junction with the Stateline Trail (16T) immediately southwest of Indian Hill, but no such junction exists. It is completely fictitious for the location shown. This spacious clearing is a very impressive location, with far-reaching views

Rugged country above Watchtower Creek, as seen from the Montana-Idaho line.

extending across the southern reaches of the Selway-Bitterroot Wilderness and well into the Frank Church–River of No Return Wilderness to the south. In the tall grass the tread seems to disappear, but a series of metal fence-posts shows the way as the trail drops sharply on switchbacks and reenters lodgepole forest. Passing a well-established private hunting camp near an unnamed headwater fork of Indian Creek, the trail makes a short ascent to reach a junction with the Sheephead Creek Trail (142ML). A wooden sign marks the juncture.

From the junction a straightforward 6.8 miles is all that lies between you and the trailhead. The descent along Sheephead Creek is a very pleasant hike, with an undulating course that alternately crosses small tributaries and wanders across open slopes overlooking the stream bottom. Campsites shown up beside the trail every so often, including one location very close to the North Fork Sheephead Creek. Beyond the North Fork you pass through heavy forest that shades the trail to its conclusion.

Option: This route can be hiked in reverse, but the ascent to the Bitterroot Divide entails an especially brutal 2,500-foot climb in only 1.1 miles!

Side trips: Depending on your aptitude for cross-country travel, you may want to visit Watchtower Lake, Cooper Point, or the nameless lake at the head of North Fork Sheephead Creek. The diversion to Cooper Point offers outstanding scenic value and both lakes offer excellent campsites for the few souls willing to make the trip.

ADDITIONAL TRAILS

Burnt Strip Ridge (5S), 3.3 miles (5.3 km). This ridgeline trail links the Indian Ridge Trail (10ML) to the west with the Cooper Point Trail (23S) to the east, forming a continuous east-west route across the Bitterroot Divide and into the Watchtower Creek drainage on the Montana side of the Bitterroots. By itself, the trail itself is not terribly interesting: It is used mostly by hunters bound for camps at the heads of Snake and Peach creeks.

Indian Ridge (10ML), 14.3 miles (23 km). Indian Ridge provides an exhausting approach route into the high country centered on Burnt Strip Mountain. Initially the going is very steep, with numerous game trails crisscrossing the tread. But the slope is fairly open and offers views comparable to those from the nearby Spot Mountain Trail (3ML). Higher up, the trail passes an outfitter's camp at the head of Jack Creek, reaching an unsigned junction with the Burnt Strip Ridge Trail (5S) at 8.6 miles. The segment going south toward Schofield Creek receives light use and has not been cut out by USFS crews in well over a decade.

Southern Nez Perce Trail (13W), 36 miles (57.9 km). This ancestral route leads west across the Selway-Bitterroot Wilderness from the Bitterroot Divide to the vicinity of Three Prong Ridge. Over the years various segments of the old Indian trail were incorporated into the modern USFS trail system, while other portions of the route were essentially left to their own devices and abandoned. The 16.2-mile segment east of Selway River sees varying degrees of maintenance as it leads along forested ridges, down into a deep canyon (Cayuse Creek), and up steep peaks, usually without the benefit of switchbacks or other such improvements. Brush and downed trees are frequent obstacles. Scenic value is highest between Nez Perce Peak and the Bitterroot Divide, as well as from the vicinity of Cayuse and Beaver Jack mountains. But if the eastern segment is merely challenging, then the 19.8-mile-long trail west of the Selway River is downright devious: the route going west from the Little Clearwater River has been abandoned by the USFS and is now blocked by hundreds of pines downed in 1996 windstorms. Several outfitters' camps in the headwaters of Lonely Creek and the Little Clearwater have been similarly deserted.

A dark historical footnote surrounds the Selway-Bitterroot segment of the Southern Nez Perce Trail. With the discovery of gold in the Idaho Territory in the early 1860s, the old Indian trail across the Bitterroots assumed newfound importance as prospectors and traders sought the most direct route between the booming gold camps at Elk City, Idaho, and Virginia City, Montana. During the summer of 1864, Lloyd Magruder and his companions were returning from Virginia City after making a healthy profit selling supplies to the miners. Four other travelers joined the Magruder party as they journeyed west.

After a few days on the trail, and shortly after fording the Selway River, the four travelers robbed and murdered Magruder and companions under cover of darkness. After burning and burying evidence of the deed, the outlaws fled to California and were later apprehended in San Francisco: Their

160

subsequent convictions in a Lewiston court resulted in the first legal hanging in the Idaho Territory. A USFS sign once marked the site of the Magruder Massacre on the lower end of the ridge that now bears his name.

Schumaker Ridge (14X), 2.7 miles (4.3 km). This trail offers a short but very steep approach route to Nez Perce Peak from the Magruder Corridor Road. Its inception along the corridor road 0.2 mile west of the Kit Carson outfitter camp is a bit sketchy and not especially obvious to hikers unfamiliar with the area. Experienced outdoorsmen will find the trail easy enough to follow as it crosses barbwire fences left over from old grazing allotments in the lower elevations. A nonsystem trail, the route was dropped from the USFS trail inventory years ago.

Cooper Point (23S), 5.5 miles (8.8 km). Connecting the Burnt Strip Ridge (5S) and Watchtower Creek (699ML) trails via Cooper Point, the trail passes through open subalpine country that burned in the 1997 Schofield Fire. It offers some spectacular views of various high summits—including the likes of Vance Mountain and Watchtower Peak—as you follow its poorly defined tread along the ridgeline. The route originally descended to reach a junction with the Canyon Creek Trail (2ML) less than 1 mile from Cooper Flat. But this segment is extremely steep and requires a difficult waist-deep ford of Canyon Creek; it was last maintained in 1993 and has since been abandoned.

Salamander Ridge (27S), 8.4 miles (13.5 km). This trail descends from the Magruder Corridor Road to the Little Clearwater River, passing a signed junction with the Lodgepole Hump Trail (61S) at 6.2 miles and crossing Salamander Creek at 7.5 miles. It crosses a network of game trails in its lower elevations and ultimately merges with the Flat Creek Trail (7ML) near an outfitter camp in the bottomlands of the Little Clearwater River. The route traverses heavy lodgepole forest over much of its length, including segments that suffered severe windthrow during 1996 windstorms. Trailhead parking is limited.

Indian Creek (32S), 11.8 miles (19 km). The trail follows Indian Creek east from its confluence with the Selway River to a hunting camp in one of its headwater forks below Indian Hill. The lower 7.2 miles between the Indian Creek Campground and the Scimitar Ridge Trail (36ML) have been abandoned: Numerous rockslides and hundreds of trees downed in a 1996 windstorm have mangled the trail beyond recognition. The upper 4.6 miles, however, remain on the USFS trail inventory. Two major outfitters' camps located near the Scimitar Ridge Trail junction are well used and stock accessible: Relocation of this trail along Indian Creek means its true layout and junction with the Indian Creek Trail varies somewhat from that depicted on the wilderness map. Upstream of the Schofield Creek confluence, the route closely follows Indian Creek through more upland forest to reach its terminus on the Bitterroot Divide.

Schofield Ridge (34S), 9.2 miles (14.8 km). This trail traverses a high ridgeline country with several open parks and some very pleasant views, especially of the Schofield drainage and surrounding peaks. Beginning across from an outfitter's camp on Schofield Creek, the trail ascends a steep, rocky slope and follows a poorly defined tread through ponderosa pine trees. (Those hiking the route from west to east should avoid the nonsystem trail leading up Schofield Creek—which looks like the better trail at its outset—and stick to the ridgeline instead.) Schofield Ridge was scheduled to be cleared a few years back but went without maintenance when the contractor mistakenly cut out the adjoining Indian Creek Trail (32S) instead. Water availability is poor.

Cayuse Mountain (35S), 4.8 miles (7.7 km). Strictly a ridgeline trail, this undulating route links the Southern Nez Perce (13W) and Stateline (16ML) trails via Cayuse Mountain. It traverses big open fir and pine parks and maintains an easy contour with frequent southerly views, entering heavier lodgepole toward its western end. A big tree with lots of chops and blazes denotes its junction with the Southern Nez Perce Trail (13W) near Cayuse Mountain. The trail receives little maintenance and may be abandoned within the next few years.

Mount Aura (40S), 11 miles (17.7 km). Leading north over Mount Aura from its junction with the Spot Mountain Trail (3ML), this trail passes outfitter camps at the heads of Eagle Creek and West Fork Crooked Creek tributaries. The route is fairly open in its higher elevations and offers views of some of the more obscure country of the Selway-Bitterroot Wilderness and roadless areas to the west, including Box Car Mountain. It then makes an extended descent as the terrain plunges toward the northeast, with the trail running right down the fall line to first ford Crooked Creek and then the Selway River upstream of their confluence. This deepwater ford is extremely dangerous during periods of high water; the USFS has no plans to construct a pack bridge in its place.

Vance Mountain (46S), 9.2 miles (14.8 km). This steep ridgeline route is one of the most obscure trails on the West Fork District. Years ago it provided an access and resupply route for the USFS lookout at Vance Point. But today the trail receives so little use and upkeep (no maintenance contracts are pending as this book goes to print) that only a few old-timers can pinpoint the whereabouts of its fainter segments with certainty. Its days as a system trail are numbered.

Lodgepole Hump (61S), 7.4 miles (11.9 km). This steep trail leads north from the Magruder Corridor Road, cresting Sabe (Sob-ee) Mountain before descending for approximately 3,850 feet to reach a junction with the Salamander Ridge Trail (27S) on Salamander Creek. There are some exceptional views of the upper Selway country from the slopes of 8,245-foot Sabe Mountain, but otherwise the route is of minimal scenic value. Used mostly by hunters bound for spike camps along Salamander Creek and the Little Clearwater River, this trail sees little backpacking activity.

Eagle Point-Parachute Ridge (70S), 0.8 miles (1.3 km). Linking the Parachute Ridge (537S) and Eagle Creek (562S) trails at the extreme western margin of the Selway-Bitterroot Wilderness, this trail apparently functioned as a cutoff route between the USFS lookouts atop Parachute Ridge and Eagle

Point many, many years ago. The route traverses heavy spruce-fir forest and, as this book goes to print, is nearly unrecognizable on the ground.

Salamander Creek (87X), 6.2 miles (10 km). This trail leads north from Horse Heaven Saddle and descends into the headwaters of Salamander Creek to reach junctions with the Salamander Ridge (27S) and Lodgepole Hump (61S) trails in just over 6 miles. It passes through an Opportunity Class I area and was abandoned by the USFS in 1992.

Bad Luck Creek (93ML), 8 miles (12.9 km). This well-maintained trail follows Bad Luck Creek upstream from the Selway River Trail (4ML) to its headwaters, crossing and recrossing the stream multiple times. The fords themselves run deep and swift through early June but are far from a deterrent by the time hunters converge on the area each September. The trail tends to be hot and brushy in its lower elevations and grows a bit sketchy as you ascend switchbacks to meet the Forest Divide Trail (710S) at the head of the drainage. Bad Luck is well named: One 35-year veteran of the Selway-Bitterroot reported encountering "the biggest rattlesnake I've ever seen" just above the trail junction along the Selway River.

North Star Creek (219S), 3.4 miles (5.5 km). North Star Creek provides an alternate stream-bottom approach to the Gardiner Peak Lookout. For the most part it traverses open, brushy terrain and is in better condition than the adjoining trail (519S) up North Star Ridge. The route is not an obvious choice for backpacking but may be of some interest to those seeking solitude—at least before hunting season starts in September. This is good rattlesnake country.

Soda Springs Creek (250X), 5.6 miles (9 km). Few other Bitterroot trails are so consistently scattershot and unfriendly to the hiker as this devious path. Beginning at an unmarked trailhead and in the midst of an old clearcut, the route quickly passes Soda Springs, an unimpressive, muddy seep enriched in sodium bicarbonate. The trail then pursues a northwesterly course parallel to Soda Springs Creek for about 4 miles. Reconnaissance on July 9, 1999, revealed hundreds of downed spruce along the upper length of the trail; as such, it is not recommended for horsemen or casual hikers.

North Star Ridge (519S), 6.3 miles (10.1 km). The trail follows the Selway River past the North Star Ranch and northeast along an overlooking ridge running toward Gardiner Peak. The ascent out of North Star drainage is extremely steep and dry, traversing brushy burned-over country with quite a few rattlesnakes. Be sure to top your water bottles before leaving North Star Creek because the ridgeline above is waterless. The route is stock passable over its entire length, although tread erosion has been a problem on some of the steeper sections.

Parachute Ridge (536S), 4.3 miles (6.9 km). This obscure route connects Parachute Ridge with the Mount Aura Trail (40S). It remains in unburned timber over most of its length and is of generally low scenic value. Water availability is very limited, and obvious trailside campsites are few and far between. The switchbacked ascent out of Eagle Creek is incredibly steep and difficult with stock. This is a very lightly traveled backcountry route: Hunters and outfitters are among its only users.

Archer Point (546X), 2.5 miles (4.0 km). This trail takes off from the Selway River Trail (4ML) at an unmarked junction north of Running Creek Ranch. The long-abandoned route follows dry ridgeline country west to Archer Point, gaining approximately 2,320 feet over the course of its ascent. This is excellent rattlesnake country, so watch your step. Archer Point was the site of a USFS lookout until 1957.

Eagle Creek (562S), 5.8 miles (9.3 km). This badly neglected route connects the Running Creek Trail (532ML) with 5,403-foot Eagle Point via Eagle Creek. Years ago the trail provided access to several USFS lookouts and fire camps in the vicinity of Parachute Ridge, but nowadays it is used almost exclusively for hunting access. It is poorly suited for recreational hiking: There is a lot of brush and downed timber to slow your progress, and the Eagle Creek ford is hazardous at high water, for both hikers and horses alike.

Forest Divide (710S), 2.3 miles (3.7 km). This short and generally unremarkable trail straddles the boundaries of the Nez Perce and Bitterroot national forests and connects the Bad Luck Ridge (52S) and Gardiner Peak (520S) trails. It sees very little use outside of hunting season but is reportedly in good shape and easy to follow.

Clearwater National Forest

Lochsa Ranger District

46 Warm Springs Creek

Highlights: Thermal-driven springs and a nice view of the Lochsa
River; quiet cedar forests and a pretty waterfall.
Type of hike: Out-and-back day hike.
Total distance: 7.2 miles or 11.6 kilometers (round trip).
Difficulty: Easy.
Best months: May through October.
Elevation gain: 1,010 feet.
Maps: Bear Mountain and Tom Beal Peak USGS quads.

Special considerations: As the trailhead signs explain, use of the Jerry Johnson Hot Springs is restricted to the hours between 6:00 A.M. and 8:00 P.M.
(PST); the USFS has wisely prohibited overnight camping here. At any given
time you can expect to share the hot springs with at least three other parties, even in the dead of winter. Jerry Johnson receives more praise than it
rightly deserves—those who regard the springs as "breathtaking" or "spectacular" have obviously seen very little of the Selway-Bitterroot Wilderness.

Trailhead access: The trailhead at Warm Springs Pack Bridge is located 55
miles west of Lolo on U.S. Highway 12. It is clearly marked and features a
wide pullout parking area with room for two dozen vehicles. You might notice license plates from far-flung states and provinces—I've seen plates from
as far away as Maine.

Keypoints:
0.0 Inception of trail at the Warm Springs Pack Bridge. Junction with the
Cooperation Ridge Trail (44S).
1.2 Trail files past Jerry Johnson Hot Springs. Bare ass alert!
1.3 Trail merges with the Stock Bypass Trail (46ML).
2.0 Notched log crossing of Cooperation Creek.

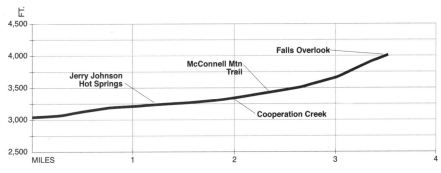

Warm Springs Creek • Bear Mountain Lookout

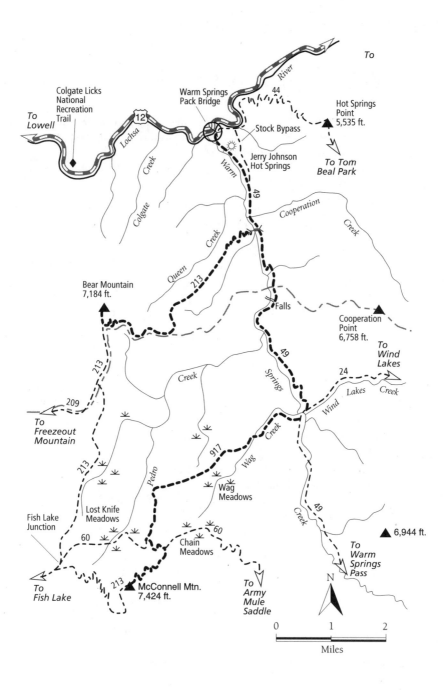

Colgate Licks
National
Recreation
Trail

Warm Springs
Pack Bridge

To
Lowell

12

Lochsa

Colgate

Creek

Warm

Stock Bypass

Jerry Johnson
Hot Springs

River

44

Hot Springs
Point
5,535 ft.

To

To Tom
Beal Park

49

Cooperation

Creek

Queen

Creek

213

Bear Mountain
7,184 ft.

Falls

Cooperation
Point
6,758 ft.

To
Wind
Lakes

213

49

Springs

24

Lakes   Creek

209

To
Freezeout
Mountain

Creek

Wind

213

917

Wag

Pedro

Wag
Meadows

Creek

49

Fish Lake
Junction

Lost Knife
Meadows

Creek

▲ 6,944 ft.

60

60

Chain
Meadows

To
Warm
Springs
Pass

To
Fish Lake

213

McConnell Mtn.
7,424 ft.

To
Army
Mule
Saddle

N

0   1   2

Miles

2.3 Junction with the McConnell Mountain Trail (213ML).

3.2 Trail enters the Selway-Bitterroot Wilderness.

3.6 Overlook of falls on Warm Springs Creek.

The hike: This exceptionally nice trail is fast becoming a victim of its own ever-growing popularity. The source of its endless attraction is Jerry Johnson Hot Springs, long a favorite stopover of passing motorists. For obvious reasons you will lose most hikers at the springs and, farther along, arrive at a nice overlook of the nameless falls on Warm Springs Creek. The falls are best exposed for photography by early afternoon, remaining in the shadows for hours after morning light first illuminates the ridges above. All forms of mechanized travel, including mountain bikes, are prohibited from using the trail, a primary wilderness-access route.

A massive cable suspension pack bridge provides a dry passage to the south side of the Lochsa River, where a USFS information board and sign mark the junction with the Cooperation Ridge Trail (44S). A right-hand turn takes you through the ranks of a fragrant cedar and grand fir forest along Warm Springs Creek. The trail here is wide, well traveled, and easy to follow. After only 25 minutes of hiking you encounter the first of eight pools comprising Jerry Johnson Hot Springs. The waters issue from an elusive subterranean source, with several of the springs steaming right beside Warm Springs Creek and others found elsewhere along the trail bubbling at only lukewarm temperatures. Beyond the uppermost spring the trail passes a group of grassy wallows frequented by local moose and soon reconnects with the stock bypass.

Following a slippery log crossing of Cooperation Creek you come to a marked junction with the McConnell Mountain Trail (213ML). Upstream of the junction, the horse-churned tread ambles through wet cedar forest with the rushing waters of Warm Springs Creek audible in the bottomland hush. The route turns uphill and gradually ascends the hillside before contouring over to reach the wilderness boundary. A footpath diverges from the mainline route at this point and leads to a good overlook of the drainage ahead.

The trail continues its hillside traverse and crosses a particularly spooky-looking forest surrounding a small rivulet, only to emerge at the falls overlook a short time later. Here the route runs atop a 200-foot-high ledge long ago blasted out to provide a safe thoroughfare through an otherwise impassable canyon. Several fine vantages of the falls are available, although they are too far removed to provide up-close viewing. The falls plummet 30 feet or more into a dark pool nestled below the cedars as the perspective continues upstream along the steep watercourse and into the progressively narrower canyon. Venturing to the foot of the falls might seem tempting, but an off-trail scramble is inadvisable due to the precipitous slope.

Side trips: Several diversions from the main trail are available. If you are interested in escaping the heavy crowds bound for Jerry Johnson, take a side trip along the Cooperation Ridge Trail (44S) from its outset at the Warm Springs Pack Bridge. Just follow the trail, which is in fair condition and remains alongside the Lochsa for the better part of a mile, as far as you like. Bear Mountain is a second possibility. Refer to the separate narrative devoted to this scenic peak and its fire lookout for more information.

47 Spruce Creek Lakes

Highlights: Pleasant subalpine scenery and a pair of high mountain lakes.
Type of hike: Out-and-back day hike or overnighter.
Total distance: 7.8 miles or 12.6 kilometers (round trip).
Difficulty: Moderate.
Best months: July through September.
Elevation gain: 1,120 feet.
Elevation loss: 1,440 feet.
Map: Ranger Peak USGS quad.

Trailhead access: Take U.S. Highway 12 to Beaver Ridge Road (369), 35.5 miles west of Lolo, and follow this rough-and-tumble mountain road for approximately 19.9 miles to reach the Beaver Ridge Lookout. The final 1.3 miles below the trailhead are steep, rocky, and unsuited for horse trailers—a vehicle with high clearance and four-wheel drive is recommended but not required. The end-of-the-road lookout marks the inception of the Spruce Creek Lakes Trail (63S) and is one of only four fire lookouts still staffed on the Lochsa Ranger District. Parking is available on a limited basis below the lookout, with a few additional possibilities elsewhere along the road below.

Keypoints:
0.0   Inception of trail below the Beaver Ridge Lookout.
0.1   Overlook of Beaver Lake.
3.9   End of trail description at the Spruce Creek Lakes.

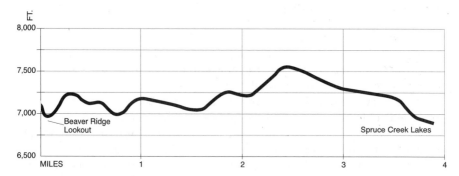

The hike: This route traverses high, scenic ridgeline country on its way to a pair of charming tarns located 2 miles west of the Bitterroot Divide. The trail receives moderate packstock use but is sometimes difficult to discern due to the prevalence of trail-eating meadows along its length. In its 1987 Forest Plan, the USFS recommended the Spruce Creek Lakes for addition to the Selway-Bitterroot Wilderness.

Spruce Creek Lakes • Siah Lake

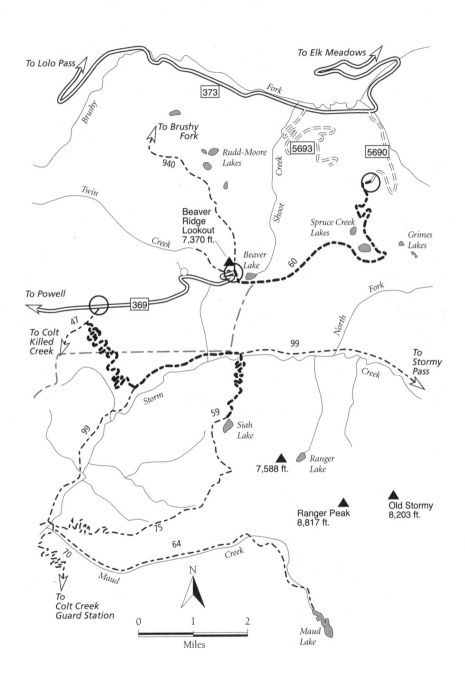

From the slopes below the Beaver Ridge Lookout, the trail assumes a generally eastern bearing and descends along the high ridgeline above Beaver Lake, which cannot be seen without a dozen-pace jaunt from the main trail. Old blazes guide the route across an undulating ridge of grassy clearings and open forest with lots of decaying blowdowns. Southerly views take in the massive flanks of 8,817-foot Ranger Peak as well as the long, heavily forested drainage through which Storm Creek flows. An occasional backward glance reveals the receding Beaver Ridge Lookout, visible at times but more often concealed behind intervening trees and topography.

The course drops across several low rock ledges as it progresses from one high saddle to the next, crossing a pair of pocket clearings populated with native grasses and other forage. These meadows would like nothing better than to consume the trail as part of its regular diet, but for the most part the route is not especially difficult to follow. You soon enter a 1994 burn area where selective immolation scorched many of the subalpine fir, spruce, and pine but spared others in their midst.

Here the tread degrades with abrupt swiftness and peters out atop the open ridge overlooking the Spruce Creek Lakes from the southwest. Only a short stroll is required to reach a beautiful vantage of the Spruce Creek Lakes, nestled in separate, steep-walled pockets some 700 feet below. Views from the precipitous overlook encompass these deep blue lakes and the equally inspiring peaks in the distance.

Option: A patient backpacker may follow the remaining trail segment as it continues down into the timbered lake basin, turns north, and travels into progressively rougher forest on its way to a rendezvous with Forest Road 5690 above the South Fork Spruce Creek. Although a shuttle arrangement is possible for a point-to-point excursion, the trail is most frequently traveled as an out-and-back hike from the Beaver Ridge Lookout. It hardly seems worth the effort to arrange a shuttle since the trail beyond the lakes has essentially been abandoned and is of low scenic value.

---

48 Walton Lakes

See Map on Page 188

Highlights:	Two large mountain lakes and two mysterious meadows.
Type of hike:	Day hike shuttle.
Total distance:	8.5 miles or 13.8 kilometers.
Difficulty:	Moderate.
Best months:	July through September.
Elevation gain:	2,440 feet.
Elevation loss:	1,520 feet.
Map:	Grave Peak USGS quad.

Trailhead access: To find the Savage Pass Trailhead, follow U.S. Highway 12 to its junction with Elk Summit Road—42.8 miles west of Lolo and 67.2 miles northeast of Lowell—and continue south to the confluence of Colt Killed Creek and the Crooked Fork. After crossing these two streams, pass a junction with Forest Road 362 and follow the road through cut-over tracts to reach the clearly marked junction with FR 360. A feeling of deepening mystery builds as the road climbs the narrow grade to 6,168-foot Savage Pass. Here a crude roadside campsite and wooden sign denote the trailhead.

For the Walton Lakes Trailhead, just east of Tom Beal Park, take FR 362 for 9 miles from its junction described above. Expect a jarring ride on this steep mountain road. The trailhead, which overlooks one of the two Walton Lakes, offers generous parking but no other facilities of any kind.

Keypoints:

- 0.0   Inception of trail at Savage Pass.
- 2.3   Trail shuffles past Sneakfoot Meadows.
- 4.1   Trail passes above Marion Meadows.
- 6.3   Outlet of the southern Walton Lake.
- 7.0   Foot of the northern Walton Lake.
- 8.5   Terminus of trail east of Tom Beal Park. Overlook of the northern Walton Lake.

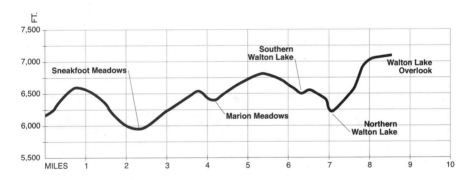

The hike: This trail traverses heavily forested ridgeline country at the northern periphery of the Elk Summit roadless area. A land of high water tables, undulating woodlands, and wet meadows, the Elk Summit has long enjoyed support for wilderness designation. Its scenic merits lie squarely within the Walton Lakes basin, the opportunity to observe local elk and moose in the marshy meadows accessed from this trail more than compensates for an initial lack of scenic interest. For this reason the description below follows the longer route from Savage Pass rather than a much shorter northwestern approach from the vicinity of Tom Beal Park. The trail is closed to all motorized vehicles.

The trail begins with a modest climb of the forested prominence west of Savage Pass. After reaching level ground the trail makes an unhurried turn to the southwest and steadily loses elevation in the process. At the foot of this slope, intermixed woodland gives way to an immature forest of lodgepole pine anchored like fenceposts in thin granitic soils. Sneakfoot Meadows remains unseen as the trail shuffles past and veers away from this mile-long marshland. The trail climbs an incoming ridge cloaked with large subalpine fir before meeting an informal junction to a hunter's camp just above Marion Meadows. Watch closely for moose and other wildlife in this spacious and sparsely timbered wetland. The trail returns to its western bearing and crosses a handful of tiny rivulets before venturing within sight of the nameless peaks overshadowing the Walton Lakes basin. Immediately after traversing an open knob dotted with Engelmann spruce, the course falls to meet the largest of the two Walton Lakes, 6.3 miles after leaving the Savage Pass Trailhead.

This large mud-bottomed lake offers good shoreline access and angling for cutthroat trout. Ancient granite faces rise from the lakeshore to form a dramatic backdrop for the blue-green waters. Campsites are well distributed throughout the area, with those near the outlet receiving the heaviest wear and tear. To minimize your impact at this popular weekend spot, please restrict your activities to sites already bare from previous use.

Leaving the southern lake's outlet, the trail rises slightly as it proceeds northwest, drops into a second basin and soon arrives beside its smaller companion. Surrounded by old stands of spruce and fir, snow cornices drape the lee flanks of a prominent ridgeline overlooking the northern Walton Lake. Fishing opportunities here are similar to those of its southern counterpart— except that shoreline brush and trees make backcasts slightly more difficult.

From the foot of the lower northern lake, the trail runs west and tackles a steep ascent of the canyon headwall via 10 switchbacks. Bracken ferns and

A steep headwall rises beyond the Walton Lakes.

Indian paintbrush show up as the main trail continues sharply uphill. Views improve considerably as the Bitterroot Divide appears to the east, where the Heavenly Twins and dozens of other major summits impale the skyline. After a climb of nearly 900 feet, the trail gains the ridge and pursues a southwest course to reach its western terminus near Tom Beal Park.

Option: Hiking the trail from west to east offers a much shorter approach to the lakes, but you'll run into far more people at the outset and will probably be less inclined to hike the entire 8.5-mile shuttle to Savage Pass.

49 Grave Peak

See Map on Page 188

Highlights:	Attractive subalpine country and spectacular views from an unusual D-6 lookout.
Type of hike:	Out-and-back day hike.
Total distance:	9 miles or 14.5 kilometers (round trip).
Difficulty:	Difficult.
Best months:	July through September.
Elevation gain:	2,510 feet.
Elevation loss:	570 feet.
Map:	Grave Peak USGS quad.

Trailhead access: Follow U.S. Highway 12 to its junction with the Elk Summit Road—42.8 miles west of Lolo and 67.2 miles northeast of Lowell—and continue south on a washboard grade to the confluence of White Sand Creek and the Crooked Fork. After crossing these two bridges, follow the road through the cut-over Plum Creek plantation to reach the marked intersection with Forest Road 360. At this intersection, turn right and follow a steep, narrow grade over Savage Pass and into the forested drainages beyond. Watch for the Kooskooskia Meadows Road (358), which appears 15 miles from US 12. Turn here and follow this rough wilderness-access road for the final 2.2 miles to its terminus (all motorized use is prohibited beyond this point). There are no formal trailhead accommodations other than a makeshift hitchrail and rather limited parking space for perhaps five or six vehicles.

Keypoints:
- 0.0 Inception of trail at the Kooskooskia Meadows Trailhead.
- 0.7 Junction with the Cedar Ridge Trail (6ML).
- 0.9 Trail reaches a nameless pond and leaves the abandoned roadbed.
- 1.0 Trail draws abreast of Kooskooskia Meadows.
- 1.3 Trail enters the Selway-Bitterroot Wilderness.
- 2.2 Junction with the Pouliot Trail (30ML).
- 2.8 Trail reaches the foot of Swamp Lake.
- 3.6 Unmarked junction with the Grave Peak Trail (905S) below Friday Pass.
- 3.7 Trail crosses the crest of Friday Ridge.
- 4.5 Trail reaches its terminus at the old Grave Peak Lookout.

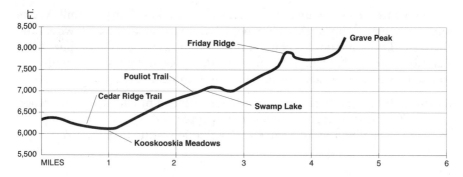

The hike: Heavy forest provides a deceptively uninteresting preamble for the Grave Peak Trail. Yet in spite of its initial appearance, the trail has much to offer visitors seeking a scenic day hike or overnight excursion. The enduring beauty of these mountains assumes an added dimension after reading *The Lochsa Story,* which recounts in part the unsuccessful efforts of trappers and prospectors to wrest legendary riches from the Bitterroot Mountains. Here indeed is a classic Bitterroot trail!

The trail starts out by following the forementioned roadbed downhill through a very heavy spruce-fir forest that limits early views of the treeless mountains in the distance to a few tantalizing glimpses. The course ambles west and passes a marked junction with the Cedar Ridge Trail (6ML) before venturing upon a nameless pool situated at the headwaters of Cedar Creek. Here the trail rendezvous with a second junction while the old road continues left to a deadend back in the trees. The main trail turns right and drops alongside Kooskooskia Meadows, a veritable marshland of weedy inlets and placid pools that are the result of an unusually high water table. It is among the reeds and scattered copses of the meadows that Grave Peak makes its initial appearance to the northwest. After following the edge of the meadows for several hundred yards, the trail begins its climb of a forested ridge to the immediate west. Another signed junction—this time for the Pouliot Trail (30ML)—appears 0.5 mile short of Swamp Lake. A subsequent descent into the Swamp Creek drainage takes the traveler through subalpine forest and brings the trail to a lonely tarn berthed in the evening darkness of Friday Ridge.

Soft lake-bottom sediments trace the passage of foraging moose across the shallows of Swamp Lake. A few fire rings scattered here and there are the only human signs. Surrounded by a sparse white pine forest, the lake's immediate surroundings offer excellent campsites; however, the would-be angler might be frustrated at the absence of fish in these barren waters.

A steep, switchbacking ascent ensues above Swamp Lake, as the trail tackles the steep eastern flanks of Friday Ridge. The climb is not without reward, however, for as the trail draws ever closer to Friday Pass, the spectacular high peaks of the Bitterroot Range make their dramatic debut on the eastern horizon. Each advancing step heralds an improved view of the landscape that so captivated prospectors and trappers a mere century ago. As the route

174

completes its final switchback, an unmarked footpath veers right from the main trail, just over 100 yards below Friday Pass. This is the trail (905S) to Grave Peak.

Leaving the mainline trail behind, a sketchy footpath leads north to a drafty defile, where grotesque granite spires add an element of strangeness to the scene. Here you enter the Wind Lakes drainage and venture within sight of the Wind Lakes—an archipelago of blue-green tarns and shallow brown sloughs—for the first time. To the northeast looms Grave Peak, its 1924-vintage lookout standing atop a well-proportioned pyramid of broken granite. With your destination now fully in view, the trail makes a partial descent into the Wind Lakes drainage, then contours north to reach a high saddle at the headwaters of a Swamp Creek tributary. From this point, a poorly defined tread guides your north across rockslides and snowfields to reach the windswept heights of the 8,282-foot summit.

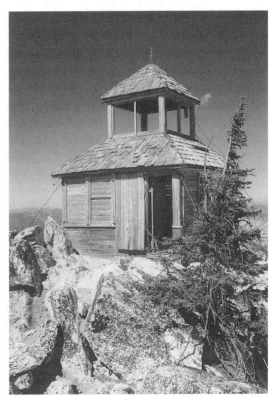

The Grave Peak lookout is one of only a handful of D-6 cupola structures that remain standing on the national forests of the Northwest. Its robust frame has withstood high winds and lightning since its retirement from active fire duty in 1968. From the lookout you gaze upon a landscape steeped in subtle mystery, with the panorama extending north to 7,950-foot Williams Peak in the Great Burn wilderness and southeast to the unmistakable shark-fin silhouette of El Capitan, some 32 miles away.

Side trips: The Wind Lakes provide a tempting side trip opportunity, as do Colt Lake and several of its unnamed counterparts in the same general vicinity.

This D-6 cupola shares the summit of Grave Peak with a lone fir on August 21, 1996.

50 Stanley Hot Springs

Highlights: Pleasant canyon scenery and a series of steaming hot springs.

Type of hike: Out-and-back day hike.

Total distance: 9.2 miles or 14.8 kilometers (round trip).

Difficulty: Moderate.

Best months: July through September.

Elevation gain: 1,760 feet.

Elevation loss: 260 feet.

Map: Huckleberry Butte USGS quad.

Special considerations: First-time visitors should note that one of the footbridges that formerly provided dry passage over Boulder Creek washed out during the winter of 1998–99, leaving a serious high-water ford in their absence. It is a structure the USFS has no immediate plans to replace. The stream is essentially impassable until early July. I strongly discourage overnight camping near the hot springs—the available sites suffer from tremendous overuse and are subject to occasional closure.

Trailhead access: Follow U.S. Highway 12 to the Wilderness Gateway Campground, located 84 miles west of Lolo and 26 miles east of Lowell. Leave the highway, cross the Lochsa River, and continue through the campground complex for 0.9 mile to reach the clearly marked trailhead parking area south of Boulder Creek. A spacious trailhead replete with restrooms and stock amenities (hitch rails and unloading ramps) is available here. Just walk downhill and cross the wooden suspension bridge over Boulder Creek to begin the hike.

Keypoints:

0.0   Inception of trail at Wilderness Gateway.
2.0   Trail enters the Selway-Bitterroot Wilderness.
4.1   Marked junction with the Rock Lake Creek Trail (221S).
4.2   Two log footbridges span Boulder Creek.
4.6   End of description at Stanley Hot Springs.

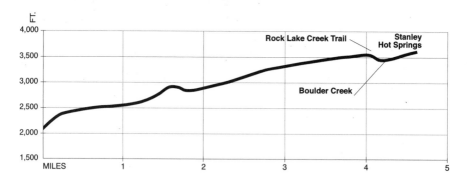

Stanley Hot Springs

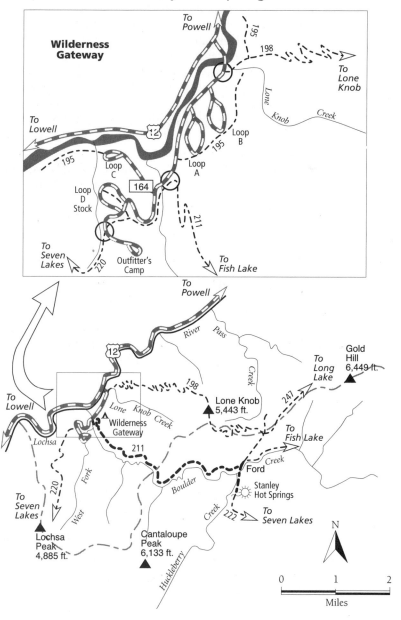

The hike: Stanley Hot Springs is far and away the most popular destination for day hikers in the Wilderness Gateway area. The trail provides good scenic value and makes a fine alternative to the ridiculously overused Jerry Johnson and Weir Creek hot springs found elsewhere along US 12. Plenty of packstock use the trail as an entry route into the Fish Lake area, so be prepared to step aside when necessary.

The trail initially follows a series of switchbacks through steep brushfields that still characterize much of the terrain razed in 1934 wildfires. Copses of birch and ash populate the mostly open hillside, and thimbleberries and ferns crowd the narrow trail. There are many good views of the lower Boulder Creek drainage, with Lochsa Peak and McLendon Butte rounding out the background scene. The route goes through heavy brushfields offering little shade but occasionally traverses stringers of heavier forest in some of shadier draws along the way. Drawing abreast of 6,133-foot Cantaloupe Peak, you enter the Selway-Bitterroot Wilderness 2 miles from the trailhead. Boulder Creek is also visible from time to time as it tosses in a flowing whitewater tapestry through the canyon below.

The trail enters heavier forest for a time, then comes to the first of several cutoff trails to Stanley Hot Springs. Any of these will take you to the Boulder Creek ford, but it is probably best to follow the main trail until the signed junction with the Rock Lake Creek Trail (221S) shows up. Just follow the arrow indicating "Huckleberry Flat" south along the well-trodden footpath that heads to Boulder Creek.

A pair of logs formerly provided dry passage across the dual channels of Boulder Creek, but where two footbridges once spanned the stream, only one now remains. The second gangplank collapsed and washed out over the winter of 1998–99, leaving only cribbing and log abutments on either side. I found the stream running dangerously high and swift on June 15, 1999; it seems doubtful that a safe crossing can be made until early July.

Once across Boulder Creek, the trail continues into deepening forest for another 0.4 mile to reach Stanley Hot Springs. The springs bleed their primordial heat in a series of thermal pools at a sustained temperature of up to 120 degrees F. Several campsites are available in the general hot springs vicinity, but they are so overused that I would recommend against an overnight stay.

51 Diablo Mountain Lookout

Highlights: Scenic views of verdant meadows, a sparkling lake, and the Bitterroot Divide.
Type of hike: Out-and-back day hike.
Total distance: 9.8 miles or 15.8 kilometers (round trip).
Difficulty: Moderate.
Best months: July through September.
Elevation gain: 1,700 feet.
Maps: Cedar Ridge and Jeanette Mountain USGS quads.

Trailhead access: Take Elk Summit Road south from its junction with U.S. Highway 12—42.8 miles west of Lolo and 67.2 miles northeast of Lowell—and follow the high-standard washboard to the confluence of Colt Killed Creek and the Crooked Fork. Continue along the main road to reach the marked

Diablo Mountain Lookout

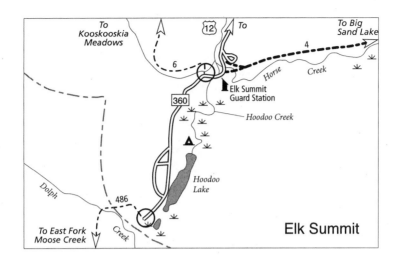

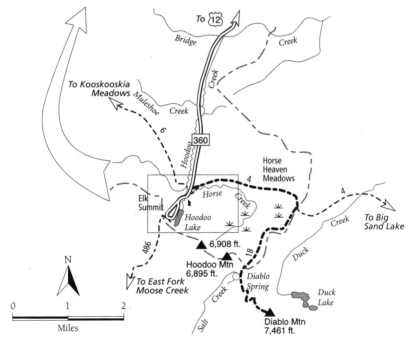

intersection with Forest Road 360. Turn right at this junction and follow the steep, narrow grade over Savage Pass and into the forested drainages beyond. You arrive at the combined Big Sand–Diablo Mountain Trailhead 18.9 miles from US 12. The trailhead features restrooms, spacious parking, and amenities such as horse ramps and hitchrails for those traveling with packstock.

(Be sure to check with USFS personnel at the nearby Elk Summit Guard Station for current trail information.)

Keypoints:
- 0.0 Inception of trail at Elk Summit.
- 2.2 Junction with the Diablo Mountain Trail (18S).
- 3.8 Trail enters the Selway-Bitterroot Wilderness.
- 3.9 Trail passes Diablo Spring.
- 4.9 Terminus of trail at the Diablo Mountain Lookout.

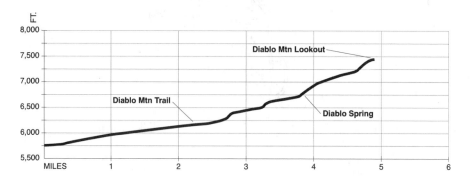

The hike: The lookout at Diablo Mountain provides a worthwhile day hike destination for travelers in the Elk Summit area. For a number of years a portion of the trail actually traversed Horse Heaven Meadows, but in 1995 this badly overgrown segment was barricaded and replaced with an alternate route that contours across a nearby hillside and instead offers a fine overlook of the meadows and their surroundings.

The trail saunters east from Elk Summit, climbing gently through pleasant woodland punctuated with mountain meadows. As it approaches the head of the drainage, you turn south to reach a marked junction with the Diablo Mountain Trail (18S) just five paces shy of the wilderness line. After following the cloaked flank of a low-lying ridge, the trail veers west for a surprisingly scenic traverse of the slopes overlooking Horse Heaven Meadows. These sylvan clearings gradually recede from view as the route makes a beeline for the high saddle at the head of Salt Creek. Directly to the west rise the tandem summits of Hoodoo Mountain.

The trail continues south and enters protected wilderness as a steep and rutted route in an open forest of subalpine fir. Soon thereafter you pass the supposed location of Diablo Spring—an intermittent water source whose whereabouts are difficult to pinpoint by late August—enroute to the ridge crest. As the route reaches the ridgeline, you gain an excellent perspective of the surrounding country—pocket bottomland meadows, deeply glaciated canyons, blue-green tarns, and stark burned forest. The trail next negotiates a final series of switchbacks that bring the journey to a swift conclusion atop the 7,461-foot peak.

Without a doubt, the Diablo Mountain Lookout boasts a panorama that at least equals those of half a dozen other active fire lookouts in the

Looking northwest toward Grave Peak from the Diablo Mountain Trail.

Selway-Bitterroot Wilderness. No fewer than a dozen major Bitterroot peaks lunge into the sky along the Montana-Idaho line; in abrupt contrast, only a handful of distinct summits rise to the west, deep within Idaho. Northerly views extend beyond a forested labyrinth to the remote mountains of the Great Burn Wilderness while the Goat Heaven Peaks hold court dead south of Diablo Mountain. Careful investigation may be necessary to locate a safe route of descent to Duck Lake, a cutthroat fishery whose green waters sparkle invitingly in the distance.

52 Lone Knob Loop

See Map on Page 202

Highlights: A challenging loop featuring fine Lochsa scenery and views into the Selway-Bitterroot Wilderness.
Type of hike: Loop (actually a lollipop).
Total distance: 10.2 miles or 16.4 kilometers (complete loop).
Difficulty: Difficult.
Best months: June through September.
Elevation gain: 3,600 feet.
Elevation loss: 3,600 feet.
Maps: Greenside Butte and Huckleberry Butte USGS quads.

Special considerations: Note that the Lone Knob Trail's location on the ground varies considerably from that shown on most government maps. The trail actually runs *atop* Lone Knob, contrary to what the USGS quadrangles and the Selway-Bitterroot Wilderness map would lead you to believe. The reason for this discrepancy is unclear.

Trailhead access: Follow U.S. Highway 12 to the Wilderness Gateway Campground, located 84 miles west of Lolo and 26 miles east of Lowell. Leave the highway, cross the Lochsa River, and continue through the campground complex for 0.9 mile to reach the clearly marked trailhead parking area south of Boulder Creek. A spacious trailhead replete with restrooms and stock amenities (hitch rails and unloading ramps) is available here. To begin the hike, walk north along the campground road for 0.8 mile to the unmarked starting point at the south end of the Lochsa River Bridge. There is no sign, but the trail is easy enough to recognize.

Keypoints:
0.0 Inception of the trail along campground road. Trail crosses Lone Knob Creek.
2.7 Trail reaches the crest of Lone Knob.
4.5 Junction with the Gold Hill Trail (247S); bear right to complete the loop.
5.1 Marked junction with the Boulder Creek Trail (211ML); keep right.
5.3 Marked junction with the Rock Lake Creek Trail (221S).
9.4 Trail returns to the Wilderness Gateway Campground.

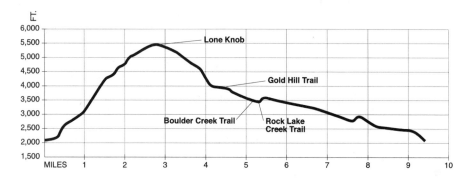

The hike: The trail over Lone Knob is rather strenuous fare for the casual hiker: The terrain is difficult, the trail is poorly defined in places, and the brushfields found on south-facing slopes can grow witheringly hot on a cloudless afternoon. Nevertheless, it is one of the very few loops in the Lochsa country that can be completed in a single day. It is best to schedule an early start so that you can tackle the steep climb from Wilderness Gateway before the hottest hours of afternoon arrive.

From its origins along the Wilderness Gateway Road, the trail enters stream-bottom forest and immediately crosses Lone Knob Creek. Thus begins the long, plodding ascent to Lone Knob. Switchbacks take you upslope at a workmanlike rate, traversing pockets of mountain birch intermingled with brush and bracken ferns. The going is fairly uneven underfoot but the trail does allow some fine views of the Wilderness Gateway and Lochsa Historical Ranger Station environs as it continues through heavy brushfields left in the wake of the Pete King Fire. Nearing the crest of Lone Knob, the trail

182

McLendon Butte guards the lower reaches of the Lochsa River near Wilderness Gateway.

reenters patchy timber before reaching an extensive brushy clearing atop the 5,344-foot point.

Lone Knob was the site of a USFS lookout some decades ago, but its low helm is now devoid of human presence. From various vantage points among the deer brush and scattered fir extend a surprisingly scenic panorama, taking in views of 6,449-foot Gold Hill as well as other peaks overlooking the Boulder Creek drainage to the south. The route here is poorly defined; indeed, were it not for orange flagging tape the trail would be far more challenging to trace.

The trail ventures into heavy forest after a time, then follows a generally easterly bearing straddling the divide between the Boulder and Pass creek drainages. In places the route descends quite steeply, and a heavy forest canopy effectively negates any scenic value. At mile 4.5 you arrive at a three-way junction located in a low, wooded saddle. (The left-hand fork continues to a dead-end above Pass Creek while the Gold Hill Trail [247S] leads up the ridge to the east.) The right-hand fork, also a segment of the Gold Hill Trail, descends through the tall trees for just over 0.5 mile to reach a marked junction with the Boulder Creek Trail (211ML). Another marked junction with the Rock Lake Creek Trail (221S) follows shortly thereafter. Disregard the several side trails cutting south toward Boulder Creek—these are cutoffs used by hikers headed for Stanley Hot Springs.

Beyond this final juncture you follow an excellent mainline trail downstream for just over 4 miles, traversing more low-elevation brushfields interspersed with islands of heavier timber. Views along the final leg take in some of the lower Lochsa peaks seen previously as well as several minor Boulder Creek tributaries—Cantaloupe and Asparagus creeks among them—across the canyon. Approaching Wilderness Gateway, the trail descends sharply on switchbacks to reach a suspension pack bridge over Boulder Creek. Cross this bridge and continue up the road to the trailhead parking area and your waiting vehicle.

Option: You can try hiking the loop counterclockwise, but doing so leaves the long, steep descent for early afternoon—the hottest hours of the day.

Side trip: Stanley Hot Springs makes a good aside as long as you are in the area and do not mind fording Boulder Creek. As with any popular day hike, it is probably best to avoid the hot springs during summer holidays and weekends, when they are most likely to be crowded.

53 Pouliot Loop

	See Map on Page 188
Highlights:	An exceptional short loop with lakeshore access and beautiful ridgeline scenery.
Type of hike:	Day hike or overnight loop.
Total distance:	11.5 miles or 18.5 kilometers (complete loop).
Difficulty:	Difficult.
Best months:	July through September.
Elevation gain:	3,670 feet.
Elevation loss:	3,670 feet.
Maps:	Cedar Ridge and Grave Peak USGS quads.

Trailhead access: Take U.S. Highway 12 to its junction with Elk Summit Road—42.8 miles west of Lolo and 67.2 miles northeast of Lowell—and continue south for 1.2 miles to the confluence of Colt Killed Creek and Crooked Fork. After crossing two bridges, follow the road through the cut-over Plum Creek plantation to reach the marked intersection with Forest Road 360. At this intersection, turn right and follow a steep, narrow grade over Savage Pass and into the forested drainages beyond. Watch for the Kooskooskia Meadows Road (358), which shows up 15 miles from US 12. Turn here and follow this rough wilderness-access road for the final 2.2 miles to its terminus (motorized access is prohibited beyond this point). There are no formal trail-head accommodations other than a makeshift hitchrail and rather limited parking space for perhaps five or six vehicles.

Keypoints:
- 0.0   Inception of trail at the Kooskooskia Meadows Trailhead.
- 0.7   Junction with the Cedar Ridge Trail (6ML).
- 0.9   Trail reaches a nameless pond and leaves the abandoned roadbed.
- 1.0   Trail draws abreast of Kooskooskia Meadows.
- 1.3   Trail enters the Selway-Bitterroot Wilderness.
- 2.2   Junction with the Pouliot Trail (30ML); bear left.
- 4.0   Trail crosses the crest of Friday Ridge.
- 5.5   Trail crosses Warm Springs Creek.
- 5.6   Junction with the Saturday Ridge Trail (89ML).
- 7.1   Junction with the Kooskooskia Meadows Trail (45ML) among the Wind Lakes; stay right.
- 7.2   Trail passes the easternmost Wind Lake.
- 7.9   Junction with the Grave Peak Trail (905S) near Friday Pass.
- 8.7   Trail reaches Swamp Lake.
- 9.3   Junction with the Pouliot Trail (30ML); bear left.
- 10.2   Trail leaves the Selway-Bitterroot Wilderness.
- 10.5   Trail returns to Kooskooskia Meadows.
- 10.6   Abandoned roadbed and nameless pond.
- 10.8   Junction with the Cedar Ridge Trail (6ML).
- 11.5   Trail completes the loop upon returning to Kooskooskia Meadows Trailhead.

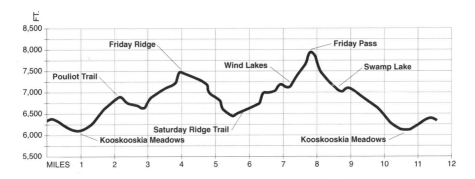

The hike: This loop makes a fine introduction to the Elk Summit country and offers considerable variety in a reasonably compact package. Over its length you encounter wet meadows, cross Friday Ridge via two high passes, and venture into the popular Wind Lakes area. The Pouliot Loop is suitable for both day hikes and overnight excursions—I recommend staying for at least a few days because of the numerous side trip possibilities.

The trail starts out by following the old roadbed downhill through a very heavy spruce-fir forest that limits early views of the treeless mountains in the distance to a few tantalizing glimpses. The course ambles west and passes a marked junction with the Cedar Ridge Trail (6ML) before stumbling upon a nameless pool situated at the headwaters of Cedar Creek. Here the trail rendezvous with a second junction while the old road continues left to a deadend back in the trees. The main trail turns right and drops alongside Kooskooskia Meadows before ascending a forested ridge to the immediate west. Another signed junction—this time for the Pouliot Trail (30ML)—appears at 2.2 miles.

From the junction the trail follows an easy contour around the hillside and then starts climbing at an increasing rate. With the increasing elevation come ever-improving views of the surrounding country, including many fine vantages of the peaks guarding the Bitterroot Divide 15 miles to the east. As you continue west, the route passes through open subalpine forest and a large boulder field to reach the crest of Friday Ridge. This high pass into Warm Springs Creek offers another fine panorama and makes a very pleasant stopover for lunch or even a short nap.

The trail dims momentarily as it cuts southwest across the backbone of Friday Ridge at an oblique angle and reenters heavy forest on the Warm Springs side. A continuous descent ensues over the next mile, during which time the trail swings north and crosses several minor rivulets to reach a series of wet pocket meadows along Warm Springs Creek. The marshy meadows and wet terrain found in this area cause the trail's location to become increasingly doubtful, but by crossing Warm Springs Creek and looking carefully on the opposite side you will find the correct route leading upstream to a signed junction with the Saturday Ridge Trail (89ML). From there a steep ascent takes you to the burned-over, boulder-strewn divide between the Warm Springs and Wind Lakes Creek drainages. Simply continue north to reach the signed junction with the Kooskooskia Meadows Trail (45ML) at a shallow woodland pond. A sign marks this junction as well.

You can lounge around the Wind Lakes basin for as long as you like—all three lakes offer good campsites and good fishing. Or you can also continue straight through to finish your hike in the same afternoon. Either way, just follow the badly eroded trail up the steep ridgeline southeast of the Wind Lakes to complete the loop. The route climbs at a fever pitch but offers excellent views to the north toward Grave Peak, at last gaining the crest of Friday Ridge after an 840-foot ascent. A large cairn marks the trail in a grassy clearing at Friday Pass. With the Bitterroot Divide once again on the eastern skyline, the trail descends sharply into the Swamp Creek drainage on a deteriorated tread and continues east to close the loop and return to the Kooskooskia Meadows Trailhead in another 3.6 miles of hiking.

Option: Hiking the loop in reverse (counterclockwise) is possible, but you are more likely to lose the trail in the wet meadows near Warm Springs Creek when traveling in this direction. This is not really a problem for patient backpackers out for an overnight trip, but losing the trail in the headwaters of Warm Springs Creek can quickly grow frustrating for those out for only a day hike.

Side trips: You should definitely schedule enough time to investigate the Wind Lakes area as well as the restored D-6 lookout site atop Grave Peak.

54 Wind Lakes

Highlights:	Three charming lakes nestled in attractive subalpine country.
Type of hike:	Out-and-back day hike or overnighter.
Total distance:	11.8 miles or 19 kilometers (round trip).
Difficulty:	Moderate.
Best months:	July through September.
Elevation gain:	1,350 feet.
Elevation loss:	1,100 feet.
Maps:	Grave Peak and Tom Beal Peak USGS quads.

Special considerations: If you have any aversion to stream crossings, be forewarned—this route includes *10* encounters with two major watercourses. Wet feet are probably unavoidable at two or three of the crossings, but a few others remain negotiable even during peak runoff. None are particularly hazardous.

Trailhead access: The trailhead at Tom Beal Park is reached by following U.S. Highway 12 to Elk Summit Road (111), whose turnoff is located 67.2 miles northeast of Lowell and 42.8 miles west of Lolo. Continue south and cross twin bridges spanning Colt Killed Creek and the Crooked Fork just upstream of their confluence. Take Forest Road 362 at its signed junction and follow this steep logging road for 10 miles to its terminus. The Tom Beal Park Trailhead rests on the divide between the Tom Beal Creek and Cliff Creek drainages, with an outhouse and parking for more than ten vehicles but no other amenities.

Keypoints:

0.0	Inception of trail at Tom Beal Park.
0.2	Trail enters the Selway-Bitterroot Wilderness.
0.3	First crossing of Tom Beal Creek.
0.7	Trail crosses Tom Beal Creek twice.
2.0	Trail completes its fourth crossing of Tom Beal Creek.
2.2	Fifth crossing of Tom Beal Creek.
2.5	Trail returns to the north side of Tom Beal Creek.
2.7	Seventh and final crossing of Tom Beal Creek.
3.0	Junction with the Wind Lakes Trail (24S).
3.1	Trail crosses Wind Lakes Creek twice.
4.7	Trail completes its third crossing of Wind Lakes Creek.
5.4	Trail reaches the lowermost Wind Lake.
5.8	Junction with the Warm Springs Trail (49ML).
5.9	End of description at the easternmost Wind Lake.

The hike: The Wind Lakes comprise one of the most compact gathering of mountain lakes on the Lochsa Ranger District. A base camp arrangement is perhaps the best way to truly appreciate the pleasant qualities of this remote country. Campsites at the lakes provide a convenient staging point for

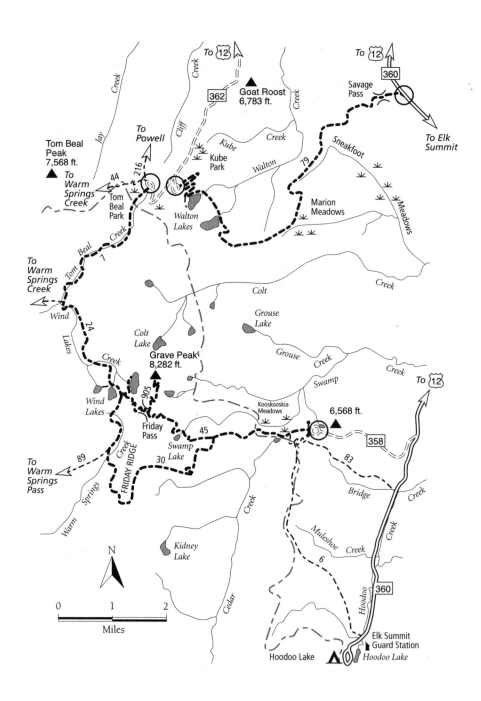

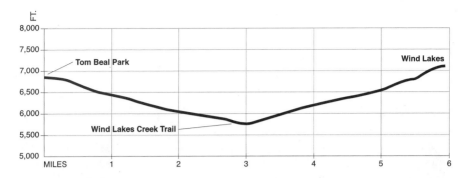

day hikes to other points of interest, with Grave Peak being the most exceptional choice.

Beginning in subalpine meadows at Tom Beal Park, the trail angles southwest and begins a slow descent into the Tom Beal drainage beyond the wilderness boundary. The route is badly furrowed from heavy horse traffic in many locations, but these are easy to detour around. It is more difficult, unfortunately, to avoid wet feet at any of the seven stream crossings you will encounter as the trail continues downstream. The creek itself is a rather docile beast, with boulder-strewn lodgepole benches overlooking meanders and cut banks along its channel. A gradual dogleg in the stream deflects the trail to a generally western course before returning to its approximate original bearing. You arrive at a signed junction with the Wind Lakes Trail (24S) 3 miles from Tom Beal Park. (Almost every nearby tree bears at least one blaze, so the junction is hard to miss even when covered with snow.) To reach the Wind Lakes, disregard the right-hand fork and continue left to ford Wind Lakes Creek. A good campsite is located on the opposite side.

The trail immediately returns to the east bank of the creek and continues upstream, traversing several timbered benches in succession and completing a tenth stream crossing as you close in on the lakes. Heavy forest limits your perspective with only a few views extending northwest to the vicinity of Cooperation Point. Reaching level ground 5 miles from the trailhead, the tread wanders over to an informal junction near a well-used campsite just north of the lowermost Wind Lake. Here a second trail diverges from the first, leading west to the smallest Wind Lake. Old spruce and fir surround the lake before you. Granite talus overlooks the scene from the south—a restful setting indeed.

The largest Wind Lake is located by following the trail around the first tarn and tackling its steep headwall to the east. Once beyond the steep pitch, you arrive at a shallow reflecting pool and a marked junction with the Warm Springs Trail (49ML). Continue left to reach the uppermost lake, only a short distance beyond. This large mosquito-infested lake is nestled in a timbered shelf southwest of Grave Peak. Anglers report catches of small brook trout in this and the other Wind Lakes. There is a good selection of campsites in the general area, many of which show signs of overuse. Please take care to leave no trace of your presence if you stay overnight.

A snowy day at the Wind Lakes.

Options: Two possible shuttle hikes are available from the Tom Beal Creek Trail (7S). The first choice involves a 13.9-mile point-to-point excursion to the Warm Springs Pack Bridge. Another possibility is to simply continue over Friday Pass from the Wind Lakes and ultimately reach the Kooskooskia Meadows Trailhead 3 miles southeast of Grave Peak. That choice involves a 10.5-mile hike with an especially attractive view from the pass. Either option requires some advance planning since two vehicles are necessary.

Side trips: There are several possible side trips from which to choose, but 8,282-foot Grave Peak is arguably the most worthwhile objective. Using the Wind Lakes as a base camp, make your way to the summit and its unusual D-6 lookout via a cross-country scramble or the Grave Peak Trail (45W) leading north from Friday Pass. For additional details concerning this peak and its lookout, see Hike 49.

55 Colt Killed Creek

Highlights:	A rushing watercourse flowing through a mostly roadless canyon.
Type of hike:	Day hike shuttle or overnight backpack.
Total distance:	12 miles or 19.3 kilometers.
Difficulty:	Easy.
Best months:	July through September.
Elevation gain:	2,820 feet.
Elevation loss:	2,060 feet.
Maps:	Grave Peak, Rocky Point, Roundtop, and Savage Ridge USGS quads.

Trailhead access: To reach the Colt Killed Creek Trailhead, take U.S. Highway 12 to its junction with Elk Summit Road, 42.8 miles west of Lolo, and continue south for 1.2 miles to the confluence of White Sand Creek and the Crooked Fork. Take Forest Road 368 east for 0.6 mile to the signed Colt Killed Trailhead. No formal facilities are available—just pull off the road and start hiking.

For the Colt Creek Trailhead, follow Elk Summit Road (111) south from US 12 to reach the marked intersection with FR 360. Turn right and follow the steep grade over Savage Pass to the junction with the Colt Creek Road (359), 11 miles from the highway. Bear left and continue down this very rough mountain road for 5.6 additional miles to the trailhead alongside Colt Killed Creek. An outhouse and ample parking are available, along with several primitive campsites located beside the stream.

Keypoints:

0.0	Inception of trail at the Colt Killed Creek Trailhead.
1.6	Trail crosses Cabin Creek.
2.5	Unmarked junction with the Roundtop Trail (57X).
2.7	Trail crosses Beaver Creek.
4.6	Junction with the Beaver Ridge Trail (47S).
7.3	Trail crosses Crab Creek.
9.3	Trail crosses Storm Creek.
12.0	Trail reaches its western terminus on FR 368.

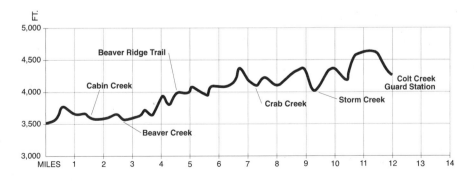

Colt Killed Creek

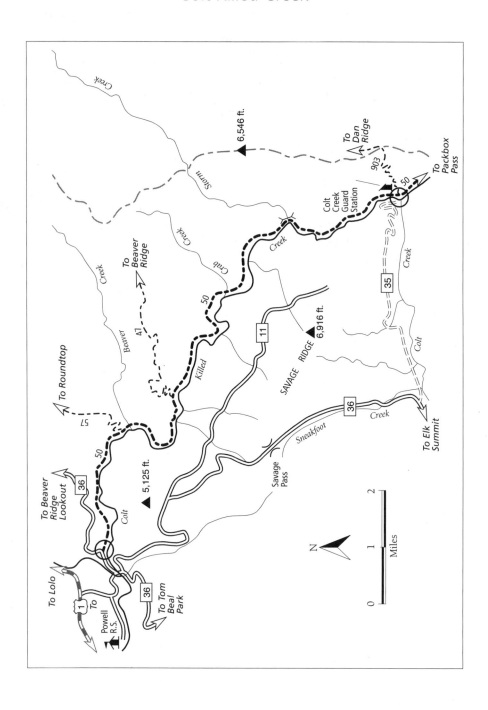

The hike: The trail along Colt Killed Creek offers an easy hike with lots of small ups and downs over its length. (Colt Killed Creek is labeled White Sand Creek on various forest maps of the area. The two are used interchangeably, although only the former is officially recognized by the U.S. Board of Geographic Names.) Its quiet beauty belies the fact that no part of the lower Colt Killed drainage falls within the Selway-Bitterroot Wilderness. Long-distance backpackers might consider this trail the first segment of a longer shuttle hike to either the Bear Creek (32.5 miles) or Big Creek (35.2 miles) trailheads on the Montana side of the Bitterroots.

From the trailhead, the route heads into the forest on a well-defined tread. The first mile offers a pleasant stroll through the trees; footpaths branch from the main trail to more closely investigate the stream. Colt Killed Creek is a swift watercourse with numerous pools and riffles that provide important spawning and rearing habitat for both resident trout and several anadromous species. In a sad consequence of the checkerboard land ownership patterns in the upper Lochsa, Plum Creek Timber Company logged the lower 2 miles of the drainage in September 1998. After crossing Cabin Creek, the trail continues upstream through more of the same before returning to woodland untouched by bulldozer and chainsaw.

Not long after leaving the last of the cut-over acreage behind, the drainage turns south and passes an obscure junction with the Roundtop Trail (57X), a long-abandoned route that once connected the Colt Killed Creek Trail to a USFS cabin at Roundtop. At Beaver Creek you will find several uprooted cedars that provide a dry passage across its main channel. The route stays close to Colt Killed Creek for a time, then begins climbing as the drainage rounds a wide U-shaped bend and swings southeast. There is a well-marked junction with the Beaver Ridge Trail (47S) at 4.6 miles.

The trail remains a healthy distance from the stream during the next 4 miles, traversing steep slopes several hundred feet above Colt Killed Creek. Scenic interest is mostly limited to the heavily forested canyon walls below Savage Ridge, although there are also views of 7,826-foot Hidden Peak at several points. Few obvious campsites are visible from the trail until you saunter within sight of a flat tent space crudely excavated into the hillside just south of Crab Creek. The route continues upstream and reaches Storm Creek after 2 more miles. If not for the excellent pack bridge, this sizable tributary would be an unsafe ford through early summer.

Beyond Storm Creek the trail climbs steadily upslope and crosses successive talus fields scattered across the canyon walls. Interspersed among these openings are stands of Douglas-fir and lodgepole pine, along with an occasional rivulet. The final mile is fairly uneventful as the trail descends slowly to a marked junction to the Colt Creek Trailhead. Just veer right from the junction and cross the high pack bridge over Colt Killed Creek to reach your waiting vehicle.

Option: Hiking this trail from south to north is slightly easier and has the added advantage of losing elevation overall. But if you cannot arrange a shuttle, try an out-and-back hike from the lower trailhead instead.

56 Cooperation Ridge

Highlights: A lightly used ridgeline route for hikers with expert
route-finding abilities.
Type of hike: Day hike shuttle.
Total distance: 12 miles or 19.3 kilometers.
Difficulty: Strenuous.
Best months: July through September.
Elevation gain: 1,550 feet.
Elevation loss: 5,360 feet.
Maps: Bear Mountain, Grave Peak, and Tom Beal Peak USGS
quads.

Special considerations: Tom Beal Park is included in this guidebook for
those of you with a penchant for "trails less traveled." It is a very demanding route, requiring stamina and excellent route-finding skills. Have your map(s)
and compass with you and plan for an early start.

Trailhead access: To reach your starting point at Tom Beal Park, take U.S.
Highway 12 to Elk Summit Road (111), whose turnoff is located 67.2 miles
northeast of Lowell and 42.8 miles west of Lolo. Continue south and cross
twin bridges spanning Colt Killed Creek and the Crooked Fork upstream of
their confluence. Take Forest Road 362 at its signed junction and follow this
steep logging road for 10 miles to its terminus. The Tom Beal Park Trailhead
rests on the divide between the Tom Beal and Cliff Creek drainages, with
an outhouse and parking for more than 10 vehicles but no other amenities.

The Warm Springs Pack Bridge is located approximately 55 miles west of
Lolo on U.S. Highway 12. It is clearly marked and features a wide pullout
parking area with room for two dozen vehicles. Additional trailhead parking and stock facilities are located just west of the lower parking lot. As the
crow flies these two trailheads are only 8 miles apart, but are separated by
a shuttle distance of nearly 24 miles.

Keypoints:
0.0   Inception of the Cooperation Ridge Trail (44S) at Tom Beal Park.
2.5   Junction with the Jay Point Trail (37W).
4.1   Junction with the spur trail (81X) to Cooperation Point.
4.3   Trail crosses the headwaters of Cooperation Creek.
6.2   Junction with the Robin Ridge Trail (938X).
7.2   Junction with the Eagle Ridge Trail (55X).
8.8   Trail runs atop Hot Springs Point.
11.7 Junction with the Warm Springs Stock Bypass Trail (46ML).
12.0 Junction with the Warm Springs Trail (49ML) on the Lochsa River.

The hike: The Cooperation Ridge Trail traverses high subalpine meadows
and ridgeline country for 12 miles along the northern periphery of the Selway-Bitterroot Wilderness. With an elevation differential of nearly 4,000 feet
between trailheads, the route presents either a calfburning ascent or knee-
jarring descent, depending on your direction of travel. From Tom Beal Park

Cooperation Ridge

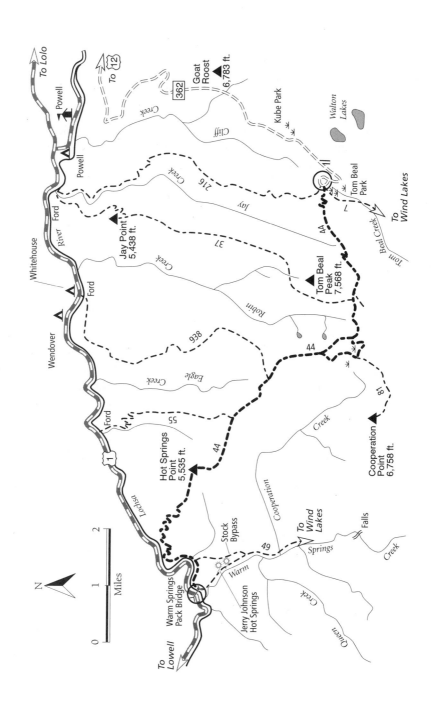

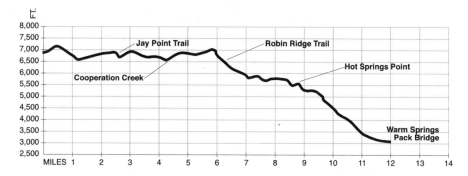

the trail may be followed for up to 4 miles without difficulty, but the route becomes a genuine bushwhack beyond Cooperation Creek. Topographic maps and compass are essential hardware. Prospective hikers who are unsure of their route-finding abilities should strongly consider an 8-mile out-and-back excursion from Tom Beal Park instead of the longer 12-mile shuttle outlined below.

From its beginnings in Tom Beal Park, the trail vaults Tom Beal Creek and follows a somewhat vague path as it climbs an open hillside to the northwest. With a fine overlook of the park environs, the trail reaches a grassy landing before turning southwest. A deeply furrowed tread traverses this south-facing hillside as it descends into a high saddle at the head of Jay Creek. To the northwest rises 7,568-foot Tom Beal Peak, whose boulder-strewn summit provides a recurring diversion for the next 3 miles. The descent continues for a time as the trail assimilates an old dozer grade. Lodgepole forest envelops the surrounding terrain, then the trail gains an incoming ridge and levels into a gentle sidehill. Openings in the trees yield a southeast glimpse to Grave Peak, where a tiny lookout is perched atop its mitered tooth. The trail continues west and soon reaches an informal junction used by outfitters to access prime elk habitat in the area. Follow the right-hand fork upslope. Straddling the wilderness boundary, the woodland canopy opens to reveal a high mountain meadow and series of mud wallows bounded by open parkland forest peppered with decaying blowdowns. The entire area, it seems, has the "feel" of elk, moose, and other big game, making it an intriguing destination during the fall hunting season.

The trail reaches another saddle in the woods above these meadows, where a signed junction with the Jay Point Trail (37W) appears; the trail leads sharply downhill into the marshy upper reaches of Robin Creek. After crossing a small stream—where the trail briefly disappears—the route renews its ascent. A series of excellent vistas draws the eye down the length of Robin Creek and north to Williams and Rhodes peaks in the Great Burn wilderness. The trail continues its climb through dry lodgepole forest, turning north with the ridgeline before it emerges from the trees. (An alternate route refrains from ridgeline exposure and instead crosses the head of Cooperation Creek near a junction with an abandoned spur trail to Cooperation Point.) This bald expanse offers another excellent panorama of the Lochsa's mountainous country, and the view of Tom Beal Peak is especially nice from this

196

A hiker takes in the view of Tom Beal Peak from the Cooperation Ridge Trail.

location. A diminutive lake resides anonymously in its own secluded basin below. Passing the rusting remnants of an old fire camp, the trail then reenters timber to the northwest.

The trail rises and falls with the topography for 2 more miles before making a sharp descent to a marked junction with the Robin Ridge Trail (938X). After crossing an old burn area, the grade slackens and a serious bushwhack begins. The going gets tough as the trail follows a poor tread marked with blazes so old as to look completely overgrown. Encroaching brush and downed trees are frequent nuisances. An unmarked but readily apparent junction with the Eagle Ridge Trail (55X) turns up some time later. At 8.5 miles you reach Hot Springs Point, an unremarkable forested knob, and continue west to a pair of artificial clearings from which USFS personnel once watched for wildfires. The poorly marked trail then drops onto the northeast ridge face and commences a grueling descent on switchbacks. Fir and pine soon give way to hemlock and cedar as you approach the Lochsa River. The trail then meanders for nearly 1 mile through wet cedar forest along the river, crossing as many as five rivulets and shaded ravines to reach the Warm Springs Pack Bridge.

Option: Hiking this trail in reverse, from west to east, is about as sensible as sinking the ship to put out the fire.

Side trip: If you are truly desperate for a side trip and have the time to spare, Jerry Johnson Hot Springs is one possible side trip. But the springs are so overrun (and overrated) that it hardly seems worth the effort.

57 Mocus Point

Highlights:	A lightly used ridgeline trail of below-average scenic value.
Type of hike:	Day hike shuttle.
Total distance:	12.5 miles or 21.1 kilometers.
Difficulty:	Strenuous.
Best months:	June through September.
Elevation gain:	3,810 feet.
Elevation loss:	4,040 feet.
Maps:	Greystone Butte and Holly Creek USGS quads.

Special considerations: Other than Eagle Mountain Creek and a small stream flowing through Indian Meadows, there are no reliable sources of drinking water convenient to the trail. Remember to top your water bottles (and your gas tank) before driving to the trailhead.

Trailhead access: The Mocus Point Pack Bridge is located 46.4 miles northeast of Lowell and 63.6 miles west of Lolo along U.S. Highway 12. USFS signs clearly mark the turnoff for motorists. The trailhead offers spacious parking, and outhouse, hitchrails and stock unloading ramps. This is a heavily used trailhead once the fall hunting season gets under way, but other-

Mocus Point

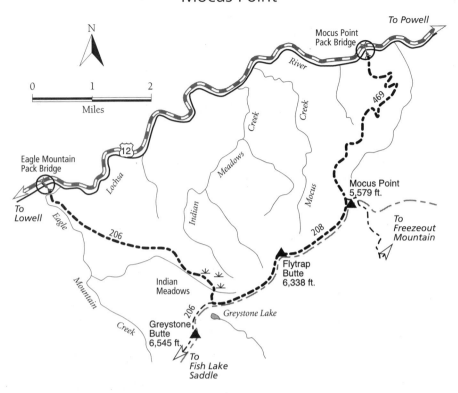

wise it is likely to be deserted compared to the nearby trailhead for Weir Creek Hot Springs.

The Eagle Mountain Pack Bridge is located approximately 38.1 miles northeast of Lowell and 71.3 miles west of Lolo on U.S. Highway 12. Like the other Lochsa River trailheads it is clearly marked and features a wide pullout area with stock unloading ramps and hitchrails. Parking for five vehicles is available.

Keypoints:

0.0	Inception of trail at the Mocus Point Pack Bridge.
4.5	Trail reaches the ridge crest west of Mocus Point. Junction with the Indian Meadows Trail (208S).
6.2	Trail reaches the crest of Flytrap Butte.
7.7	Junction with the Eagle Mountain Trail (206ML); bear right.
8.0	Trail reaches Indian Meadows.
12.2	Trail crosses Eagle Mountain Creek.
12.5	Terminus of trail at the Eagle Mountain Pack Bridge.

The hike: Prior to 1973 this trail was used primarily by USFS resupply parties headed up to the lookout at Mocus Point; today, with the lookout long gone, it is used mostly by hunters bound for spike camps in the Selway-Bitterroot Wilderness. It does not provide sweeping mountain panoramas, nor does it lend itself to convenient camping possibilities—the only sites

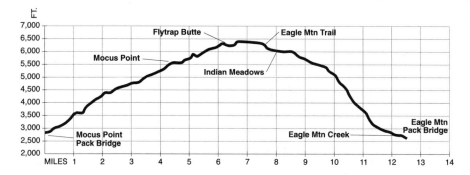

worth mentioning occur near Indian Meadows. It does, however, offer a reasonable degree of seclusion. Hiking this trail is not a bad way to spend an
afternoon in the woods.

From the Mocus Point Pack Bridge the trail begins its long, plodding ascent toward the ridge above. It enters stands of hemlock and western red cedar
on the flat south of the Lochsa River, then starts climbing on switchbacks.
The familiar sounds of a busy highway prevail in the background for the first
mile; other than northerly glimpses toward Ashpile Peak there is little to see.
Heavy brushfields provide the first unobstructed views east, with Bear Mountain being the most recognizable landmark on the horizon. After crossing several of these brushy pockets, you make your way to a junction with the Indian
Meadows Trail (208S) just west of 5,579-foot Mocus Point. USFS signs mark
both the trail junction and the Selway-Bitterroot Wilderness boundary. Disregard the left fork, which follows a poor trail over Mocus Point before descending into the Sponge Creek drainage, and veer right instead.

The trail straddles the wilderness boundary as it follows the ridgeline southwest for the next 3 miles. Heavy lodgepole forest effectively minimizes any
scenic value; decades of heavy stock use have eroded trenches to a depth of
3 feet in the decomposed granite tread. The route goes over 6,338-foot Fly-
trap Butte and surmounts a second forested prominence before descending
to a saddle north of Greystone Lake. Here you will find a marked junction
with the Eagle Mountain Trail (206ML). Stay right to complete the hike.

From the saddle, the trail bends northwest and quickly crosses a small
stream above Indian Meadows. The meadows themselves are not as intriguing
as the name might suggest—they consist merely of a lodgepole park with
a few boggy areas and mostly open understory. (Two large outfitter camps
located nearby see little use outside of the fall hunting season.) You continue to descend toward the Lochsa River and enter a running series of brushfields less than 1 mile beyond the outfitter camps. Various viewpoints along
the way offer views of 6,659-foot Castle Butte to the northwest as well as
Greystone Butte to the southeast.

The trail literally dives off the end of the ridge, dropping so steeply on
its furrowed tread that at times it is difficult to control your descent. Although the route traverses hot south-facing slopes most of the time, it sometimes ventures into timber on the opposite side of the ridge where the
surroundings are a full 20 degrees cooler. After reaching a good overlook,

200

you continue the knee-jarring descent to reach a log crossing of the lively stream. From there the trail contours around the sidehill and switchbacks down through river-bottom forest to reach the Eagle Mountain Pack Bridge. At the Lochsa River, pause and reflect. And if you like what you see, stop and relax before heading home for the day.

Option: Hiking this trail in reverse is substantially more difficult due to the lack of tree cover on the south-facing slopes above Eagle Mountain Creek. On a hot summer afternoon, this ascent is murderous. Bring plenty of water and get an early start if you decide to try it.

58 Old Man Point

Highlights:	A lightly traveled spur trail offering pleasant views and isolation.
Type of hike:	Out-and-back day hike.
Total distance:	13.4 miles or 21.6 kilometers (round trip).
Difficulty:	Strenuous.
Best months:	July through September.
Elevation gain:	4,280 feet.
Elevation loss:	1,410 feet.
Map:	Huckleberry Butte USGS quad.

Trailhead access: Take U.S. Highway 12 to the Wilderness Gateway Campground—located 84 miles west of Lolo Pass and 26 miles northeast of Lowell—and cross the Lochsa River. Follow signs for "trailhead parking" across the bridge spanning Boulder Creek. The trailhead includes two connected parking lots with complete stock facilities and restrooms. To avoid any needless confusion, follow the Lochsa Peak Trail (220ML) from the signpost at the stock unloading facilities, in the lower trailhead lot.

Keypoints:
0.0 Inception of trail at Wilderness Gateway.
3.0 Junction with the Old Man Point Trail (243S). Trail enters the Selway-Bitterroot Wilderness.

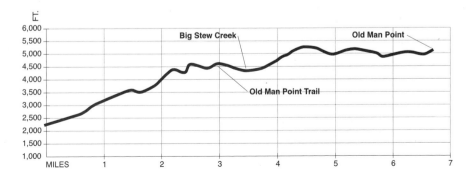

Lone Knob Loop • Old Man Point

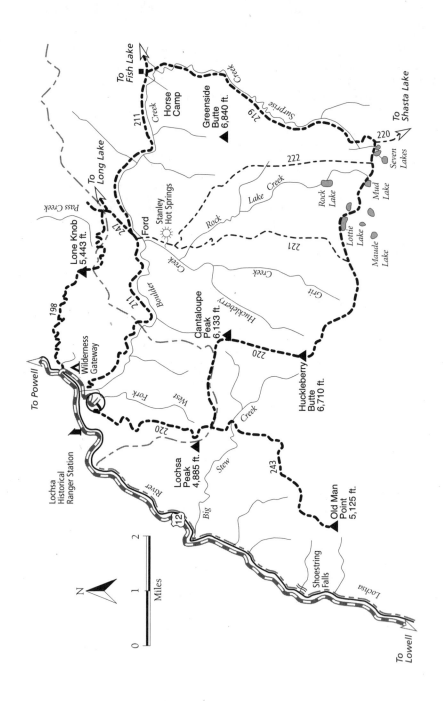

3.5   Trail reaches a wet crossing of Big Stew Creek.

6.7   Terminus of trail atop Old Man Point.

The hike: Old Man Point is one of the many inconspicuous 5,000-foot mountains that surround the lower Lochsa River. Although it lacks the scenic qualities of other peaks in the Wilderness Gateway area, Old Man Point remains an intriguing choice for quiet wilderness seclusion. Many poignant reminders of the 1934 Pete King Fire still haunt the landscape along this trail, such as the pockets of fire-blackened snags that loom like specters in the Big Stew drainage.

The trail initially climbs a fern-cloaked ridgeline west of the Wilderness Gateway Campground and emerges at a fine overlook of the Lochsa River and its immediate surroundings. With a soft but uneven dirt trail underfoot, you amble south through shady cedars and moist hardwoods. After vaulting several small brooklets, the trail traverses a sunny hillside whose southeast gaze includes the West Fork Boulder Creek drainage and Cantaloupe Peak. The trail maintains a steady ascent and soon reaches a small clearing in an otherwise wooded saddle just southeast of 4,885-foot Lochsa Peak. Here the trail forks: The route to Old Man Point veers right while the Lochsa Peak Trail (220ML) continues left, bound for the Seven Lakes basin. An inconspicuous signpost propped up against a nearby tree denotes the wilderness boundary.

Shortly after passing the first clearing, the trail saunters within sight of a second. As this opening disappears behind you, the trail makes a sharp descent into the Big Stew drainage. After a time the trail leaves heavy forest and returns to a gentle contour, while the ominous din of Big Stew Creek continues to grow. You soon draw abreast of the frothing brook and follow it upstream to a shallow crossing. The stream—which cannot be forded sans water contact until after mid-July—flows in the morning shadows of 6,710-foot Huckleberry Butte, an unassuming peak standing above the head of the drainage.

The trail resumes its climb beyond Big Stew Creek and eventually reaches several pleasant though unspectacular vistas of the Lochsa's mountainous terrain. Encroaching brush, occasional downed trees, and a few badly flooded stretches are frequent features along the final 2 miles of trail. Atop a forested saddle north of Old Man Point, the trail passes a primitive campsite used by outfitters during the fall hunting season. Soon thereafter the trail reaches its terminus atop Old Man Point. Although the peak once served as a USFS lookout site, there is little to see from the summit because of intervening larch and Douglas-Fir; however, the mountain does offer a few cursory glimpses of the distant and spectacular Selway Crags on the far southeast horizon.

59 Bear Mountain Lookout

See Map on Page 166

Highlights: A seldom-visited fire lookout with an exceptional view.
Type of hike: Out-and-back day hike.
Total distance: 15 miles or 24.1 kilometers (round trip).
Difficulty: Strenuous.
Best months: July through September.
Elevation gain: 4,250 feet.
Elevation loss: 120 feet.
Maps: Bear Mountain and Tom Beal Peak USGS quads.

Special considerations: Use of Jerry Johnson Hot Springs is restricted to the hours between 6:00 A.M. and 8:00 P.M.; overnight camping is forbidden.

Trailhead access: Take U.S. Highway 12 to the Warm Springs Pack Bridge, which spans the Lochsa River some 55 miles west of Lolo and 55 miles northeast of Lowell. Parking sufficient for two dozen vehicles is available beside the highway. Information concerning day use restrictions in the Warm Springs drainage is posted at either end of the bridge.

Keypoints:

0.0 Inception of trail at the Warm Springs Pack Bridge. Junction with the Cooperation Ridge Trail (44S).

1.2 Trail files past Jerry Johnson Hot Springs. Always a full moon here.

1.3 Trail merges with the stock bypass trail.

2.0 Notched log crossing of Cooperation Creek.

2.3 Junction with the McConnell Mountain Trail (213ML). Pack bridge spans Warm Springs Creek.

6.8 Trail reaches a signed junction to McConnell Mountain; bear right.

7.5 Terminus of trail at Bear Mountain Lookout.

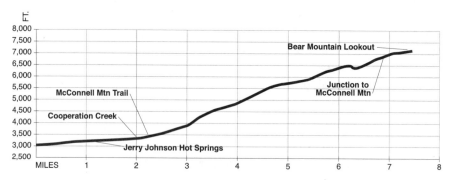

The hike: The McConnell Mountain Trail provides arduous passage to a mountain outpost that—according to one veteran fire watchman—typically sees fewer than two dozen visitors each summer. Though not exceptionally high, the summit of Bear Mountain offers a striking panorama of the surrounding country. Water is unavailable over long segments of the trail, which is well maintained in spite of the light traffic.

After crossing the Lochsa River you meet a junction with the Cooperation Ridge Trail (44S) and then wander through the ranks of fragrant cedar and hemlock for a mile to reach the Jerry Johnson Hot Springs. These waters issue from a series of deep fissures and collect in an archipelago of rock-lined pools—some alongside the trail and others well below—before disappearing into Warm Springs Creek. Just above the uppermost spring the trail passes a group of grassy wallows frequented by local moose, reconnecting with the stock bypass a short while later. Following a log crossing of Cooperation Creek the traveler reaches a marked junction with the McConnell Mountain Trail (213ML). Here a cable-anchored pack bridge provides high clearance over Warm Springs Creek.

Thus begins the most arduous segment of this trail, with switchback after steep switchback ushering the traveler ever higher through incredibly dense forest toward the crest of an unseen ridge. This rather featureless climb persists for another mile prior to gaining the ridgeline. After a time the trail reaches a burned-over pocket marking the easternmost extent of the 8,200-acre Freezeout Fire of 1994. The effect of this blaze is particularly striking as the course traverses a stark tract where the flames reached peak intensity and reduced green trees to acre after acre of blackened snags. Untouched forest momentarily reclaims the surroundings as the trail returns to its western heading and begins a brief descent that offers the first glimpse of Bear Mountain. After crossing a narrow saddle the trail begins its final climb toward the summit, reaching a signed junction to McConnell Mountain before leaving most of the timber—burned or otherwise—behind. Once out of the trees the trail proceeds north through extensive beargrass spreads high above the head of Queen Creek to reach the summit structures.

Bear Mountain Lookout has maintained its silent vigil over the surrounding Lochsa breaklands since 1951. A rustic storage cabin of much earlier vintage still stands nearby. Montane peaks and stony massifs extend to the limits of visibility in all four compass directions, and one could spend

Bear Mountain lookouts.

many an afternoon without ever being able to identify them all. The tranquillity at Bear Mountain Lookout belies the tempest wrought over so much of the landscape by the 1994 Freezeout Fire, whose fiery advance consumed much of the nearby forest but left the lookout buildings untouched.

60 Big Sand Lake

Highlights: A large upland lake with excellent angling and wildlife viewing opportunities.
Type of hike: Out-and-back day hike or overnighter.
Total distance: 15.2 miles or 24.5 kilometers (round trip).
Difficulty: Easy.
Best months: June through September.
Elevation gain: 590 feet.
Elevation loss: 1,060 feet.
Maps: Cedar Ridge and Jeanette Mountain USGS quads.

Trailhead access: Take Elk Summit Road south from its junction with U.S. Highway 12—42.8 miles west of Lolo and 67.2 miles northeast of Lowell—and follow the high-standard washboard to the confluence of Colt Killed Creek and the Crooked Fork. Cross the dual bridges, then follow the road through cut-over tree farms to reach the marked intersection with Forest Road 360. Turn right at this junction and follow the steep, narrow grade over Savage Pass and into the forested drainages beyond. The combined Big Sand–Diablo Mountain Trailhead is located at the first of three trailhead loops in the vicinity of Hoodoo Lake, 18.9 miles from US 12. It features restrooms, spacious parking, and amenities such as horse ramps and hitchrails for those traveling with packstock. (Pay a visit to the nearby Elk Summit Guard Station for current trail information.)

Keypoints:
- 0.0   Inception of trail at Elk Summit.
- 2.2   Junction with the Diablo Mountain Trail (18S). Trail enters the Selway-Bitterroot Wilderness.
- 3.5   Trail crosses Duck Creek.
- 4.4   Junction with the Big Sand Creek Trail (1ML); stay right.
- 4.6   Trail fords Big Sand Creek.
- 6.0   Junction with the Little Dead Elk Trail (5W).
- 6.1   Trail crosses Cold Creek.
- 7.0   Trail reaches the foot of Big Sand Lake.
- 7.6   End of description at the head of Big Sand Lake. Junction with the Frog Peak Trail (906S).

The hike: This trail offers access to Big Sand Lake, Elk Summit's single most popular destination. The lake is as popular a stopover for moose as it is for backcountry hikers: It is one of the very few places left outside a national park where you can regularly fish within four or five casting distances' of

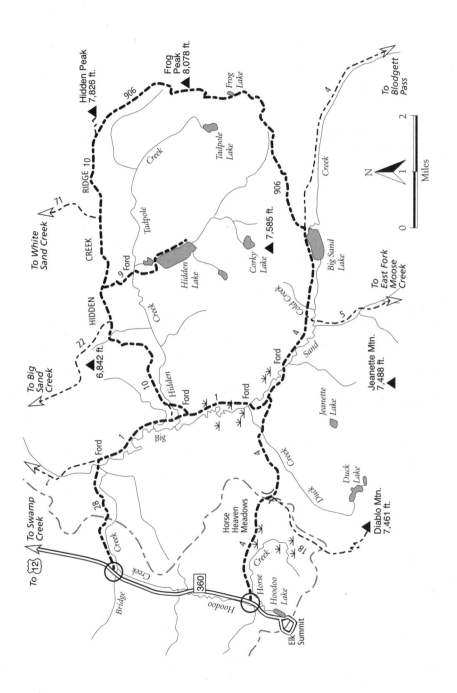

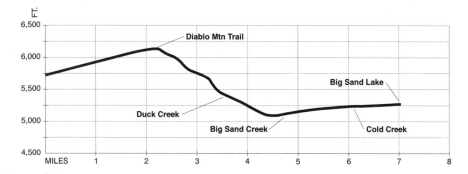

the ungainly creatures. Those traveling at a steady but unhurried clip should expect to reach the foot of Big Sand Lake in about three hours; even slower hikers can reach it in less than four.

The trail runs east from Elk Summit, climbing gently through woodland punctuated with pleasant pocket meadows for the first mile or so. Side trails lead down to Horse Heaven Meadows at several points, but the main route continues through the trees and bends south as it approaches the head of the Horse Creek drainage. A sign denotes the junction with the Diablo Mountain Trail (18S) just five paces shy of the wilderness boundary.

From here the trail enters the Big Sand watershed, following tread so torn up from packstock use that major reconstruction will someday be necessary to repair the damage. The route descends across a small boulder field on its way to Duck Creek, where a jumble of exposed boulders allows a dry crossing by midsummer. The trail continues over protruding roots and rotting puncheon walkways to a marked junction with the Big Sand Creek Trail (1ML). A heavily used camping area with good access to Big Sand Creek lies on the wooded flat a short distance beyond this junction.

At mile 4.4 the route reaches its first and only ford of Big Sand Creek. The stream here is broad and fairly shallow; however, there is no obvious way across that does not involve wet feet until late summer. Once on the opposite side, you venture into terrain that burned in the 1994 Big Sand Fire. The trail continues through burned timber alternating with green forest for the next few miles. In one of the most extensively blackened areas, the route reaches a cairn-marked junction with the Little Dead Elk Trail (5W) before crossing Cold Creek less than 1 mile short of Big Sand Lake. Green spruce and fir reclaim the surroundings as you approach its large blue expanse at 7 miles.

Big Sand Lake occupies a long, timbered upland valley. Rupe Peak and other high mountains provide splendid background scenery, and the trail, which continues past the head of the lake to Blodgett Pass, offers good access to the shoreline and to several campsites near the inlet and outlet. The lake attracts large numbers of elk and moose that are frequently sighted swimming in its shallows and feeding along its shores. Excellent fishing for cutthroat trout complements the picture. Big Sand Lake derives its name from the extensive beaches found near its inlet, whose sands were in turn derived from the decomposition of Idaho batholith gneisses and granodiorites over geologic time.

Option: If you dislike the idea of retracing your steps back to the trailhead at Elk Summit and are willing to arrange a shuttle, try hiking the continuous route east over Blodgett Pass and downstream to the Blodgett Canyon Trailhead. This 23.8-mile hike is best suited for a three-day backpack, but you should definitely try to schedule an extra day to visit Blodgett Lake—a short side trip on the Montana side of the Bitterroots.

Side trips: Several nice day hikes are available from a base camp at Big Sand Lake. The two best choices are Blodgett Pass and Frog Lake.

▲ The trail to **Blodgett Pass** follows a well-defined but severely eroded tread upstream for 5.6 miles, passing through heavy stream-bottom forest interspersed with brushy avalanche slopes and stands of lodgepole pine. There is little in the way of striking scenery for the first 3 miles, but the view improves dramatically as you ascend the final four switchbacks to reach the pass. To the northwest are views of the bare ridge running between Blodgett and Shattuck mountains, while Blodgett Lake and the full length of Blodgett Canyon unfold before you on the Montana side of the Bitterroots. Experienced mountaineers might try for the summit of 8,648-foot Blodgett Mountain by following a rugged route along the Bitterroot Divide and around the backside (southwest) flank of the peak. All told, the 11.6-mile round trip to the pass makes a fine day hike from your camp at Big Sand Lake.

▲ The **Frog Peak Trail (906S)** begins from a signed junction just six paces above the spur trail at the head of Big Sand Lake. It climbs continuously through the 1994 burn on switchbacks for the first few miles, then

Sandy fingers extend into the water at the inlet of Big Sand Lake.

209

reaches a pass into the headwaters of Hidden Creek. The trail next descends through silent forest for a time before beginning its ascent anew. (Do not bother looking for the old cutoff trail to Hidden Lake—it traverses marshy terrain and has seen no maintenance since the 1960s). From there the trail climbs to an open park on the Big Flat–Hidden Creek divide and runs north to a high pass above Frog Lake. A very steep descent takes you to several excellent campsites located very close to the inlet of this small, shallow body of water. Frog Lake is a lovely place to visit in the waning weeks of summer, after the biting insects have died off but before the onset of the fall hunting season. Its quiet charm is reserved for those lonely souls willing to make the difficult 7.6-mile round trip from Big Sand Lake.

61 Siah Lake

See Map on Page 169

Highlights:	A bright mountain lake with ample wildlife viewing opportunities and good fishing.
Type of hike:	Out-and-back day hike or overnighter.
Total distance:	15.4 miles or 24.8 kilometers (round trip).
Difficulty:	Difficult.
Best months:	July through September.
Elevation gain:	1,780 feet.
Elevation loss:	2,180 feet.
Map:	Ranger Peak USGS quad.

Trailhead access: There are two different ways to reach the Siah Lake Trailhead. The first is to take U.S. Highway 12 to Elk Summit Road—42.8 miles west of Lolo and 67.2 miles northeast of Lowell—and continue south for 1.2 miles to the confluence of Colt Killed Creek and the Crooked Fork. From there, follow Forest Road 368 east for 16.8 miles to the Siah Lake Trailhead, denoted by a forest sign and a primitive roadside campsite. The alternative is to turn onto the Beaver Ridge Road (369) at its junction with US 12, 35.5 miles west of Lolo, and follow the twisting mountain road for 12.8 miles to the same. The trail starts out along an old roadbed leading southwest past Beaver Meadows. Parking is limited to only three or four vehicles at the trailhead itself; just pull off the road wherever you can find room. No other facilities are present.

Keypoints:

0.0 Inception of trail near Beaver Meadows.
0.5 Signed junction with the Beaver Meadows Trail (77S); bear left. Trail enters the Selway-Bitterroot Wilderness.
3.2 Junction with the Storm Creek Trail (99ML).
5.7 Junction with the Siah Lake Trail (59S). Trail fords Storm Creek.
7.7 End of description at Siah Lake.

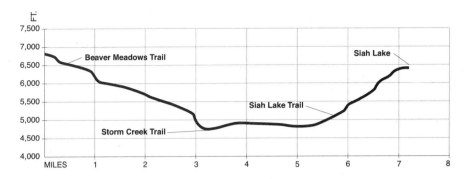

The hike: The trail to Siah Lake offers a challenging hike for folks looking to spend an afternoon or weekend at a pretty lake in the woods. Its configuration is somewhat unusual in that you begin high on Beaver Ridge, drop sharply into Storm Creek, and climb to almost the starting elevation on the opposite side of the canyon. The overall effect of this V-shaped profile makes the hike every bit as rigorous on the return trip as the initial hike into the lake. The trail is generally in good shape and holds up well to the heavy horse traffic it receives.

The trail starts out along an old roadbed and ambles gently downhill for the first 0.5 mile. A sign clearly marks the junction of the Beaver Meadows (77S) and Beaver Ridge (47S) trails; keep left and continue downhill. The trail descends into the Storm Creek drainage, passing through open forest with nice views of the surrounding country. At first the switchbacked descent is quite gradual but gets increasingly steep as you approach the stream bottom. The descent is slow and jarring; it takes about an hour to reach the unmarked junction with the Storm Creek Trail (99ML). There is a makeshift campsite available here; stay left for Siah Lake.

The Storm Creek bottomlands make for a very pleasant hike over the next 2 miles. Rivulets invade the tread from time to time, but the trail is otherwise in good shape (in fact, not a single downed log blocked the trail when I hiked it on September 29, 1999). Spruce-fir forest and recurrent clearings provide a varied landscape through which the trail passes. Watch for elk and white-tailed deer in these open areas and on the many gravel bars along the stream. At 5.7 miles you reach the junction with the Siah Lake Trail (59S). Though unmarked, the junction shows up in a grassy clearing with an unobstructed line-of-sight view to Storm Creek.

From the junction, the trail to Siah Lake goes south across Storm Creek, crossing at a shallow gravel channel that never exceeds ankle depth in late summer. Beyond the crossing you begin a prolonged ascent toward the unseen lake, alternately passing through open stands of larch and fir and thickets of tag alder and other low brush. Views of the Storm Creek drainage, though infrequent, are good. You reach Siah Lake after 2 miles of continuous climbing.

Siah Lake is a secluded body of water tucked away in a basin just below the main subsidiary ridge extending east to the flanks of Ranger Peak and the Bitterroot Divide. It is a rather charming locale, in spite of the fact that several campsites have been degraded through inappropriate excavation and leveling to accommodate wall tents and the like. Please make an effort to minimize your impact on these delicate sites and the nearby lakeshore. Siah Lake is worth visiting for the scenery alone, but also happens to offer good cutthroat fishing as well.

Option: A base camp at Siah Lake makes an excellent springboard for mountaineers interested in climbing 8,817-foot Ranger Peak, an impressive summit located along the Bitterroot Divide less than 3 miles to the south-east. The peak is very seldom climbed via its western ridge, but the ascent hinges more on sheer determination than technical expertise. Vestiges of an old spur trail lead as far as the saddle south of Ranger Lake. From there just follow the main subsidiary ridge southeast to the windswept summit.

Side trip: If you are out for more than a day hike and have a few extra hours to spare, why not hike up Storm Creek another mile or two? The trail passes through alternating forest and parks and is well maintained as far as the confluence of Storm Creek's main (north and south) forks. I stumbled across a large hunting camp while hiking this area one September afternoon: nearly a dozen wall tents and a huge stack of firewood stood at the margins of a spacious stream-bottom meadow, as did a makeshift corral and flagpole. What can I say? This is the only time I have ever seen the Stars-and-Stripes flown with the Stars-and-Bars in the backcountry.

62 Dan Ridge Loop

Highlights:	A lightly used loop for experienced hikers only.
Type of hike:	Day hike or overnight loop.
Total distance:	16 miles or 25.7 kilometers (complete loop).
Difficulty:	Strenuous.
Best months:	July through September.
Elevation gain:	3,980 feet.
Elevation loss:	3,980 feet.
Maps:	Savage Ridge and White Sand Lake USGS quads.

Special considerations: This is a demanding hike, to say the least, and in places the trail is impossible to locate with certainty. Only those individuals who possess the skills necessary to find and follow a faint trail for considerable distances should even consider it. *Do not* attempt this trail without both topographic maps and compass!

Trailhead access: Take U.S. Highway 12 to its junction with Elk Summit Road, 42.8 miles west of Lolo, and continue south to the confluence of Colt Killed Creek and the Crooked Fork. After crossing two bridges, follow the road through cut-over commercial timberland to reach the marked intersection with Forest Road 360. Turn right and follow the steep, narrow grade over Savage Pass to reach the marked junction with FR 359—some 11 miles from

Dan Ridge Loop • Hidden Peak • White Sand Lake

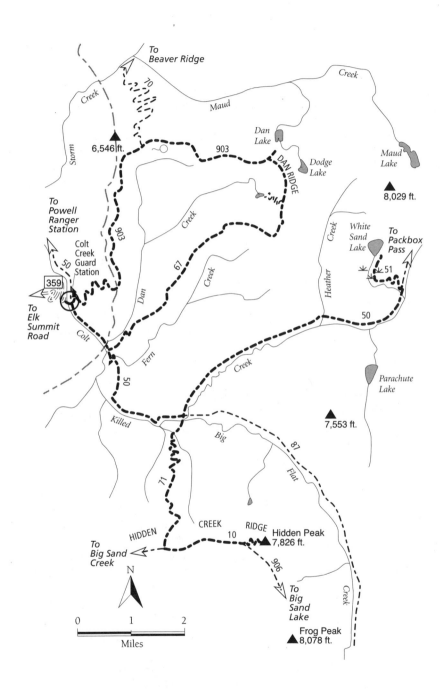

the highway. Bear left and continue down this very rough mountain road for 5.6 additional miles to the trailhead alongside Colt Killed Creek. An outhouse and ample parking are available, along with several primitive campsites located beside the stream below.

Keypoints:
- 0.0 Inception of trail at Colt Creek Trailhead.
- 0.1 Trail passes the Colt Creek Guard Station and corral. Junction with the Dan Ridge Trail (903S).
- 2.7 Trail enters the Selway-Bitterroot Wilderness.
- 5.7 Junction with the Maud–Dan Ridge Trail (70S).
- 5.8 Trail passes a mountain spring.
- 8.4 Site of abandoned Dan Ridge Lookout. Trail joins the Fern Ridge Trail (67X).
- 14.7 Fern Ridge Trail (67X) merges with the Colt Killed Creek Trail (50ML).
- 14.8 Trail crosses Dan Creek and exits the wilderness.
- 16.0 Trail completes its loop at the Colt Creek Guard Station.

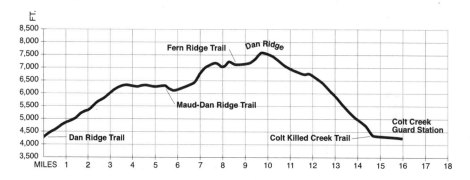

The hike: Here is a strenuous loop hike that ventures into some of the Bitterroots' wildest and least-visited backcountry, offering an unusually attractive vantage east toward the austere Bitterroot Divide. The description outlined below follows the route in a clockwise direction, beginning with the reasonably intact Dan Ridge Trail (903S) and returning to the vicinity of Colt Killed Creek via the Fern Ridge Trail (67X).

Beginning in the cool bottomlands beside Colt Killed Creek, the trail crosses the stream on a high wooden pack bridge, then turns right and continues for a short distance to the combined Colt Creek Guard Station and corral. The Dan Ridge Trail (903S) veers left at a marked junction just south of this structure. The mountainside becomes progressively steeper as the route cuts sharply upslope on a haphazard path that zigzags through stands of larch, Engelmann spruce, and Douglas-fir. Gradually the low din of water rushing through the canyon below gives way to the lonely hush of an autumn wind issuing through ridgeline timber. The ascent is inexorable and difficult, passing an old metal sign that indicates a water source some 150 yards off the trail.

Upon reaching the ridge crest, you enter the Selway-Bitterroot Wilderness and hurriedly turn north to follow a substantially easier grade. With little in the way of scenic views, the next 3 miles pass rather quickly as the well-defined tread makes its way through a hallway of evergreens to rendezvous with the Maud–Dan Ridge Trail (70S). This unsigned but readily apparent junction shows up as the trail reaches a saddle just above a pocket meadow visible through the trees—site of an outfitter's camp that is generally occupied by Labor Day each year. A single spring issues from an unseen source farther along the trail, which crosses several boggy sections before renewing its ascent. Reminders of days gone by soon appear alongside the trail, where abandoned porcelain insulators and bundles of wire are all that remain of an old telephone line that once provided communication to the Dan Ridge Lookout. These vestiges of human activity litter the trail at odd intervals, still awaiting removal from the wilderness.

The route reaches the first of many scenic vistas atop a boulder-covered ridge about 2.5 miles east of the spring. Northeast views extend along the Maud Creek drainage and to the massive gray summit of Ranger Peak. Lower ridges and mountains rise from forested uplands in the opposite direction, with 8,282-foot Grave Peak providing the most recognizable landmark on the southwest horizon. Directly ahead stands the forest-and-talus prominence of Dan Ridge. The trail becomes increasingly illegible as it approaches the former Dan Ridge Lookout site, once perched atop its northernmost promontory.

Reaching the long-abandoned lookout site requires a short uphill jaunt along a very poor and indistinct spur trail. Surrounded by the stumps of trees felled to accommodate the USFS outpost, Dan Ridge Lookout operated from 1934 to 1973. Reconnaissance on September 1, 1998, revealed charred timbers and four concrete footings as the only surviving traces of the L-4 structure. The mountainous panorama that unfolds to the east, however, has remained essentially unchanged in the years since the lookout's demise. Tooth-shaped Dan Lake lies directly below while the deeper and more reclusive Dodge Lake retains its own secrets farther southeast.

The Fern Ridge Trail (67X) leads southeast from an obscure trail junction below the old lookout site. A gradual descent takes the route through heavy timber, following occasional blazes as it circles around high above the head of Dan Creek on the 7,100-foot contour—high enough to clear the steepest terrain but low enough to avoid extensive talus fields found on the higher slopes. This difficult-to-follow segment improves from time to time, but if its location is in doubt, you can just scramble to Dan Ridge and follow it south toward Point 7,598. (Unsuspecting visitors may be fooled into following a blazed route that switchbacks down to the vicinity of a nameless lake at the headwaters of Dan Creek. Woodsmen probably established this trail to patrol their trap lines during the early 1900s, but it is not the correct route, nor is it depicted on any current map.) For its part the main trail continues south and reaches a high divide between the Dan and Heather creek drainages, then climbs steeply uphill to reach its apex near Point 7,598. Views from these precipitous heights take in much of Heather Creek and regal mountains such as the Heavenly Twins and Sky Pilot.

Having attained its maximum elevation, the route enters burned-over country as it turns west and proceeds through a stark environment with sharp contrast between the white bedrock and blackened fir. Often the trail's whereabouts are difficult to decipher and it drops through the burn, following charred blazes all the while. Reentering stands of living trees from time to time, the route continues its descent before returning to another burned section razed during the 1994 Fern Creek Fire. In an unlikely reversal of fortunes, the route regains its lost definition upon leaving the burn behind and continues a sharp descent on an obvious trail blocked with occasional downed timber. Many of the surrounding larch and fir bear the scars of lightning strikes—wounds that spiral down the length of the tree and are slow to heal. Some authorities have speculated that perhaps a magnetic anomaly within the underlying ridge is responsible for this unusual concentration of strikes. The trail once again grows indistinct as it approaches the canyon floor, forcing you to watch for old blazes and sawn logs as visual cues. At last the trail emerges from brush and thickets to reach an unmarked junction with the Colt Killed Creek Trail (50ML) about 1.4 miles upstream of the Colt Creek Guard Station. Turn right to return to the trailhead.

An unavoidable early-season ford of Dan Creek quickly follows, and the stream bottom trail leaves the wilderness behind. Another mile of uneventful travel alongside Colt Killed Creek brings the trail to the Colt Creek Guard Station and draws this loop to a close.

Option: Hiking this loop in reverse (counterclockwise) is a good idea if you want to treat Dan Ridge as a day hike. Most hikers don't relish the thought of following a faint trail in fading daylight, so plan to tackle the Fern Ridge segment first thing in the morning. Keep your eyes peeled—the junction of the Fern Ridge Trail (67X) is unmarked and easy to miss.

A wildfire burns in the headwaters of Heather Creek on September 1, 1998.

63 Hidden Lake

See Map on Page 207

Highlights: A large mountain lake with good campsites and excellent cutthroat fishing.
Type of hike: Out-and-back day hike or overnighter.
Total distance: 17.4 miles or 28 kilometers (round trip).
Difficulty: Moderate.
Best months: July through September.
Elevation gain: 1,330 feet.
Elevation loss: 1,070 feet.
Maps: Jeanette Mountain and Savage Ridge USGS quads.

Special considerations: This trail requires three significant fords that can cause problems for parties attempting the hike to Hidden Lake in early summer. It is best to wait until late July to make the trip; I had no difficulty with any of the fords on August 22, 1999. Those traveling on horseback should note there is no grazing for stock at either of the two main campsites at Hidden Lake. A third site suffered from chronic overuse and was razed by USFS and volunteer personnel in August 1999.

Trailhead access: Take the Elk Summit Road south from its junction with U.S. Highway 12—42.8 miles west of Lolo and 67.2 miles northeast of Lowell—and follow the high-standard washboard to the confluence of Colt Killed Creek and the Crooked Fork. Cross the dual bridges, then follow the road through cut-over forest to reach the marked intersection with Forest Road 360. Turn right at this junction and follow the steep, narrow grade over Savage Pass and into the forested drainages beyond. Some 16.1 miles after leaving the pavement on US 12 you arrive at the signed pullout at the Bridge Creek Trailhead. A stock unloading ramp and hitchrail are available, as is limited roadside parking for three or four vehicles. Please do not block the unloading ramps when you pull off the road.

Keypoints:
  0.0   Inception of trail at the Bridge Creek Trailhead.
  1.0   Trail enters the Selway-Bitterroot Wilderness.
  2.1   Trail crosses Bridge Creek.
  2.2   Trail reaches the banks of Big Sand Creek.
  2.3   Junction with the Big Sand Creek Trail (1ML); stay right.
  4.0   Junction with the cutoff trail up Hidden Creek Ridge.
  4.4   Junction with the Hidden Peak Trail (10S).
  6.7   Signed junction with Swamp Ridge Trail (22S).
  7.3   Trail passes outfitter camp.
  7.4   Unmarked junction with the Hidden Lake Trail (9S).
  8.2   Trail crosses Hidden Creek.
  8.7   End of description at the foot of Hidden Lake.

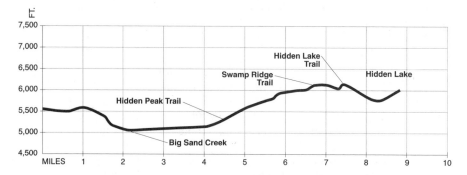

The hike: The hike to Hidden Lake provides a pleasant summer foray into some nice country. Much of the trail leading to the lake is of rather low scenic value, although the destination more than compensates for any perceived shortcomings. Experienced hikers with an early start might treat Hidden Lake as a long day hike, but staying overnight is the best way to fully appreciate its beauty. Chances are good you will not be alone.

The trail leads downhill from its inception, initially passing within sight of several wet meadows gathered along Bridge Creek. In its early miles the route fails to conserve on elevation gain and loss as it repeatedly rises and falls for no apparent reason. The overall descent continues until you pass a primitive camping area just west of Bridge Creek. Ironically enough, this stream must be forded—there is no bridge. A second knee-deep ford follows close on the heels of the first at Big Sand Creek, which flows lazily through a spacious streamside meadow. Just beyond another obvious campsite east of the crossing is a signed junction with the Big Sand Creek Trail (1ML).

The main trail continues through timber for the next several miles, gaining very little elevation in the process. Other than a few isolated boulder fields and cliffs, there is little to see. At 4 miles you reach an unmarked cutoff trail up Hidden Creek Ridge. (Stay left at this obvious junction unless you would prefer to ford Hidden Creek twice.)

A steady ascent ensues as the route begins to pick up elevation and ties in with the Hidden Peak Trail (10S). The climb toward Hidden Creek Ridge is long and tiring, alternately traversing young lodgepole forest interspersed with older spruce and fir. Few sources of water are convenient to the trail and—almost without exception—heavy tree cover precludes scenic views of any kind. The route follows a northeasterly tack past a marked junction with the Swamp Ridge Trail (22S), then reaches an obvious outfitter camp in a wooded saddle at 7.3 miles. The small perennial stream found here provides the first reliable source of drinking water since leaving the vicinity of Hidden Creek nearly 3 miles back.

Only a short distance east of the outfitter camp you arrive at an unmarked but well-defined junction with the Hidden Lake Trail (9S). From the junction the tread descends steadily across timbered terrain to reach Hidden Creek at 8.2 miles. Crossing the watercourse requires either a tricky boulder hop

Big Sand Creek runs slow and deep above its confluence with Bridge Creek.

or a shallow ford. Once on the opposite side you continue south through bottomland forest and pass a small outlying lake to the east. The trail brings you to a nice camping area near the foot of Hidden Lake.

Given its considerable size, Hidden Lake's name seems an unlikely paradox—when standing on its shoreline, nothing about it seems hidden or even low-key. This large, relatively low-elevation lake offers several good campsites along its lower end, including one location very close to the outlet. Hidden Lake is home to a self-sustaining population of red-bellied cutthroat trout and freshwater crawdads. Older maps show a connecting trail leading along the eastern lakeshore and upstream and to a junction near the head of the drainage, but the USFS long ago abandoned this marshy upper segment.

64 Hidden Peak

See Map on Page 213

Highlights: An exceptional, close-up view of the Bitterroot Divide and numerous high granite peaks.
Type of hike: Out-and-back day hike or overnighter.
Total distance: 18.4 miles or 29.6 kilometers (round trip).
Difficulty: Strenuous.
Best months: July through September.
Elevation gain: 3,690 feet.
Elevation loss: 120 feet.
Maps: Blodgett Mountain, Jeanette Mountain, Savage Ridge, and White Sand Lake USGS quads.

Special considerations: Experienced and well-conditioned hikers can tackle Hidden Peak as a day hike, but since the trailhead involves a long (2-hour plus) drive for most people, treating this as an overnighter is perhaps a better choice. The sole source of difficulty along the trail is the ford of Colt Killed Creek, which must be crossed without the benefit of any bridge or downed trees. No water source is convenient to the trail over its final 5 miles, so filter several extra bottles' worth before starting the long climb out of Colt Killed Creek.

Trailhead access: Take U.S. Highway 12 to its junction with Elk Summit Road, 42.8 miles west of Lolo, and continue south to the confluence of Colt Killed Creek and the Crooked Fork. After crossing two bridges, follow the road through cut-over commercial timberland to reach the marked intersection with Forest Road 360. Turn right and follow the steep, narrow grade over Savage Pass to reach the marked junction with FR 359, 11 miles from the highway. Bear left and continue down this very rough mountain road for 5.6 more miles to the trailhead alongside Colt Killed Creek. An outhouse and ample parking are available, along with several primitive campsites beside the stream below.

Keypoints:
- 0.0   Inception of trail at Colt Creek Trailhead.
- 0.1   Trail passes the Colt Creek Guard Station and corral. Junction with the Dan Ridge Trail (903S).
- 1.2   Trail enters the Selway-Bitterroot Wilderness and crosses Dan Creek.
- 1.3   Unmarked junction with the Fern Ridge Trail (67X).
- 1.4   Trail crosses Fern Creek.
- 3.8   Junction with the Big Flat–Hidden Ridge Trail (71ML). Trail fords Colt Killed Creek.
- 7.2   Junction with the Hidden Peak Trail (10S); keep left.
- 8.8   Marked junction with the Frog Peak Trail (906S) below Hidden Peak.
- 9.2   Terminus of trail at the old lookout site atop Hidden Peak.

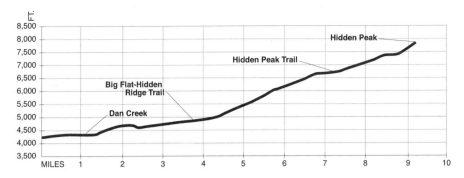

The hike: Hidden Peak is among the lesser-known lookouts of the Selway-Bitterroot Wilderness, but what it lacks in widespread recognition it more than makes up for in scenic value. The trail is in good condition and remains easy to follow at all times, with all junctions clearly marked and few obstructions to slow you down. The hike described below provides the shortest of several possible approach routes to the peak; even at that, it is still a long haul to the lonely lookout perched atop its summit.

Beginning at the pack bridge over Colt Killed Creek, the trail crosses the stream and veers right at a marked junction. You pass the Colt Creek Guard Station and a marked junction with the Dan Ridge Trail (903S) and follow the boulder-studded watercourse upstream to the Selway-Bitterroot Wilderness boundary at Dan Creek. As it briefly switchbacks toward Fern Creek, the route passes the Fern Ridge Trail (67X), which cuts back upslope from an unmarked junction. Beyond Fern Creek the trail ascends a forested swale, then changes its heading to a more easterly direction upon rejoining Colt Killed Creek.

On its way upstream the trail traverses forest burned in the 1999 wildfire season. (I hiked this trail on September 5, 1999, while the fire was still burning high on the hillside well above the trail. When I returned five weeks later, large swaths on both sides of the trail had been charred and smoky pall hung over the still-smoldering forest, illustrating how dramatically trail conditions can change in only a short time.) Easy hiking continues until you reach a large, well-established campsite on a lodgepole flat just across from the signed junction with the Big Flat–Hidden Ridge Trail (71ML). I recommend staying overnight here so that you can get an early start for the push to Hidden Peak the next morning.

The trail makes a tricky high-water crossing of Colt Killed Creek, passes an obvious outfitter's camp off to the left, and starts the plodding ascent to Hidden Creek Ridge. Heavy forest largely precludes sweeping vistas; steep terrain makes for slow going as you make your way through spruce and fir forest checkered with younger stands of lodgepole. The worst of the grind is over once you reach the signed three-way junction with the Hidden Peak Trail (10S) atop Hidden Creek Ridge at 7.2 miles. Bear left for the lookout.

The trail continues east on a good tread, climbing gradually along the crest of Hidden Creek Ridge. You arrive at a junction with the Frog Peak Trail (906S) less than 0.5 mile short of your destination. The final pitch to Hidden Peak is steep and eroded, switchbacking through increasingly open forest toward the unseen summit structure. The old lookout at last appears on the slightly lower northern knob of the peak, standing there resolute and dignified in spite of its age.

From Hidden Peak Lookout you gaze upon a bright land infused with light and color—the windswept crest of the Bitterroot Divide provides an especially inspiring focus. High peaks rise in every direction: Most (such as 8,078-foot Frog Peak) lie wholly inside Idaho, whereas others (including 8,984-foot Castle Crag) peer over the divide from Montana. The second-generation L-4 lookout has stood on its masonry foundation since 1961, when it was constructed by the USFS to replace the original structure. It was withdrawn from active duty in 1979 and was subsequently abandoned. These days it is not unusual for six or seven months to pass without the summit seeing a single human visitor, which in part explains its state of disrepair. Creaking stairsteps, broken railings, missing shutters, shattered windows—such are the trappings of neglect.

This abandoned L–4 lookout stands among the fir at Hidden Peak.

65 White Sand Lake

See Map on Page 213

Highlights: An excellent, easy-to-follow trail with a gentle gradient and lots of wildlife.
Type of hike: Out-and-back overnighter.
Total distance: 21.4 miles or 34.4 kilometers (round trip).
Difficulty: Moderate.
Best months: July through September.
Elevation gain: 2,870 feet.
Elevation loss: 160 feet.
Maps: Savage Ridge and White Sand Lake USGS quads.

Trailhead access: Take U.S. Highway 12 to its junction with Elk Summit Road, 42.8 miles west of Lolo, and continue south to the confluence of Colt Killed Creek and the Crooked Fork. After crossing two bridges, follow the road through cut-over commercial timberland to the marked intersection with Forest Road 360. Turn right and continue on the steep, narrow grade over Savage Pass to reach the marked junction with FR 359, 11 miles from the highway. Bear left and continue down this very rough mountain road for another 5.6 miles to the trailhead alongside Colt Killed Creek. An outhouse and ample parking are available, as are several primitive campsites beside the stream below.

Keypoints:
- 0.0   Inception of trail at Colt Creek Trailhead.
- 0.1   Trail passes the Colt Creek Guard Station and corral. Junction with the Dan Ridge Trail (903S).
- 1.2   Trail enters the Selway-Bitterroot Wilderness and crosses Dan Creek.
- 1.3   Unmarked junction with the Fern Ridge Trail (67X).
- 1.4   Trail crosses Fern Creek.
- 3.8   Marked junction with the Big Flat-Hidden Ridge Trail (71ML). Junction with the Big Flat Creek Trail (87X).
- 7.2   Trail crosses Heather Creek.
- 8.7   Marked junction with the Garnet Creek Trail (43X).
- 9.0   Trail crosses Colt Killed Creek.
- 9.1   Junction with the White Sand Lake Trail (51S).
- 10.7 End of trail description at White Sand Lake.

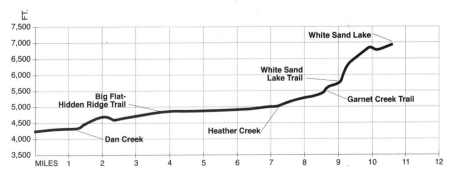

The hike: This excellent trail offers access to a beautiful but shallow mountain lake well suited for a summer visit. The route is easy to follow and in good condition over its entire length, and except for the final mile to White Sand Lake, the grade is quite gentle. White Sand Lake is one of the more secluded lakes in the high Bitterroots but has attracted increasing attention from stock users in recent years, including those who make their way to the lake from base camps on the Montana side of the Bitterroots.

Beginning in the cool bottomlands along Colt Killed Creek, the trail crosses the stream on a high wooden pack bridge, then turns right and continues for a short distance to the combined Colt Creek Guard Station and corral. From the Guard Station you continue past a marked junction with the Dan Ridge Trail (903S) and follow the boulder-studded watercourse upstream to the Selway-Bitterroot Wilderness boundary at Dan Creek. The route remains in heavy stream-bottom forest, and, as it briefly switchbacks toward Fern Creek, you sidestep the Fern Ridge Trail (67X) at an unmarked junction. Beyond Fern Creek the trail ascends a forested swale but changes its heading to a more easterly direction upon rejoining Colt Killed Creek. The easy hiking continues among trees burned in a 1999 wildfire until you reach a signed junction with the Big Flat–Hidden Ridge Trail (71ML) and an unmarked junction with the Big Flat Creek Trail (87X) at 3.8 miles. An excellent campsite is available nearby.

Upstream of these two junctions, the trail wanders northeast through a montane valley characterized by heavy forest and occasional pocket meadows. These middle reaches of the Colt Killed drainage are as flat as any in the Bitterroot Mountains and make for very easy hiking. The spruce and fir largely preclude scenic vistas save for a few views of the surrounding mountainsides and of Colt Killed Creek itself, which pools in shady meanders and rushes quietly across shallow gravel bars. The grade steepens as you approach Heather Creek, where four separate channels inconveniently spill across the tread. One mile north of Parachute Lake you encounter an obvious horse camp beside the trail; a footpath heads south from the trail, but it is unclear whether it goes all the way to the lake. The elevation gain continues as you pass a signed junction with the trail up Garnet Creek (43X) and press on to the junction with White Sand Lake Trail (51S) some 9.1 miles from the trailhead. The junction occurs just after you cross Colt Killed Creek opposite a large horse camp along the trail—it is marked only by a blaze but is easily recognizable.

From here the route climbs steeply to the lake basin, crossing brushy timbered terrain and with a partial view south to Parachute Lake across the canyon. Turning north, you cross a marshy expanse along Colt Killed Creek and continue on a moderate incline to the lake. White Sand Lake occupies a burned-over basin that is neither entirely cirque nor shelf; its surface sparkles like mercury when struck by sunlight. The immediate shoreline consists of coarse granitic sand while aquatic vegetation and cutthroat trout inhabit the depths. There are campsites on around, but a makeshift camp can be improvised on the sandy beach if need be. Chances are you will not have the lake to yourself but will instead be forced to share the backcountry accommodations with moose that are frequently sighted feeding in the shallows.

Options: Ambitious backpackers may treat White Sand Lake as the first leg of longer shuttle hikes to either the Big Creek or Bear Creek trailheads (26.1 and 24.2 miles, respectively) on the Montana side of the Bitterroot Divide.

66 Hidden Creek Ridge

See Map on Page 207

Highlights:	Intriguing ridgeline country with dramatic views of the Bitterroot Divide and several excellent side trip opportunities.
Type of hike:	Five-day backpacking shuttle or base camp.
Total distance:	25 miles or 40.2 kilometers.
Difficulty:	Strenuous.
Best months:	July through September.
Elevation gain:	5,210 feet.
Elevation loss:	4,990 feet.
Maps:	Blodgett Mountain, Cedar Ridge, and Jeanette Mountain USGS quads.

Special considerations: The hike described below requires at least four major fords along its length, none of which is unusually hazardous but all of which can cause problems in early summer. Drinking water availability ranges from poor to nonexistent over long segments of this trail; the stretch between the Hidden Lake junction and Frog Peak is virtually bone dry by late August, so fill your water bottles whenever you get the chance. Campsites are similarly hard to come by along this stretch.

Trailhead access: To find the Bridge Creek Trailhead, take the Elk Summit Road (111) south from its junction with U.S. Highway 12 some 42.8 miles west of Lolo and 67.2 miles northeast of Lowell. Follow the high-standard washboard to the confluence of Colt Killed Creek and the Crooked Fork, cross the dual bridges, and continue through cut-over forest to reach the marked intersection with Forest Road 360. Turn right at this junction and follow the steep, narrow grade over Savage Pass and into the forested drainages beyond. Some 16.1 miles after leaving the pavement on US 12 you arrive at the signed pullout at the Bridge Creek Trailhead. A stock unloading ramp and hitchrail are available, as is limited roadside parking for three or four vehicles. Take care not to block the unloading ramps when you pull off the road.

The combined Big Sand–Diablo Mountain Trailhead is located 18.9 miles from US 12 via Elk Summit Road described above. The trailhead turnout (marked along the road as "Loop A") consists of a large parking area with restrooms, horse ramps, and hitchrails. Numerous trucks and horse trailers crowd this otherwise spacious trailhead during summer holidays and the fall hunting season.

Keypoints:

- 0.0   Inception of trail at the Bridge Creek Trailhead.
- 1.0   Trail enters the Selway-Bitterroot Wilderness.
- 2.1   Trail crosses Bridge Creek.
- 2.2   Trail reaches the banks of Big Sand Creek.
- 2.3   Junction with the Big Sand Creek Trail (1ML); stay right.
- 4.0   Junction with the cutoff trail up Hidden Creek Ridge.
- 4.4   Junction with the Hidden Peak Trail (10S).
- 6.7   Signed junction with Swamp Ridge Trail (22S).
- 7.3   Trail passes an old outfitter's camp.
- 7.4   Unmarked junction with the Hidden Lake Trail (9S).
- 8.8   Marked junction with the Big Flat–Hidden Ridge Trail (71ML).
- 10.4   Marked junction with the Frog Peak Trail (906S) below Hidden Peak.
- 12.6   Trail passes below summit of Frog Peak.
- 13.6   Trail reaches Frog Lake.
- 15.9   Trail reaches pass into Big Sand Creek.
- 17.4   Junction with the Big Sand Lake Trail (4ML).
- 18.0   Trail passes the foot of Big Sand Lake.
- 18.9   Trail crosses Cold Creek.
- 19.0   Junction with the Little Dead Elk Trail (5W).
- 20.4   Trail crosses Big Sand Creek.
- 20.6   Junction with the Big Sand Creek Trail (1ML); bear left for Elk Summit.
- 21.5   Trail crosses Duck Creek.
- 22.8   Junction with the Diablo Mountain Trail (18S). Trail leaves the Selway-Bitterroot Wilderness.
- 25.0   Terminus of trail at Elk Summit.

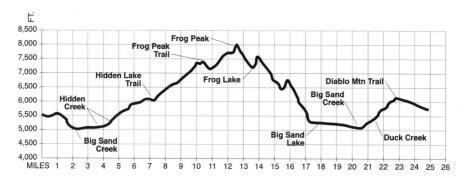

Suggested itinerary: There are two or three different ways to divvy up this hike, but the most efficient way to maximize your enjoyment of the country is to schedule a four- or five-day backpack. Doing so allows you to integrate must-see side trips such as Hidden Lake and Hidden Peak into your overall itinerary. Under such an arrangement Hidden Lake is the obvious destination for the first afternoon, followed by Frog Lake the next day, and a layover at Big Sand Lake for the third night out. This leaves an easy final leg back to Elk Summit for the fourth and final day.

| First day | — | Bridge Creek Trailhead to Hidden Lake, 8.7 miles. |
| Second day | — | Hidden Lake to Frog Lake, 7.5 miles. |

| Third day | — | Frog Lake to Big Sand Lake, 3.8 miles. |
| Fourth day | — | Big Sand Lake to Elk Summit, 7.6 miles; or to Bridge Creek Trailhead, 9.4 miles. |

The hike: Hidden Creek Ridge is one of the more interesting backpacking trips on the Lochsa Ranger District. The hike incorporates a little bit of everything: lively streams and pretty lakes; scenic parks and high ridgelines; good fishing and excellent wildlife viewing. This hike ranks among my all-time personal favorites—give it a try and see what you think.

The trail leads downhill from its inception and quickly passes a gathering of wet meadows along Bridge Creek. In these early miles the route fails to conserve on elevation gain and loss as it repeatedly rises and falls for no apparent reason. The overall descent continues until you reach a shallow ford of Bridge Creek. Crossing this shallow, gravelly channel is little cause for alarm. A second knee-deep ford follows close on the heels of the first at Big Sand Creek, which flows lazily through a spacious streamside meadow. Just beyond another obvious campsite east of the crossing is a signed junction with the Big Sand Creek Trail (1ML). The main trail continues upstream through timber for the next several miles, gaining very little elevation in the process. At 4 miles you reach an unmarked cutoff trail up Hidden Creek Ridge. (This trail bypasses two fords of Hidden Creek.)

A steady ascent ensues as the route first merges with the Hidden Peak Trail (10S) and then starts gaining elevation at an increasing rate. The route follows a northeasterly bearing past a marked junction with the Swamp Ridge Trail (22S) to reach a large outfitter's camp nestled in a wooded saddle along the ridge. The small perennial stream found here is one of the few reliable sources of drinking water along the entire Hidden Creek Ridge segment of the hike. Only a short distance east of the outfitter's camp you arrive at an unmarked but well-defined junction with the Hidden Lake Trail (9S). Hidden Lake is a delightful side trip, and you should make every effort to include it in your itinerary.

The main trail follows a steady incline east for the next 3 miles, passing a signed three-way junction with the Big Flat–Hidden Ridge Trail (71S) along the way. Beyond this junction the route follows the crest of Hidden Creek Ridge to a junction with the Frog Peak Trail (906S), just west of the fire lookout atop Hidden Peak. Shuck your pack at the junction sign and follow the spur trail to the old lookout site for a spectacular view of the Bitterroot Divide—the vantage more than justifies its short 0.4-mile diversion.

From the junction below Hidden Peak, the route leaves Hidden Creek Ridge and doglegs southeast. After a brief descent through lodgepole forest the trail begins its ascent anew. The uphill effort culminates in improving scenic value as the trail enters a subalpine park straddling the saddle between the Tadpole and Big Flat Creek watersheds. The high helm of 8,078-foot Frog Peak looms directly above, its northern ridge draped beneath cornices that shrink throughout the summer but never melt completely. Cairns mark the route as you cross the foot of this snowfield and follow the talus-strewn northern ridge of Frog Peak, exactly as portrayed on the Blodgett Mountain quadrangle.

The steep ascent has its rewards, revealing the sparkling surface of Tadpole Lake to the west, as well as the lonely lookout atop Hidden Peak to the north. The route climbs steeply to the 8,000-foot level but stops short of venturing clear to the summit. From here the well-defined tread descends down the backside of Frog Peak, traversing rough country high above Big Flat Creek. Views from these slopes are absolutely breathtaking and encompass a generous swath of the Bitterroot Divide. The descent continues into timber, then enters burned forest immediately north of Frog Lake. Watch for blazes on the dead trees to find the correct route to this tiny pool nestled in the middle of nowhere.

Frog Lake is a very pleasant surprise. In spite of its small size and shallow depth, this lake is no mere mudhole. Instead, it is rather picturesque—a few stony islands protrude from its surface and there are some nice views of the Bitterroot Divide from various points along its shores. A choice campsite is available right beside the inlet but sees very little use. Perhaps the hordes of mosquitoes force backpackers to look elsewhere for a place to stay overnight.

The trail tackles an extremely steep pitch via switchbacks above Frog Lake, then descends through mostly open country to the south. More beautiful views of 8,648-foot Blodgett Mountain and other nameless peaks of similar stature await you from these slopes. The route descends to an open saddle on the divide between the Big Flat and Hidden Creek drainages, then takes an abrupt westerly swing and reenters heavy forest in the headwaters of Hidden Creek. For the next mile you pass through old spruce-fir forest loaded with downfall and heavy brush. Just as the going gets a bit tedious, the trail makes a short climb to a burned-out saddle between Hidden and Big Sand drainages. Three high granite peaks—Rupe, Shattuck, and Blodgett—rise in order of increasing height along a single subsidiary ridge of the Bitterroot Divide while Big Sand Lake makes its initial appearance in the valley below. A steep, switchbacked descent leads through the wreckage of the 1994 fire. The lake grows larger by the minute until unburned forest rescinds the view near the signed junction with the Big Sand Lake Trail (4ML). A sign marks this junction, which takes off just six paces from a spur trail to campsites clustered around the head of the lake.

Big Sand Lake occupies a remote upland valley. Early trappers and prospectors built the first permanent structures here in the 1890s, but today visitors camp in their own temporary lodgings at either end of the lake. Big Sand attracts large numbers of elk and moose that are frequently sighted swimming in its shallows and feeding along its shores; excellent fishing for cutthroat trout provides an added incentive for those inclined to linger for a few days longer.

The trail continues west for 7 miles from the foot of Big Sand Lake to its terminus at the combined Big Sand–Diablo Mountain Trailhead. The three junctions that occur along this segment are well marked, so there is little chance of getting lost. For further details on these final 7 miles, refer to the Big Sand Lake narrative (Hike 60).

Options: To maximize scenic value and minimize backtracking, I recommend hiking this trail exactly as described. A figure-8 arrangement is also possible; in addition, the hike can be easily modified to form a loop from either trailhead. The bottom line here is that it hardly matters *how* you hike the trail so long as you see the spectacular country near Frog Peak.

In a related note, I do not recommend trying to shorten this hike by taking the old connecting trail between Hidden and Big Sand lakes. The USFS abandoned this route many years ago: It is swampy, brushy, and very difficult to find and follow.

Side trips: Three excellent side trips will increase your overall satisfaction with this hike. These include Hidden Lake, the abandoned fire lookout atop Hidden Peak, and the Diablo Mountain Lookout. All three are highly recommended, and separate narratives are devoted to each elsewhere in this book.

ADDITIONAL TRAILS

Little Dead Elk (5W), 2.8 miles (4.5 km). This trail runs south from the Big Sand Lake Trail (4ML) to a wooded saddle atop the Lochsa-Selway Divide. Its junction with the Big Sand Lake Trail occurs in a stretch of burned-over forest, but otherwise the route traverses heavily timbered country. The trail is rather swampy along the lower reaches of Little Dead Elk Creek and has a tendency to disappear among the undergrowth and downed trees. But for those willing to persist, there is a good campsite and flowing spring in the swale on the Lochsa-Selway Divide. Beyond the

Spectacular country as seen from the southern slopes of Frog Peak.

saddle, the trail descends sharply into the Dead Elk Creek drainage on the adjoining Nez Perce National Forest.

Cedar Ridge (6ML), 4.8 miles (7.7 km). The trail provides a crossover route between Elk Summit and the popular Wind Lakes area. Beginning just across the road from the Elk Summit Guard Station, the route ascends a forested prominence as it runs northwest through heavy upland forest to reach a junction with the Kooskooskia Meadows Trail (45ML) in just under 5 miles. The trail itself is easy enough to follow, but scenic views are quite limited. A sign marked the junction with an abandoned route (83X) down Bridge Creek when I last hiked this trail in 1999.

Swamp Ridge (22S), 5.7 miles (9.2 km). This hike consists of two distinctly different but continuous trails running east from Elk Summit Road (360) and over the crest of Hidden Creek Ridge. The trail is maintained as a secondary route as far east as Big Sand Creek, where it meets the incoming Big Sand Creek Trail (1ML) at a wide, slow-moving ford. Beyond this waist-deep crossing, the trail's less favorable complexion becomes apparent: Encroaching brush and more than 370 downed trees cause problems for hikers and render it all but impassable to stock.

Colt Lake (23X), 4.4 miles (7.1 km). This trail leads west from the Elk Summit Road (360) to its terminus near Grouse Lake. Most of this old fire-access route traverses rolling upland forest of low scenic value. The trail offers proximity to a handful of backcountry lakes on its way west, but the very few hikers who venture this way report difficult bushwhacking and hundreds of downed trees. But once you make it to Grouse Lake, the forest opens up to the point that cross-country hiking to Colt Lake is relatively straightforward. The trail has gone without maintenance for well over a decade; the trailhead has been unmarked since 1993.

Lewis & Clark (25ML), 7.0 miles (11.3 km). This newly constructed trail connects four popular USFS campgrounds along the upper Lochsa River and closely parallels the route traveled by the Corps of Discovery on September 14, 1805. It was developed to provide an easy, low-elevation hike for area campers. It follows the river downstream from White Sand Campground, crossing US 12 to reach its western terminus at Wendover Pond. The route is scenically varied and includes a stretch of riverside trail below Powell Campground as well as various overlook points and a nice cedar grove near Papoose Creek. Plans are in the works to mark a series of waypoints along which you may take a self-guided tour with an accompanying brochure.

Jay Point (37S), 8.2 miles (13.2 km). This trail follows a rough tread across the Lochsa River and to a signed junction with the Cooperation Trail (44S) southwest of Tom Beal Peak. It is very lightly used. Most hikers are either intimidated by the river ford or are simply unable to find the crossing, located slightly west of Powell Campground. (At one time a tramway spanned the river at this point, but it is long gone.) Once across the Lochsa, you pass a junction with the Cliff Ridge Trail (216X) and ford Jay Creek before making a very steep ascent to the lookout. The route was maintained as far as

Jay Point in 1993, but the upper segment has gone without maintenance for much longer and is choked with lots of brush and downed timber. The L–4 lookout at Jay Point is no longer manned during the summer months.

Fish Lake Crossover (39S), 1.0 mile (1.6 km). Runs south from the Fish Lake Guard Station and airstrip to a signed four-way junction with the Wounded Doe Ridge Trail (644W) on the Lochsa-Selway Divide. Located in heavy timber, this short connecting trail is unremarkable in itself but does offer possibilities for extended day hikes from a base camp at Fish Lake.

Beaver Ridge (47S), 10.5 miles (16.9 km). This hike follows a forested ridgeline from the Beaver Ridge Road (369) to a junction with the Colt Killed Creek Trail (50ML) above the Colt Killed Creek. It is generally unremarkable fare and overall is not as appealing as other ridgeline trails on the district. Heavy spruce-fir forest precludes scenic views and the tread grows increasingly steep and deteriorated as you hike from east to west. The trail is closed to motorized use over its entire length.

Eagle Ridge (55X), 3.6 miles (5.8 km). A crossover route connecting U.S. Highway 12 and the Cooperation Ridge Trail (44S), this primitive route has been abandoned by the USFS and was deleted from the 1999 Selway-Bitterroot Wilderness map. The trail requires a dangerous ford of the Lochsa River and is almost completely overgrown in the lower elevations; however, its junction with the Cooperation Ridge Trail (44S) was clearly recognizable when I passed through the area on July 16, 1998.

Roundtop (57X), 3.2 miles (5.1 km). This hike leads from Colt Killed Creek to the former site of a USFS fire lookout at Roundtop. Its take-off point along the Colt Killed Creek Trail (50ML) is unmarked and nearly impossible to pinpoint; numerous logging spurs and skid roads now crisscross the upper reaches of this long-abandoned route.

Army Mule (60S), 10.8 miles (17.4 km). Connects Fish Lake Saddle with the Warm Springs Trail (49ML) via Army Mule Saddle. The segment through Lost Knife Meadows is maintained to mainline standards, while the remainder receives upkeep as a secondary trail. Much of the route traverses forested country on the Lochsa-Selway Divide, but there are also some exceptional views, including dramatic ridgeline landscapes between Chain Meadows and Army Mule Saddle. Even so, it attracts little notice from backpackers and is mostly used by horsemen bound for outfitter's camps at Chain Meadows, Lost Knife Meadows, and Fish Lake Saddle.

Maud Creek (64X), 7.0 miles (11.3 km). This trail runs upstream from Maud Creek's confluence with Storm Creek to its headwaters at Maud Lake. Years ago it was used by trappers and outfitters as a crossover route into Montana via the high pass east of Maud Lake. Although currently considered a non-system trail, the USFS may resume maintenance if and when resources become available. A trail survey on August 22, 1999 revealed 230 trees downed over its length. There was no evidence of recent camping at the lake.

Maud-Dan Ridge (70S), 4.0 miles (6.4 km). This connects the Storm Creek (99ML) and Dan Ridge (903S) trails via a steep, twisting path running through heavy timber. Trail crews rerouted and reconstructed much of the original tread and added plenty of wide-radius switchbacks in 1997. Even so, it is easy to lose the trail for any number of similar-looking footpaths leading through swampy meadows near the confluence of Maud and Storm creeks, where five different trails converge in close proximity to a commercial outfitter's camp.

Maud Ridge (75S), 5.8 miles (9.3 km). This route follows a timbered ridgeline extending east from Maud Creek's confluence with Storm Creek. It consists of a steep 2,760-foot ascent with lots of tight switchbacks in its lower miles and a relatively flat stretch midway up the ridge. Toward the upper end a series of springs and small rivulets provide sources of drinking water, but you will find little in the way of scenic interest. The Ranger Peak quadrangle shows a short spur trail continuing east along the ridge to a deadend southwest of Ranger Lake, but that particular route is not an official USFS trail and is not maintained as such.

Cooperation Point (81X), 1.7 miles (2.7 km). This unremarkable trail leads west from a junction with the Cooperation Ridge Trail (44S) to its terminus at Cooperation Point, site of an L-4 lookout until 1950. Heavy forest cloaks the entire route leading to the old lookout site.

Saturday Creek (82W), 3.6 miles (5.8 km). Connects the Wind Lakes (24S) and Saturday Ridge (89ML) trails via Warm Springs Pass. Its boggy tread fords Saturday Creek repeatedly and at one crossing actually proceeds to follow the stream channel itself upstream for more than 50 yards before emerging on the opposite side. Saturday Creek is bordered by a series of pocket meadows and watery glades along its length, which in turn are surrounded by spruce-fir forest. Stock users should stay clear of this route unless prepared to cut out or bypass scores of blowdowns.

Upper Bridge Creek (83X), 2.5 miles (4 km). This hike leads west from Elk Summit Road (360) to a signed junction with the Cedar Ridge Trail (6ML), as shown on the Cedar Ridge and Grave Peak quadrangles. It is actually a continuation of the Lower Bridge Creek Trail (28S) running east to Big Sand Creek. Unlike its lower counterpart, however, this upper segment receives no significant use and is of minimal scenic value.

Big Flat Creek (87X), 6.5 miles (10.5 km). This relict route leads upstream from an unsigned junction at the confluence of Colt Killed Creek and Big Flat Creek. The 1970 Selway-Bitterroot Wilderness map shows the trail continuing to a dead end among a series of avalanche chutes about 1 mile northeast of Frog Lake. But recurring avalanches and blowdowns from a 1988 wildfire in the upper reaches of the drainage have all but erased any trace of the trail for its final 3 miles. Expect difficult going.

Saturday Ridge (89ML), 5.9 miles (9.5 km). This trail connects the Warm Springs Trail (49ML) with the Wind Lakes via Warm Springs Pass. It passes through heavy lodgepole forest checkered with stands of spruce and fir and traverses some boggy timbered terrain in the vicinity of Warm Springs Pass, where it ties in with the old trail (82W) down Saturday Creek. The trail is well defined and offers pleasant though unspectacular views of the surrounding country.

Sponge Creek (209W), 14.2 miles (22.8 km). The hike consists of two dissimilar but roughly equidistant segments linking the Eagle Mountain (206ML) and McConnell Mountain (213ML) trails via Freezeout Mountain. The western segment begins at a signed junction with the Eagle Mountain Trail and continues downstream along Sponge Creek for 5.8 miles, where it ties in with the Indian Meadows Trail (208S) near an old outfitter's camp. This portion of the trail is easily followed from either of these two endpoints, but its middle reaches along Sponge Creek are in poor repair and are scheduled for maintenance in 2000. The remaining 8.4-mile eastern segment over Freezeout Mountain had been abandoned for a number of years prior to the 1994 Freezeout Fire; in its aftermath, many hundreds of broken and uprooted trees killed in the 8,200-acre blaze now block the route and in some places resemble a jumble of jackstraws. The Freezeout Mountain segment of the trail will likely disappear completely in a matter of years.

Cliff Ridge (216X), 7.2 miles (11.6 km). This hike traces a forested ridgeline south from the Lochsa River to its terminus at Tom Beal Park. This is a steep, rough trail following a marginal tread over its entire length. It has seen little or no maintenance for well over a decade, and windstorms during the winter of 1996–97 left dozens of blowdowns across the trail, including many large-diameter cedars in the lower elevations. The USFS has no plans to maintain or otherwise upgrade this trail anytime soon.

Jay Point Crossover (218X), 2.9 miles (4.7 km). This is a very poor trail, unmarked and obviously abandoned. It passes through stands of cedar and grand fir from its inception along Forest Road 362. Dozens of wind-felled cedars blocked most of the route on October 19, 1999. There are a few rotting puncheon walkways, but the trail goes through the toe of several clearcuts and grows progressively more indistinct as it travels west opposite the USFS ranger station complex at Powell.

Wounded Doe Ridge (644W), 9.5 miles (15.3 km). This route connects the Eagle Mountain (206ML) and Boulder Creek (211ML) trails via Wounded Doe Ridge. Straddling the Lochsa-Selway Divide over much of its length, the trail varies widely in appearance and scenic value. The high country of Wounded Doe Ridge, for instance, offers very pleasant hiking: open subalpine forest with scenic views near and far. But north of California Point the trail grows increasingly difficult to pick out and follow because it is so overgrown and deteriorated from lack of upkeep. Watch for old blazes to stay on course.

Savage Ridge (909S), 2.5 miles (4 km). Here you travel east along the crest of Savage Ridge to the horizontal control station and long-razed USFS lookout site at point 6,916. The downed lodgepole that accumulate on this lightly used trail are cut out every few years. The USFS is considering plans to extend this trail to the Colt Creek Trailhead to improve the connectivity of the trail network. Although the trail is closed to motorized use, the trailhead at Savage Pass is clearly marked.

Hungry Creek (910X), 5.2 miles (8.4 km). This non-system trail connects the Maple Lake Trail (939ML) with the Warm Springs Trail (49ML) via Hungry Creek. Going north from Maple Lake, the route traverses open subalpine country with plentiful views. It offers access to Hungry Lake and the Porphyry Lakes via unmaintained spur trails bailing off to either side. But once you cross the Lochsa-Selway Divide and begin the descent into Hungry Creek, the tread promptly disappears.

Crab Creek (914S), 4.4 miles (7.1 km). This connecting trail links the Colt Killed Creek Trail (50ML) with the Storm Creek Trail (99ML). It is maintained mostly through the efforts of an outfitter and is very lightly used outside of hunting season. The scenery is not unduly impressive, but Crab Creek and its tributaries provide reliable water for thirsty horses and hikers.

Robin Ridge (938X), 5.8 miles (9.3 km). Here is yet another ridgeline route leading from the Lochsa River to the Cooperation Ridge Trail (44S). Accessing the trail requires first knowing just where it takes off near Wendover Campground (Loop B) and then making a dangerous deepwater ford of the Lochsa River before starting up the steep, timbered slope on the opposite side. An obsolete fire-suppression trail, it receives virtually no use (or maintenance, for that matter) and was abandoned by the USFS years ago.

Rudd-Moore Lakes (940W), 6.4 miles (10.3 km). This route follows subalpine country north from the Beaver Ridge Lookout to its terminus along Forest Road 112 and the Brushy Fork of the Lochsa. It is used primarily as an approach route to the Rudd-Moore Lakes, although it does not access them directly. The trail is poorly defined though passable in its upper elevations and stays within 100 yards of the main subsidiary ridge leading north toward the lakes. (There are several different routes to the lakes, with roundabout approaches from ridgelines to the east and west of the lakes being slightly preferable to a more direct descent down the headwall in between.) Beyond the Rudd-Moore Lakes, the route traverses Plum Creek timberlands and a confusing network of logging roads as it descends into the Brushy Fork drainage; these lower miles have seen no USFS maintenance in recent memory.

Lolo National Forest

Missoula Ranger District

67 Skookum Butte

Highlights:	A far-reaching panorama from the Skookum Butte Lookout.
Type of hike:	Out-and-back day hike.
Total distance:	2.2 miles or 3.5 kilometers (round trip).
Difficulty:	Easy.
Best months:	July through September.
Elevation gain:	930 feet.
Map:	West Fork Butte USGS quad.

Trailhead access: Follow U.S. Highway 12 west from Lolo for 10.5 miles to Elk Meadows Road (451). Turn south, cross the bridge over Lolo Creek, and continue on this high-standard road for 10.8 miles to the Montana-Idaho stateline atop the Bitterroot Divide. Follow the road into Idaho for 0.4 mile, then turn right onto Forest Road 5959. Continue for another 0.7 mile to reach the signed trailhead turnout. There is sufficient space for six or seven vehicles. You will find no other amenities.

Keypoints:
- 0.0 Inception of trail along FR 5959.
- 1.0 Junction with the Lost Park Trail (1S) below Skookum Butte.
- 1.1 Terminus of trail at Skookum Butte Lookout.

The hike: Skookum Butte is one of the more interesting day hikes in the heavily logged Elk Meadows area. A modified L-5 lookout still stands atop its natural summit fortifications, which require only 45 minutes to reach via the route described below. The mountaintop scene shows off a formidable array of high peaks as well as some of the Bitterroots' lower and lesser-known summits.

The trail sets out along an abandoned jeep road and ventures west at a slight grade and into heavy forest. At a signless post, the route cuts left and leaves the old roadbed behind. After crossing a small rivulet just south of a marshy meadow lying a stone's throw within Montana, the trail switchbacks into the timber. You soon pass through a large cut-over tract owned by the Plum Creek Timber Company and cross a spur logging road coming in from the north. Views from the clearing take in the logged-over headwaters country of the Brushy Fork and the high mountains beyond, including 7,812-foot Rocky Peak.

Skookum Butte

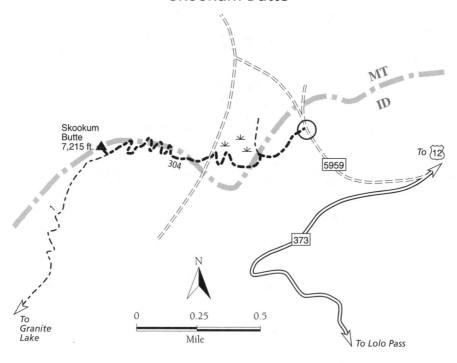

Reentering spruce and fir above the far end of the clearing, the trail continues steadily upslope on switchbacks. An increasing number of silver fire-killed snags appoint the landscape as the trail draws closer to the interstate summit. When you finally emerge from the trees, the trail circles over at the foot of a large summit boulder field to a crudely marked junction with the Lost Park Trail (1S). That route departs the summit for Granite Lake and beyond, but the remaining segment to Skookum Butte continues through the rocks to reach the weatherbeaten lookout atop its 7,215-foot platform.

Skookum Butte Lookout stands squarely atop the most rugged boundary between any two states in the Union.

In 1998 the lookout was still open to the general public, but its interior is spartan. The summit view is far-reaching, encompassing Grave Peak to the southwest, the mighty Mission Range to the far northeast, and a healthy swath of the Bitterroots in between. Mounts Jumbo and Sentinel—both familiar Missoula landmarks—are also in sight, although the city itself remains unseen in the valley below.

Option: If you are out for a longer day hike, consider hiking southwest to Granite Lake via the Lost Park National Recreation Trail. The route incurs a drop of 1,260 feet over approximately 1.5 miles from its junction near Skookum Butte. Do not expect unblemished surroundings or wilderness solitude—the lake rests squarely on Plum Creek timberland.

68 Lolo Peak

Highlights: Attractive high-elevation scenery and a northeast view of Missoula.
Type of hike: Out-and-back day hike or overnighter.
Total distance: 9.2 miles or 14.8 kilometers (round trip).
Difficulty: Difficult.
Best months: July through September.
Elevation gain: 3,770 feet.
Elevation loss: 490 feet.
Map: Carlton Lake USGS quad.

Special considerations: This hike description leads to the *true* northern summit of Lolo Peak, elevation 9,096 feet. Many hikers incorrectly refer to Peak 8,694, north of Carlton Lake, as Lolo Peak's "north summit" when in fact it is significantly lower and separated from the true peak by nearly 1 full mile.

Trailhead access: The Mormon Peak Road (612) exits U.S. Highway 12 some 3.8 miles west of Lolo. Upon crossing a single-lane bridge over Lolo Creek drive 8.7 steep miles on an improved gravel road to the Lolo Peak trailhead. Take care not to block the road or other vehicles at this congested switchback, which is marked with a sign but lacks any other facilities.

Keypoints:
   0.0   Inception of trail at the Lolo Peak Trailhead.
   0.6   Junction with the Mill Creek Trail (1310S).
   2.4   Trail gains the crest of Carlton Ridge.
   2.5   Vista Point and overlook of Carlton Lake.
   2.6   Route merges with the One Horse Lakes Trail (326W).
   3.2   Trail crosses the irrigation dam at Carlton Lake.
   3.3   Trail reaches the Selway-Bitterroot Wilderness.
   4.6   Northern summit of Lolo Peak.

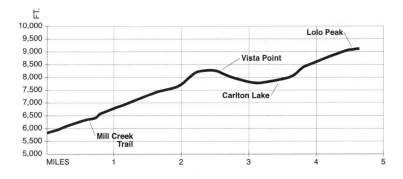

Lolo Peak • Lantern Ridge
South Fork Lolo Creek to Bass Creek

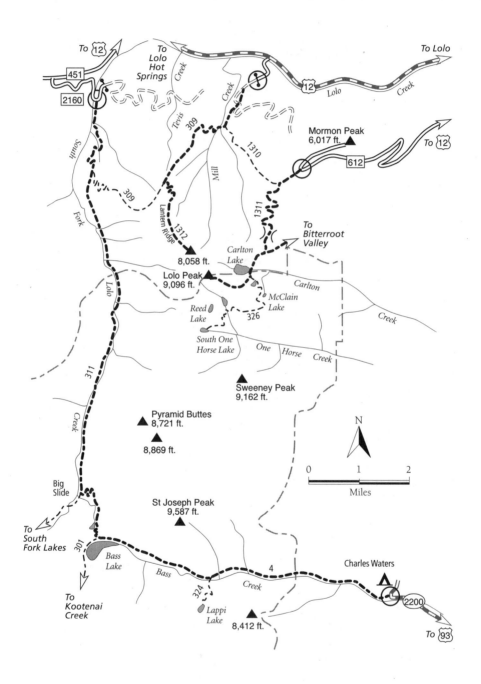

The hike: Lolo Peak guards the northern limits of the Selway-Bitterroot Wilderness just 15 miles southwest of Missoula. This nontechnical summit—the northernmost of the 9,000-foot Bitterroot peaks—provides a fine vantage for outdoor enthusiasts beginning in early July each summer. Yet one should not dismiss the mountain's wild character because of its heavy use and proximity to a major population center, for beyond the peak lies the most extensive wilderness complex in the contiguous United States— 4 *million* acres of primeval wildlands known collectively as the Greater Salmon–Selway ecosystem.

The trail wanders like a rudderless boat upslope from the trailhead to a rendezvous with the Mill Creek Trail (1310S). Beyond this junction the trail continues through a dark hallway of conifers and ventures across a steep hillside far above the still forests of a Mill Creek tributary. Alpine larch replace subalpine fir as the dominant species while openings in the forest canopy allow glimpses of Missoula and its attendant foothills to the northeast. Having finished with switchbacks, the trail reaches level ground just west of a high saddle leading into the Carlton drainage. After a stopover at Vista Point—where a sign prematurely announces the trail terminus—the route descends among phalanxes of creaking silver snags to link up with the incoming One Hose Lakes Trail [326W]. At this point the rock-strewn trail proceeds in a southwestwardly direction toward Carlton Lake, with the sound of cascading water heralding the approach of an unseen waterfall off to the left. Straight ahead looms the 9,096-foot northern crown of Lolo Peak.

Nestled at the headwaters of its namesake drainage, Carlton Lake offers temperamental fishing for cutthroat and rainbow trout. Anglers should have a DEET-based repellant on hand to fend off the mosquitoes, which were quite bad during my first visit. After crossing an unsightly irrigation dam at the foot of the lake, the final climb to Lolo Peak begins in earnest. (The unkempt One Horse Lakes Trail [326W] continues past fishless Little Carlton Lake, destined for the secluded tarns of One Horse Creek.)

Although the terrain suggests several possible routes of ascent, a ridgeline approach from the east is the most popular choice. An alternate line of attack gains the summit following a very steep ascent of sliding talus debris on the north face. Either route offers its own scenic rewards culminating in an unobstructed mountainscape at the summit. Beyond Missoula the huge peaks of the Mission Range disappear into the distance while the isolated flanks of 7,995-foot Squaw Peak curve to a point slightly west of north. In the opposite direction rises the 9,139-foot southern helm of Lolo Peak, whose rust-colored flanks stand emblazoned with glowing white snowfields scattered about like so many shards of shattered porcelain.

Side trip: If you find Carlton Lake a bit too crowded, a side trip to One Horse Lakes might prove worthwhile. From the wilderness boundary sign near Carlton Lake, the route follows a generally poor trail past Little Carlton and McClain lakes—shallow, mosquito-infested waters—and enters the One Horse drainage at a wooded pass. From this point you continue to South One Horse Lake and the terminus of Trail 326W. Those willing to venture from the main trail can also survey North One Horse Lake, a shallow tarn with a

Carlton Lake and the northern summit of Lolo Peak.

tiny wooded islet, as well as Reed Lake, a substantially deeper body of water backed up behind an old stone dam.

69 Lantern Ridge

See Map on Page 238

Highlights: A lightly used route with exceptional views of Missoula and Lolo Peak.
Type of hike: Out-and-back day hike or overnighter.
Total distance: 12 miles or 19.3 kilometers (round trip).
Difficulty: Strenuous.
Best months: July through September.
Elevation gain: 4,440 feet.
Maps: Carlton Lake and Dick Creek USGS quads.

Special considerations: The USFS has officially abandoned the Old Lolo Peak Trail (1312X). Portions of this nonsystem trail are nearly illegible on the ground and require faint trail expertise to follow for any distance. If your own route-finding abilities are in doubt, just turn around before you venture very far from recognizable tread—this is one area where a lost trail can lead to serious problems.

Trailhead access: Follow U.S. Highway 12 west from Lolo for 6.5 miles to reach Mill Creek Road. Turn south and continue over Lolo Creek and through rural residential property to the Mill Creek Trailhead after another 0.6 mile. A gated road closure greets you at this dead-end trailhead below the Elk Snout Ranch, and a painted wooden sign for trails 309S and 1310S stands along the road beyond. The trailhead is entirely undeveloped and lies on a county right-of-way, with parking for only two or three vehicles. Do not block the road.

Keypoints:
0.0   Gated terminus of the Mill Creek Road. Inception of the Mill Creek Trail (1310S).
0.5   Trail veers left to bypass switchbacks along the road.
1.5   Junction with the Lantern Ridge Trail (309S). Trail crosses Mill Creek.
3.8   Junction with the Old Lolo Peak Trail (1312X); bear left.
6.0   Approximate trail terminus at the old Lantern Ridge lookout site.

The hike: This challenging out-and-back course traverses a variety of landscapes, including heavy forest, stark clearcuts, and high ridgeline country, north of Lolo Peak. Missoula and its surrounding mountains are occasionally visible as you follow the trail to a long-abandoned lookout site at the crest of Lantern Ridge. Surviving evidence of the structure was largely absent at the time of my September 28, 1998 visit.

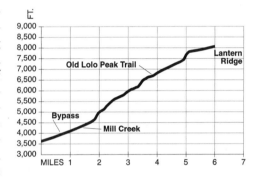

The trail begins by following the closed-off portion of the Mill Creek Road through a large cut-over tract. (A public access gate permits the entry of stock and mountain bikes.) After about 0.5 mile, watch for a signless but well-defined trail cutting left from the logging road. This is the Mill Creek Trail (1310S), which continues south to bypass a major switchback along the road before reentering stream-bottom forest and reaching a large wooden sign at its junction with the Lantern Ridge Trail (309S).

Taking the right-hand fork, you soon come to a stout bridge over Mill Creek. After crossing this rushing watercourse and a smaller companion tributary, the trail emerges in clearcut surroundings once again and begins a steep, loose-dirt ascent out of the drainage. Switchbacks cut across the open hillside as the route intersects five logging spurs—all closed to motorized traffic. The lack of trees permits pleasant though unspectacular views, extending north to the low summits of the Grave Peak Range and northeast to Lolo and the Sapphire Mountains beyond. Directly to the south rises the northern summit of Lolo Peak, its high helm towering over the headwaters of Mill Creek.

The trail remains easy to follow as it leaves commercial timberland behind and enters a dark lodgepole forest. This is perhaps the single most taxing portion of the trail, consuming another 900 vertical feet without any diversionary view or other scenic interlude. Some time later, and about 3.8 miles from the trailhead, you arrive at a marked junction with the Old Lolo Peak Trail (1312X). A time-faded trail sign immediately below this junction still bears an inscription for "Cedar-Mill Creek Trail 323." Bear left at this junction.

Heavy forest keeps the trail shaded as it pursues a lengthy series of switchbacks, ascending continuously all the while. The tread steadily gains elevation among the fir and pine until the route ventures east to the canyon rim. Here you will find an impressive northeast view of the Missoula area and the massive Mission Range towering in the distance. Freshly cut blazes and a clearly defined tread follow the ridge farther upslope and into an atmosphere of rarified air, where the whitebark pine forest surrenders its first close-up view of Lolo Peak—still 1 mile to the southeast. Just as the trail reaches level ground along the crest of Lantern Ridge, the tread becomes progressively more evasive. It is easily lost in the thin soils and among the competing game trails that crisscross the ridgeline. A resourceful outdoorsman can trace the route as far south as Lolo Peak, but a high knob atop Lantern Ridge (elevation 8,058 feet) is probably the most logical turnaround point. Another fine view of the Missoula Valley and Mission Range awaits you from this site of lonely splendor.

Options: Depending on your abilities and personal preference, Lantern Ridge may be treated as an approach route to 9,096-foot Lolo Peak. This rigorous day hike requires an early-morning start. The final ascent is quite scenic but requires a difficult 1,100-foot talus scramble.

Side trips: Connecting trails to the South Fork of Lolo Creek (309S) and Lolo Peak (1310S) provide several variations from the Lantern Ridge route described above. They are as follows:

▲ **Lantern Ridge Trail (309S)** continues west from its junction with the Old Lolo Peak Trail (1312X) and maintains a modest ascent for about 1 mile, crossing two rivulets above the head of Cedar Creek before reaching its apex just shy of the 7,000-foot contour. Here you will find a second marked junction for Lantern Ridge, but this alternate route up the ridge was abandoned years ago. The trail begins a gentle descent along a northwest bearing before dropping more steeply via switchbacks. A marked junction with the South Fork Lolo Creek Trail (311ML) appears at the upper end of large clearcut, and you can follow this good trail north to its origins at the South Fork Lolo Creek Trailhead. This demanding shuttle incurs an elevation gain of 3,380 feet and measures 9.1 miles from start to finish.

▲ **Mill Creek Trail (1310S)** continues southeast from its signed junction with the Lantern Ridge Trail (309). There is little in the way of scenic interest as the trail climbs through forest or along the margins of clearcuts. You reach a marked junction with the Lolo Peak Trail (1311ML) after some 2.3 miles and a 2,790-foot ascent from the Mill Creek Trailhead. Simply turn left and follow the trail northeast to the Lolo Peak Trailhead to complete the 4.4-mile shuttle.

70 South Fork Lolo Creek to Bass Creek

See Map on Page 238

Highlights: A challenging and lightly used trail through a remote wilderness canyon.
Type of hike: Three-day backpacking shuttle.
Total distance: 19.8 miles or 31.9 kilometers.
Difficulty: Strenuous.
Best months: July through September.
Elevation gain: 4,440 feet.
Elevation loss: 4,500 feet.
Maps: Dick Creek and Saint Joseph Peak USGS quads.

Special considerations: Although the route remains easy enough to follow for the first 9 miles, serious route-finding difficulties may be encountered as the trail leaves the stream bottom and begins the prolonged ascent to a nameless lake near the headwaters. It is all too easy to take the wrong trail by mistake or to lose the tread completely if you have not been through this area before.

Trailhead access: To reach the South Fork Lolo Creek Trailhead, follow Elk Meadows Road (451) from its marked junction with U.S. Highway 12, 10.5 miles west of Lolo. This wide country road is usually well maintained but subject to heavy traffic from area logging operations, graders, and other recreationists. After approximately 2.5 miles of travel, the South Fork Lolo Creek Road (2160) veers left at a signed junction. Turn here and follow this narrow, winding road for 2 more miles to reach the marked USFS trailhead alongside the South Fork Lolo Creek. Do not park immediately at the trailhead, but instead continue to the generous parking area just below the road a short distance beyond. A stock unloading ramp, hitchrail, and several primitive campsites are available nearby.

For the Bass Creek Trailhead, take the Bass Creek Road from its intersection with U.S. Highway 93, 4 miles south of Florence. This paved road continues west and crosses a narrow bridge over Bass Creek to reach the Charles Waters Campground after 2.5 miles. Parking is available at the upper end of the recreation area near the trail's outset.

Keypoints:

0.0	Inception of trail at the South Fork Lolo Creek Trailhead.
0.6	Trail crosses Cedar Creek and enters clearcuts.
2.3	Junction with the Lantern Ridge Trail (309S).
3.7	Trail crosses Lantern Creek.
3.9	Trail crosses Middle Creek.
4.3	Trail fords Falls Creek.
5.1	Trail enters the Selway-Bitterroot Wilderness.
5.5	Trail crosses Meadow Creek.
5.7	First ford of the South Fork.

7.5	Trail returns to the east bank of the South Fork.
9.9	Trail crosses the Big Slide and starts up toward the pass into Bass Creek.
11.5	Trail reaches a nameless tarn.
11.8	Trail merges with the Bass Creek Trail (4ML) at the pass into Bass Creek.
12.0	Junction with the Bass Pass Trail (301X) above Bass Lake; stay left.
12.5	Trail leaves the foot of Bass Lake.
13.7	Subalpine avalanche meadows.
15.0	Unmarked junction with the Lappi Lake Trail (324W).
17.4	Trail leaves the Selway-Bitterroot Wilderness.
18.0	Trail passes an old log dam and reservoir.
19.8	Charles Waters Memorial Campground.

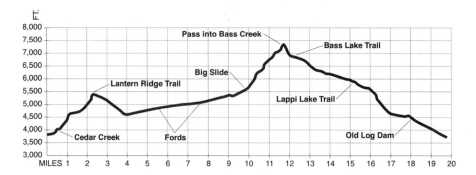

The hike: The South Fork Lolo Creek Trail (311ML) provides a lengthy alternate route into the Bass Lake area. Light recreational traffic is a general rule, though the drainage experiences a marked increase in use as hunters venture into the drainage each autumn. In order to really enjoy the country you should schedule a three-day excursion. This itinerary is easily extended if you wish to spend an extra day or two in the popular Bass Lake area or desire greater seclusion at Lappi Lake.

The trail begins with a gentle streamside ascent through an intermixed forest of deciduous and coniferous species. Upon passing several crude campsites along the log-strewn South Fork, the trail crosses Cedar Creek and turns east to climb the slopes above its moss-covered boulders and fragrant softwoods. Entering an extensive clearcut, the trail switchbacks steeply uphill, crossing no fewer than five logging spurs on its way to a marked junction with the Lantern Ridge Trail (309S) at the margin of the uppermost clearcut. Northerly views from this point take in the low summits of the Grave Creek Range, a 15-mile-long subrange of the Bitterroots located due west of Missoula.

Leaving commercial timberland behind, the trail enters fir-pine forest and resumes a modest ascent. The trail soon reaches a grove of stately ponderosa pines. A short footpath leads downhill through the trees to a bedrock outcrop from which you can gauge the immense extent of the South Fork Lolo Creek drainage and view a succession of high Bitterroot peaks arrayed over its eastern rim. The trail descends at a gradual rate beyond this park and completes simple crossings of Lantern and Middle creeks. An encounter is also made with Falls Creek, a substantially larger watercourse crossed via downed logs. Upon crossing Meadow Creek, the trail emerges in a delightful pocket meadow situated alongside the slow-moving South Fork. Private hunting parties occupy the campsites here each fall, and for good reason—this is prime big-game habitat. Elk, moose, and white-tailed deer haunt these meadows during the early morning hours.

Reentering woodland at the far end of the meadows, the trail negotiates a tricky log crossing over the South Fork. Talus clearings and steep brush-fields interrupt uneventful hiking over the next 2 miles until the trail returns again to the gravel streambank, 7.5 miles from the trailhead. There is no shortage of possible log crossings at this shallow ford. Several more tedious miles pass underfoot as the trail navigates uneven terrain in the silent bottomlands. Then, without warning, the course reaches a large mountain meadow with views of the peaks standing guard over the South Fork's headwaters. Known informally as the Big Slide, this narrow clearing is a welcome departure from otherwise heavy forest that concealed a large outfitter's camp on August 17, 1998. A large blaze at the far end of the clearing marks the trail to Bass Lake. First-time visitors might inadvertently follow the original course of the South Fork Lolo Creek Trail (311W) as it continues upstream, crosses the South Fork, and ventures into the basin beyond. This primitive route traverses wild country and was reportedly last maintained by USFS crews into the 1960s. Although a resourceful wilderness traveler can follow the remaining vestiges of this trail as far as the South Fork Lakes, the task at hand is probably beyond the abilities of most novice hikers.

The route to Bass Lake requires a strenuous ascent and switchbacks steeply uphill following blazes, cairns, and sawn logs cut out by an industrious trail crew. In places the wind-felled firs are stacked like Lincoln logs. Be especially careful to follow the proper route, because to lose the trail here requires cross-country bushwhacking through a frightful jungle of brush and blowdowns.

The relentless climb out of the stream bottom becomes quite tiresome as the trail crosses a final open brushfield, briefly continues the ascent, and happens upon a small, nameless lake sheltered in an unusual place—just below the South Fork Pass. Good campsites are on hand at this location, and the lake itself, though fishless, provides a nice setting for silent reflection. The trail reaches the pass into Bass Creek after an additional 500-foot ascent. The long expanse of Bass Lake unfolds in the canyon below; its stony promontories and deep blue waters lend a pleasant counterpoint to the surrounding natural fortifications. The trail follows a dropping course and reaches a marked junction with the Bass Pass Trail (301X) amid the trees.

From Bass Lake you can continue downstream to the Charles Waters Memorial Campground, nearly 8 miles distant. This is an easy downhill stretch that for the most part follows an old roadbed. Refer to the Bass Creek narrative for a detailed description of this drainage.

Option: Hiking the trail in reverse is a possibility, but you face an uphill climb after leaving the wilderness and continuing downstream toward the

South Fork Lolo Creek Trailhead. I personally prefer the north-to-south direction for this reason alone. Those interested in attempting this as a day hike should plan on getting under way at daybreak.

ADDITIONAL TRAILS

Lost Park (1S), 6.5 miles (10.5 km). This National Recreation Trail straddles the Bitterroot Divide between Lost Park and Skookum Butte. Beginning near Lost Park Meadows some 4 miles east of Lolo Pass, the route crosses Lost Park Creek and closely follows the divide before dropping into Idaho above Granite Lake. From there the trail continues east to a marked junction with the Skookum Butte Trail (304ML) below the old Skookum Butte Lookout. The segments on USFS land are maintained to secondary standards, but the Plum Creek sections are so badly overcut that the trail is sometimes easy to lose among the many slash piles and spur logging roads.

Granite Lake (303S), 2.0 miles (3.2 km). This trail leads south from the gated terminus of Forest Road 461 to Granite Lake, a small body of water lying barely within Idaho. The trail follows the road along the headwaters of the East Fork Lolo Creek for the better part of a mile before entering an old Plum Creek cutting unit. Bear right and continue south on the spur logging road to reach the Granite Lake Trail, which leaves the road near the edge of the unit boundary and climbs toward a forested saddle on the Bitterroot Divide. Cut-over forest surrounds Granite Lake: Plum Creek's chainsaws have stripped all merchantable timber to within 50 feet of the lakeshore.

246

Nez Perce National Forest

Moose Creek Ranger District

71 Coquina Lake

See Map on Page 31

Highlights: An easily accessible mountain lake with numerous campsites and excellent fishing.
Type of hike: Out-and-back day hike or overnighter.
Total distance: 5.2 miles or 8.4 kilometers (round trip).
Difficulty: Easy.
Best months: July through September.
Elevation gain: 880 feet.
Elevation loss: 160 feet.
Map: El Capitan USGS quad.

Special considerations: Coquina Lake is one of the most frequented destinations in the Bear Creek Pass area, second only to Fish Lake in popularity. One dozen tents occupied campsites along its shores during my visit on the afternoon of July 18, 1999. Coquina is also the site of a large outfitter's camp during the summer months, which seems both surprising and a bit ridiculous in light of its modest distance from a major USFS trailhead.

Trailhead access: Take the Lost Horse Road (429) west from its junction with U.S. Highway 93, 9 miles south of Hamilton. Follow this recently improved gravel road west for 17.7 miles to the Lost Horse Guard Station. Here the road forks: Disregard the road to Twin Lakes and instead follow signs for Bear Creek Pass. The road continues south and crosses the Bitterroot Divide to reach the trailhead loop after another 1.2 miles. A USFS information board denotes the trail's point of departure near the southwest end of the loop. Parking space is well distributed throughout the general vicinity, with both an outhouse and packstock amenities (hitchrails and ramps) located nearby.

Keypoints:
0.0 Inception of trail at Bear Creek Pass.
0.9 Trail passes above Lower Bear Lake.
1.0 Trail enters the Selway-Bitterroot Wilderness.
1.6 Unmarked junction to Coquina Lake; bear right.
1.8 Abandoned earthen dam at Upper Bear Lake.
2.6 End of description at Coquina Lake.

The hike: Perhaps as a precautionary measure against overuse, most forest maps omit the spur trail to Coquina Lake. But on the ground it is clearly recognizable and offers access to one of the most attractive destinations within a few hours' travel of Bear Creek Pass. The round trip makes a lovely day

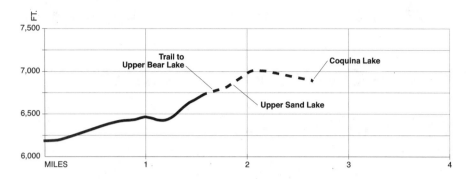

hike, well suited for folks looking for a moderate day hike with good scenic value and excellent fishing for rainbow trout.

The trail initially meanders southeast through boulder-studded forest, crossing several horse-churned segments before emerging into open terrain below the wilderness boundary. Attractive views of distant granite peaks continue as you enter designated wilderness and traverse open slopes well above Lower Bear Lake and its surrounding meadows. A westward glance takes in the upper canyon of Bear Creek, with the rock-strewn prominence of Elk Ridge arrayed along its southern rim. As you continue southeast, the trail reenters subalpine forest and tackles yet another series of switchbacks beside Bear Creek. You arrive at an unmarked junction to Upper Bear Lake at 1.6 miles.

Following a well-defined tread, the trail crosses Bear Creek and continues upstream to reach Upper Bear Lake. This shallow lake was the site of a shrewd water diversion scheme devised by Montana irrigators in the early 1900s. Bitterroot Valley residents constructed an earthfill dam and ditch to direct the lake's outflow over Bear Creek Pass and into Montana. The waterworks attracted little notice at first but were later breached when state and federal authorities caught wind of the scheme. Today the low earthen dam, overgrown and long abandoned, still huddles beneath fir and pine at the foot of the lake. Several good tent spaces are present around the shoreline, and moose are frequently seen feeding here each morning. The fishing is no great shakes.

The trail continues southwest from the dam area and ascends gently to a wooded bench before dropping into the Coquina Lake basin. For the most part the route is obvious and—whenever the trail traverses segments of exposed bedrock—there are cairns to guide you. Coquina Lake is a rather small body of water overlooked from three directions by nameless peaks still veiled with melting snowfields in July. Interconnected footpaths wrap around the lakeshore and offer access to overused campsites scattered along its perimeter. Coquina Lake offers excellent fishing for fat rainbow trout and possibly a few rainbow-cutthroat crossbreeds.

Boulders dot the shoreline of Coquina Lake.

72 Spruce Lake

See Map on Page 31

Highlights: A very rough trail to a
seldom-visited subalpine lake.
Type of hike: Out-and-back day hike or overnighter.
Total distance: 6.4 miles or 10.3 kilometers (round trip).
Difficulty: Difficult.
Best months: July through September.
Elevation gain: 1,320 feet.
Elevation loss: 850 feet.
Maps: El Capitan and Hunter Peak USGS quads.

Trailhead access: Take Lost Horse Road (429) west from its junction with U.S. Highway 93, 9 miles south of Hamilton. Follow this good gravel road west for 17.7 miles to the Lost Horse Guard Station. Here the road forks: Disregard the road to Twin Lakes and instead follow signs for Bear Creek Pass. The road continues south and crosses the Bitterroot Divide to reach the trailhead loop after another 1.2 miles. A sign for the Bear Creek Trail (516ML) marks its origin along an old roadbed at the northern end of the loop. Parking space is well distributed throughout the general vicinity, with an outhouse and packstock amenities both located nearby.

Keypoints:
- 0.0 Inception of trail at Bear Creek Pass.
- 0.2 Junction with the Spruce Creek Trail (559S).
- 0.5 Trail crosses Bear Creek.
- 1.3 Trail enters the Selway-Bitterroot Wilderness.
- 2.0 Trail passes a nameless lake.
- 2.6 Pass into the Spruce Creek drainage.
- 3.2 End of description at the foot of Spruce Lake.

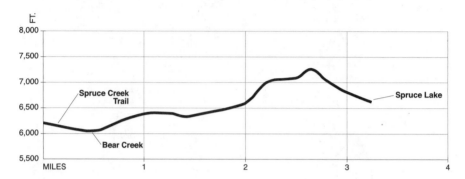

The hike: This rough trail leads to Spruce Lake, a little-known tarn located just 2 air miles southwest of Bear Creek Pass. Hikers disinclined to share the likes of Fish and Coquina lakes with dozens of other people should instead consider a trip to this decidedly out-of-the-way destination. The trail's poor condition accounts for its generally light use—much of the route suffers from benign neglect, with flooded tread and blowdowns being frequent obstacles along the way. It is slow going.

From the signed trailhead at Bear Creek Pass, the trail follows a westerly course and soon meets the Spruce Creek Trail (559S). Taking the left-hand fork, the route continues its descent over the protest of downed trees and shallow pools of standing water to reach Bear Creek. Fallen logs provide dry passage over this stream. Switchbacks take the trail to a higher bench covered in spruce and subalpine fir. There is a wilderness sign at 1.3 miles. After another slight descent, you cross the outlet stream flowing from Coquina Lake and leave the stream bottom behind.

The trail then begins a sustained climb and passes within sight of a nameless lake; talus aprons and couloirs rise to a snow-draped headwall overlooking this small body of water. Views continue to improve until at last the route skirts a boulder field just below the pass into Spruce Creek. Here you can gaze upon the broad upper reaches of Bear Creek and look north into Montana and the headwaters of the Lost Horse drainage. The trail unveils a ghostly perspective from atop the 7,300-foot pass into Spruce Creek, where a 1998 wildfire razed the subalpine forest on the south-facing slopes below. Several excellent campsites are available at the pass, provided you know the way to a pair of springs nearby.

Spruce Lake remains out of sight for a short time as the route follows switchbacks sharply downhill through the fire-killed snags. The tread is quite

250

Spruce Lake sits below the nameless peaks of Elk Ridge.

steep and rough underfoot, but fortunately the grade eases somewhat before returning to green forest near the foot of the lake. Spruce Lake is a narrow green tarn wedged between spruce-fir forest and a towering headwall.
There are some good campsites here should you decide to spend the night.

73 Gedney Creek

Highlights:	A lightly used trail with pleasant views and early-season access.
Type of hike:	Out-and-back day hike.
Total distance:	7.8 miles or 12.6 kilometers (round trip).
Difficulty:	Easy.
Best months:	April through November.
Elevation gain:	680 feet.
Elevation loss:	160 feet.
Map:	Selway Falls USGS quad.

Trailhead access: From Lowell take the Selway River Road (223) southeast along the river, following the paved road through a rural residential area for the first 6.8 miles. A narrow forest road takes up where pavement leaves off, but you're likely to find it very slow going: Portions of the road are so heavily pockmarked as to resemble the surface of the moon. The class III potholes persist as you continue upstream to the unmarked trailhead pullout some 17.7 miles east of Lowell. Situated beside the bridge over Gedney Creek, amenities include an outhouse and parking for perhaps five vehicles. Additional parking space is available nearby.

Keypoints:
  0.0   Inception of trail along the Selway River Road.
  3.9   End of description at Gedney Creek crossing.

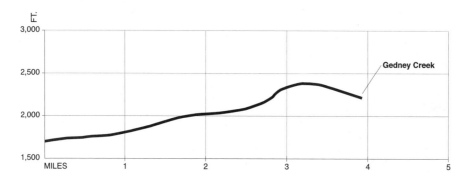

The hike: At first glance the Gedney Creek drainage is of little apparent interest to the hiker—there are no obvious attractions or scenic landmarks along its lower miles. Yet this lightly used route offers its own diversions and delivers a sense of seclusion not found on other stream-bottom trails in the area. Its quiet beauty is borne in the hush of steep brushfields and the sight of twisted snags, a landscape still recovering in the aftermath of the 1934 Pete King Fire.

Gedney Creek

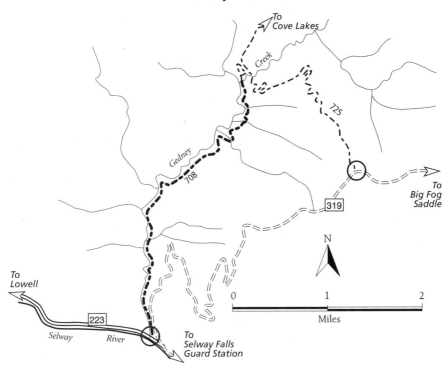

The trail starts north along Gedney Creek, rising and falling as it makes its way through stands of cedar and hemlock. Maintenance appears infrequent: Grass grows in the mostly dirt surface of the trail and a few instability-prone stretches have slumped downslope. Gedney Creek maintains an audible presence at all times. This large stream is actually wide and swift enough to attract a few adventurous kayakers in late spring.

High water overtakes one segment of the trail in late spring, beyond which you begin a steady ascent onto the slopes overlooking the stream bottom. A backward glance reveals the forested lower reaches of Gedney Creek, with 5,069-foot Falls Point rising beyond the canyon entrance. A gentle bend carries the trail into a northeasterly bearing as a succession of burnedover ridgelines plunge into drainage from the west. Several of these still bristle with snags left standing in the wake of the 1934 conflagration.

Crossing intermittent brooklets from time to time, you continue the moderate ascent through timbered terrain before emerging onto a broad, open slope once again at 3.5 miles. Here the trail contours across the hillside several hundred feet above a large horseshoe-shaped bend in the watercourse. After a brief descent the trail arrives at the confluence of Gedney Creek and its larger West Fork. Steep brushfields gaze down on the one serviceable camp-

Gedney Creek runs high and swift in late May.

site found here. Beyond this point the trail makes a difficult high-water ford of Gedney Creek and begins a murderous 5,140-foot climb toward Gedney Mountain, still some 4 miles away.

Option: You can follow the Gedney Mountain Trail (708W) northeast for 6.7 miles to the vicinity of Cove Lakes, nestled among the Selway Crags. Portions of this northern segment, no longer maintained, are in poor repair and require considerable expertise to find and follow—not that many ever try.

74 Cupboard Creek

Highlights:	A quiet retreat along the wild and scenic Selway River, featuring shaded cedar groves and big sand beaches. A popular trail with backcountry horsemen.
Type of hike:	Out-and-back day hike or overnighter.
Total distance:	12 miles or 19.3 kilometers (round trip).
Difficulty:	Easy.
Best months:	April through November.
Elevation gain:	140 feet.
Elevation loss:	100 feet.
Maps:	Fog Mountain and Selway Falls USGS quads.

Cupboard Creek

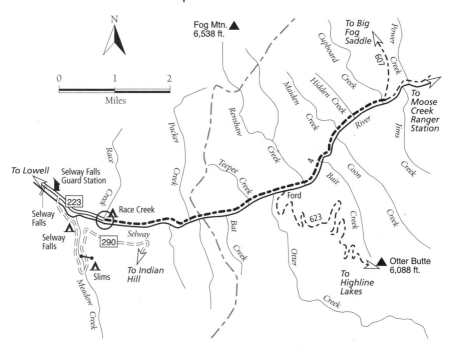

Special considerations: The Selway River breaks are prime rattlesnake country. Watch your step and keep an eye out if small children or the family dog is along. Temperatures along the river routinely push 90 degrees F during the summer months, so get an early start and keep your water filter handy.

Trailhead access: From Lowell take Selway River Road (223) upstream along the river, following a good paved road through a rural residential area for the first 6.8 miles. A narrow and horribly potholed road takes up where pavement leaves off, continuing beside the river to reach the Race Creek Trailhead 19.7 miles east of Lowell. This end-of-the-road staging area features a small campground, pit toilets, and parking for more than two dozen vehicles. Be sure to sign the trail register before starting your hike.

Keypoints:
- 0.0   Inception of trail at Race Creek Campground.
- 1.6   Trail crosses Packer Creek and enters the Selway-Bitterroot Wilderness.
- 2.8   Trail crosses Teepee Creek.
- 3.3   Unmarked junction with the Otter Butte Trail (623W).
- 3.9   Trail reaches Renshaw Creek.
- 5.1   Trail crosses Maiden Creek.
- 5.4   Trail crosses Hidden Creek.
- 6.0   End of description at pack bridge over Cupboard Creek. Unmarked junction with Big Fog Saddle Trail (607W).

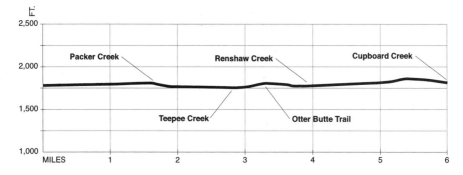

The hike: This low-elevation trail features a meandering and gently undulating course with consistently good scenic value and early-season accessibility that is all too rare in northern Idaho. Suitable for hikers of all ages and abilities, the round trip makes an excellent introduction to the wild country of the lower Selway River. One visit to the area may even convince you to hike the 49.5-mile-long river trail in its entirety, as discussed in Hike 76, Selway River.

The trail starts out as a well-maintained tread leading upstream through the forest. Interspersed among the Douglas-fir and ponderosa are pockets of hemlock and western red cedar, which take root along the lower reaches of most tributaries flowing from the southern flanks of Fog and Big Fog mountains. You enter the Selway-Bitterroot Wilderness just beyond Packer Creek. Numerous side trails cut away from the main route in its early miles; most lead to sand beaches that make idyllic stopovers for an afternoon of fishing. Anglers hook into some large cutthroat trout in the deeper holes of the Selway during late summer, but catch-and-release regulations currently apply.

All along the lower Selway River are traces of the conflagration that swept through this country in 1934. Gray snags set off the scene along the trail, heavy brushfields demarcate the worst of the firestorm, and groves of hardwoods compete with softwoods on the north-facing slopes across the river. The fire's onslaught was fickle in the extreme, reducing centuries-old evergreens to ash while sparing swaths of timber on neighboring hillsides by some strange twist of fate. The resulting mosaic pattern is still evident many decades after the fact, and will remain so for years to come.

An unmarked junction with the Otter Butte Trail (623W) turns up at 3.3 miles. This steep route leads south across the Selway to the crest of 6,088-foot Otter Butte, a remote peak that was the site of a USFS fire lookout until 1955. Slow moving though it is, the river ford remains prohibitively deep through midsummer.

The main trail continues upstream and soon reaches a squared-off log crossing over Renshaw Creek. Here you will find a selection of nice campsites beneath shady cedars or on a sand beach close by. The rhythmic sound of rushing water gives these sites a restful quality; indeed, I have slept more soundly along the Selway than anywhere else in the wilderness.

Departing Renshaw Creek the trail ascends gently above the river, turns slightly northeast, and maintains a gradual contour for the better part of the next 2 miles. On its way upstream you traverse ledges of bedrock dropping abruptly to the river, offering views of both the watercourse and the high ridgelines to the east. The outcropping rocks consist largely of metasediments—sedimentary rocks altered by heat, pressure, and other metamorphic processes to form contorted masses resembling taffy.

After crossing Maiden and Hidden creeks—both running dry by midsummer—the trail presses on to reach Cupboard Creek at 6 miles. Situated among the ponderosas are several good campsites, and from the beach you can survey Cupboard Creek, one of the many class III rapids found on the Selway River. Take your choice—relax here for an hour or two and return to the trailhead or overnight along the creek and continue farther upstream the following day.

75 Lower Meadow Creek

Highlights:	A lovely national recreation trail along one of the Selway River's largest tributaries.
Type of hike:	Out-and-back overnighter.
Total distance:	27 miles or 43.4 kilometers (round trip).
Difficulty:	Moderate.
Best months:	April through November.
Elevation gain:	2,810 feet.
Elevation loss:	1,550 feet.
Maps:	Anderson Butte, Selway Falls, and Vermilion Peak USGS quads.

Special considerations: One unique feature of this trail is the Meadow Creek Guard Station, available for private rental if reservations are made. The well-equipped station offers cabin accommodations for eight—indoor plumbing and a propane-powered refrigerator are among the amenities included at no extra charge. The current fee stands at $25 per night. Those interested in renting the guard station should contact Fenn Ranger Station for further details.

Trailhead access: From Lowell take Selway River Road (223) southeast along the river, following a good paved road through a rural residential area for the first 6.8 miles. A narrow and horribly potholed forest road takes up where pavement leaves off, continuing beside the river to reach the spectacular and seemingly unnavigable Selway Falls 18.2 miles east of Lowell. Just beyond Selway Falls Guard Station, veer right and follow the single-lane bridge over the river before proceeding for another 1.5 miles to Slims Campground. Nestled among cedars and flowering dogwoods next to Meadow Creek, this spacious trailhead includes an outhouse, stock unloading ramps, and two trailer pullouts. There is also parking for as many as 20 vehicles.

Lower Meadow Creek

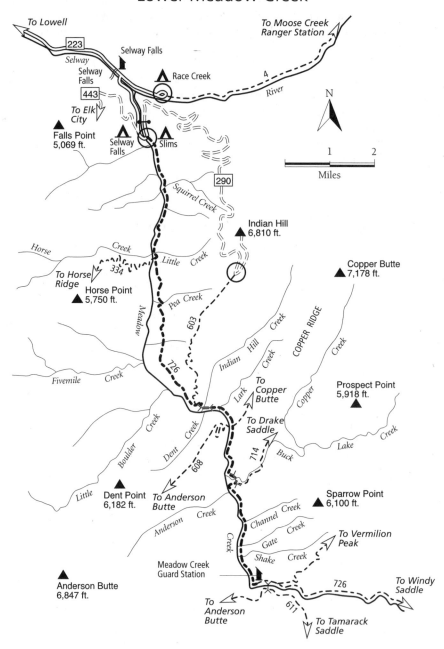

Keypoints:

- 0.0   Inception of trail at Slims Campground.
- 1.3   Trail crosses Squirrel Creek.
- 1.7   Trail vaults Rabbit Creek.
- 3.1   Junction with the Horse Point Trail (334X) at Little Creek.

4.4	Trail crosses Pea Creek.
5.0	Trail crosses Reverse Creek.
6.6	Trail meets Pell Creek.
6.9	Spur trail to Tom's Cabin site.
7.8	Junction with the Indian Hill Trail (603S).
8.0	Trail makes a crossing of Indian Hill Creek.
8.6	Trail crosses Lark Creek.
9.2	Unmarked junction with Dent Ridge Trail (608X).
10.0	Junction with the defunct Copper Butte Trail (604X).
10.3	Trail crosses Buck Lake Creek. Unmarked junction with the Buck Lake Creek Trail (714W).
11.6	Trail arrives at Channel Creek.
12.3	Trail crosses Gate Creek.
12.5	Trail crosses Shake Creek.
13.5	End of description at Meadow Creek Guard Station.

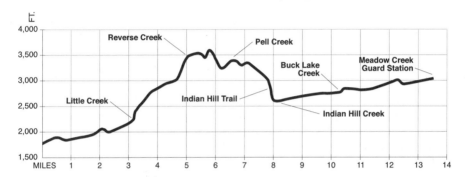

The hike: This popular national recreation trail showcases the tranquil beauty of the Meadow Creek roadless area, a labyrinth of forested canyons contiguous with the southwestern margin of the Selway-Bitterroot Wilderness. The first 3 miles provide an exceptionally pleasant day hike and are generally snow-free from April to November. Those interested in a more rigorous out-and-back hike may continue upstream to the historic Meadow Creek Guard Station, available for public use by reservation, 13.5 miles from Slims Campground.

Beneath a lush forest canopy of old-growth cedar and hemlock, the trail begins its southerly course alongside Meadow Creek. Resembling a river in its own right, this sizable stream remains a constant presence in these early miles, rushing across gravel bars and half-submerged logs and collecting in deep pools on its way downstream. Moss and maidenhair ferns drape metasedimentary bedrock exposed along the well-constructed tread; large flecks of muscovite mica sparkle in the soil underfoot. The Pacific yew, whose leathery bark was sought to synthesize the cancer-fighting drug Taxol, sends its roots into the rocky streambank.

The trail remains in excellent condition as you cross both Squirrel and Rabbit creeks and close in on the pack bridge spanning Little Creek. A marked junction with the now-defunct Horse Point Trail (334X) is posted here, but even those with advanced faint-trail skills have little chance of finding it.

Located just over 3 miles from the trailhead, Little Creek serves as a logical turnaround point for most day hikers—here, too, a well-defined side trail ventures down to a series of deep pools in Meadow Creek. Several campsites, overused and offering little privacy, are visible from this footpath.

Leaving the bottomland environs behind, a series of switchbacks forces the trail into a more aggressive posture and begins a 1,400-foot ascent of the canyon slopes. Heavy forest surrenders grudgingly few views of the drainage. (In one shady draw the trail comes across an eerie scene in which a black recess in the rock stares out from behind the veil of a carefully juxtaposed rivulet.) Pea and Reverse creeks provide the only direct gauge of progress as you follow the undulating trail across slopes so steep that any off-trail scrambling would seem a hopeless cause. Numerous interconnecting game trails crisscross the path from every direction, but the proper route remains obvious and easy to follow at all times. As the trail draws abreast of Fivemile Creek—a large Meadow Creek tributary feeding in from the west—openings in the trees permit the first impression of the plunging canyon landscape. With a good view of 5,750-foot Horse Point receding to the northwest, you slowly descend among towering ponderosas to reach a signed junction with the Indian Hill Trail (603S). The trail then drops abruptly via switchbacks to an excellent pack bridge over Indian Hill Creek.

Returning to the company of Meadow Creek once again, the trail sweeps past a well-established outfitter's campsite and quickly doglegs south. (Forest maps indicate a junction for the Dent Ridge Trail [608X] beyond Lark Creek, but the precise take-off point is elusive.) As you walk among the silent cedars, a growing sense of mystery and seclusion heightens with each passing finger ridge and inflection in the watercourse. Posted to a tree some 10 miles from the trailhead is a nearly illegible metal sign indicating the junction with the long-abandoned Copper Butte Trail (604X). Upon reaching the pack bridge at Buck Lake Creek you may notice yet another (unmarked) trail junction—deadfall and other debris now accumulate on the still-visible tread of the old Buck Lake Creek Trail (714W), which continues upstream and out of sight. The final 2 miles below the guard station involve generally pleasant hiking, with occasional overlooks of the stream bottom and only a few small brooklets to cross. Traversing blasted ledges high above Meadow Creek, the route abruptly doglegs east to reach an open landing and site of the Meadow Creek Guard Station. Timbered ridges overlook the lonely outpost from every direction.

Constructed in 1923, the station house is only one part of a larger complex that includes a bunkhouse along with a tack shed, corral, wood shed, and outhouse. Old cedars shade much of the guard station, but there is more than enough open space to permit spectacular stargazing—only the glow of an evening campfire will distract your eyes. Please note that camping and grazing livestock are prohibited in the guard station area.

Option: From the guard station you may choose to continue as far upstream as you like on the excellent Meadow Creek Trail. There is nothing particularly remarkable to distinguish this upper 13-mile segment from that seen previously, but it is worth a look all the same.

The Meadow Creek Guard Station.

Side trips: Opportunities for side trips in the Meadow Creek area are quite limited due to the extremely rugged terrain and generally poor condition of most adjoining trails. Even so, from a base camp at the guard station you might pursue a strenuous day hike to the fire lookout atop 6,847-foot Anderson Butte via the Butte Creek Trail (809S). A hike to Vermilion Peak via the Vermilion Peak Trail (609S) is another possibility.

76 Selway River

Highlights:	A weeklong odyssey along one of the Northern Rockies' wildest rivers.
Type of hike:	Six-day backpacking shuttle or base camp.
Total distance:	49.5 miles or 79.6 kilometers.
Difficulty:	Moderate.
Best months:	May through October.
Elevation gain:	2,680 feet.
Elevation loss:	3,970 feet.
Maps:	Burnt Strip Mountain, Dog Creek, Fog Mountain, Gardiner Peak, Mink Peak, Moose Ridge, Selway Falls, Shissler Peak, and Spot Mountain USGS quads.

Special considerations: Due to the rocky, open terrain that predominates along much of this low-elevation trail, the Selway River country is a notoriously hot late-summer hike. An early start on the trail is the best way to

Selway River

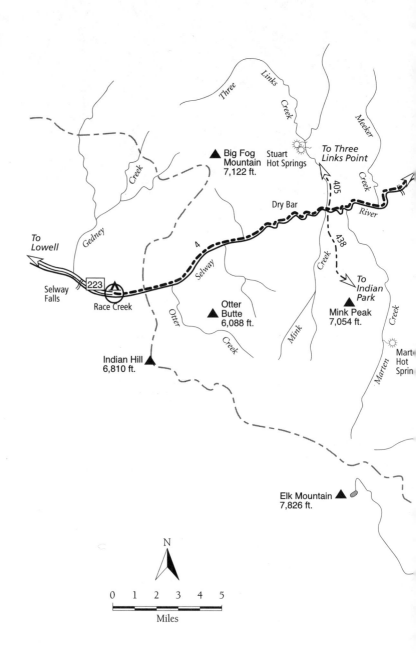

Three Links Creek

Meeker Creek

Big Fog Mountain
7,122 ft.

Stuart Hot Springs

To Three Links Point

405

Dry Bar

River

To Lowell

Gedney Creek

4

Selway

438

Mink Creek

To Indian Park

Selway Falls

223

Race Creek

Otter Butte
6,088 ft.

Otter Creek

Mink Peak
7,054 ft.

Marten Creek

Mart Hot Sprin

Indian Hill
6,810 ft.

Elk Mountain
7,826 ft.

N

0 1 2 3 4 5
Miles

Selway River

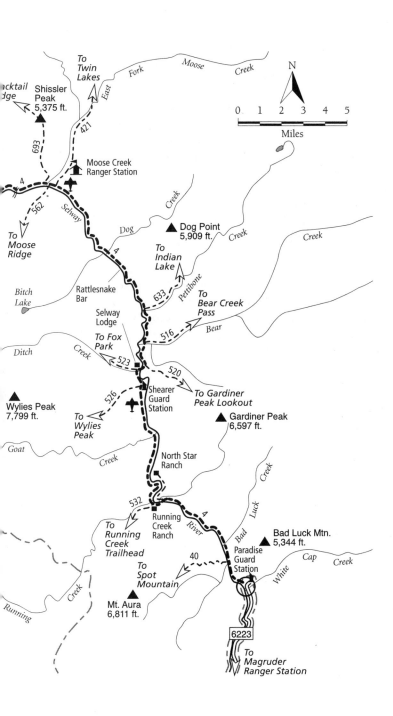

beat the heat short of swimming in the river itself. The low-lying river breaks are home to a large number of rattlesnakes, so have a snakebite kit on hand and know how to use it.

Trailhead access: One of most sobering realities of hiking the Selway River Trail is the sheer distance of the shuttle involved. It takes approximately *six hours* to cover the 245-mile route between Race Creek and Paradise via Lolo Pass, making the logistical difficulties almost as challenging as the hike itself!

To reach Paradise Landing, take U.S. Highway 93 to its junction with Montana Highway 473, 4.4 miles south of Darby. Continue southwest for 14.3 miles to Nez Perce Road (468) and veer right. Follow this high-standard gravel road across the Bitterroot Divide at Nez Perce Pass and downstream to the Selway River launch site at Paradise Landing, 46 miles from MT 473. Plentiful parking is available by continuing along the road for an additional 0.2 mile to reach the Paradise Campground and Guard Station.

For the Race Creek Trailhead, follow U.S. Highway 12 to Lowell, Idaho, and take the Selway River Road (223) upstream along the river. The road follows a good paved surface through a rural residential area and past Fenn Ranger Station in its first 6.8 miles, after which a narrow and horribly potholed road takes up where the pavement leaves off. The road plods along the river to reach the Race Creek Trailhead 19.7 miles east of Lowell. This end-of-the-road staging area features a very small campground, pit toilets, and parking for more than two dozen vehicles. An information board and trail register are located here.

Keypoints:

0.0	Inception of trail at Paradise Landing.
0.1	Trail enters the Selway-Bitterroot Wilderness.
1.5	Unsigned junction with the Mount Aura Trail (40S).
2.2	Junction with the Bad Luck Creek Trail (93ML).
2.3	Trail fords Bad Luck Creek.
3.9	Trail draws abreast of Waldo Bar.
6.5	Trail crosses Gardiner Creek.
6.7	Junction with the Elevator Mountain Trail (521S). Pack bridge over the Selway River; stay left.
6.8	Trail reaches the Running Creek Ranch.
6.9	Junction with the Running Creek Trail (532ML). Pack bridge over Running Creek.
7.6	Unmarked junction with the Archer Point Trail (546X).
11.2	Junction with the Archer Mountain Trail (529S) above Goat Creek.
13.4	Stock bypass trail at the Shearer airstrip.
13.9	Junction with the Wylies Peak Trail (526ML).
14.0	Trail reaches the Shearer Guard Station at Elk Creek.
14.8	Pack bridge over Ditch Creek.
14.9	Junction with the Ditch Creek Trail (523ML). Trail passes through the Selway Lodge inholding.
15.0	Trail crosses the Selway River via pack bridge. Junction with the Gardiner Peak Trail (520S).
16.2	Unmarked junction with the Crow Ridge Trail (518X).

16.3   Pack bridge and junction with the Bear Creek Trail (516ML).

18.5   Pack bridge over Pettibone Creek. Junction with the Pettibone Creek Trail (633S).

20.4   Trail crosses Cow Creek to reach a junction with the Dog Point Trail (435W).

20.5   Trail crosses Glacier Creek.

21.0   Trail passes Rattlesnake Bar.

22.3   Pack bridge over Dog Creek.

25.0   Trail boldly meets Hell Creek.

25.5   Trail crosses Hopwood Creek.

27.2   Junction with the East Fork Moose Creek Trail (421ML) near Moose Creek.

27.9   Trail passes the Moose Creek airstrip.

28.1   Junction with the Moose Ridge Trail (562ML).

28.2   Pack bridge over Moose Creek. Junction with the Big Rock Trail (693ML).

28.6   Unmarked junction with the Goat Mountain Trail (444X) just past Divide Creek.

29.2   Trail crosses Jake Creek.

31.3   Marked junction with the Halfway Creek Trail (447W). Pack bridge over Halfway Creek.

31.9   Trail enters the Cedar Flats.

33.6   Marked junction with the Meeker Ridge Trail (458S).

33.8   Pack bridge over Meeker Creek.

34.9   Trail crosses Tango Creek.

37.0   Junctions with the Three Links Creek (405ML), Mink Peak (438ML), and Sixtytwo Ridge (606S) trails. Pack bridge over Three Links Creek.

38.3   Trail crosses Bar Creek.

38.8   Trail draws abreast of Dry Bar.

40.1   Trail crosses Pinchot Creek.

41.0   Trail crosses Cascade Creek.

41.9   Pack bridge over Ballinger Creek.

42.9   Trail crosses Power Creek.

43.4   Junction with the Big Fog Saddle Trail (607S).

43.5   Pack bridge over Cupboard Creek.

44.1   Trail crosses Hidden Creek.

44.4   Trail crosses Maiden Creek.

45.6   Trail reaches Renshaw Creek.

46.2   Junction with the Otter Butte Trail (623W).

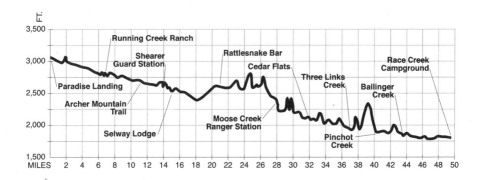

46.7   Trail crosses Teepee Creek.

47.9   Trail vaults Packer Creek and leaves the Selway-Bitterroot Wilderness.

49.5   Terminus of Selway River Trail at Race Creek.

Suggested itinerary: Experienced backpackers can tackle the river trail in as few as three days. But having gone through the considerable effort of planning this hike and arranging its 245-mile shuttle, I would recommend a trip of at least five days, averaging just under 10 miles per day. Be sure to schedule extra time if you are interested in any of the plentiful side trips.

Some hikers are frustrated to learn there are no designated campsites along the Selway River. With few exceptions, however, excellent campsites are well distributed along the trail—those at Pinchot Creek, Cedar Flats, Bear Creek, and the dry benches opposite North Star Ranch are among the better examples. Two segments of the river trail seemed devoid of good campsites when I hiked it from June 22 to 24, 1999. The first "dry spell" occurs between Paradise Landing and Running Creek: the second, between Bear Creek and the Moose Creek Ranger Station. In both cases high water likely concealed potential campsites along the river. Late summer sees many informal campsites reappear beside the river as subsiding water levels expose numerous sand spits and bars along its banks.

First day	—	Paradise Landing to Running Creek, 6.9 miles.
Second day	—	Running Creek to Bear Creek, 9.4 miles.
Third day	—	Bear Creek to Moose Creek, 11.9 miles; or to Cedar Flats, 15.6 miles.
Fourth day	—	Moose Creek to Pinchot Creek, 11.9 miles.
Fifth day	—	Pinchot Creek to Cupboard Creek, 3.4 miles; or to Race Creek Trailhead, 9.4 miles.

The hike: Here is an epic journey unlike any other in the Selway-Bitterroot Wilderness. Over its nearly 50-mile distance along the Selway River, this mainline trail crosses two USFS ranger districts on two national forests, transecting some of the wildest remaining country in the lower 48 states. At the Moose Creek Ranger Station, in the very heart of the wilderness, it is approximately 25 miles by trail to the nearest gravel road.

The river is a scenic attraction in itself and offers rafting enthusiasts some of the finest technical whitewater in the Pacific Northwest. Rapids occur intermittently over the length of the Selway, but the biggest water is limited to a 5-mile stretch downstream of Moose Creek. Some of the more memorable rapids found in this area, such as class IV + Ladle and Little Niagara, are terrifying to behold in early summer. To provide high-quality floating opportunities and prevent overcrowding, the USFS manages the Selway River under a limited permit system from May 15 through July 31. Under these restrictions only one launch per day is allowed at Paradise Landing.

Private inholdings and other outposts of civilization give the river a unique quality not found elsewhere in the wilderness; the considerable up-and-down configuration of the trail delivers a sense of challenge and variety that keep things interesting. In recognition of these outstanding characteristics, Congress extended federal protection to the Selway River with passage of the Wild and Scenic Rivers Act of 1968.

From the boat launch facility at Paradise Landing, the trail ambles downstream into increasingly open terrain contrasting sharply with that on the opposite side of the river. The route rises and falls as it crosses the toes of several minor ridges and draws abreast of Crooked Creek, the first significant tributary flowing into the Selway from the west. An archaic junction with the Mount Aura Trail (40S) is located in this area—an obscure turnoff that very few visitors bother looking for. Bald knobs and bare ridges define the rugged terrain ahead and at 2.2 miles you come to a signless junction with the trail up Bad Luck Creek (93ML). The remains of a collapsed pack bridge over this stream soon follow.

From time to time the canyon narrows enough to force the route onto ledges high above the rushing waters. These rises coincide with changes in the cadence of the river, whose rhythm intensifies in the tightly confined channel below. Little level ground is available and, except for a few marginal possibilities in the vicinity of Waldo Bar, campsite selection is extremely limited in these early miles.

After a wet crossing at Gardiner Creek, the trail circles over to reach a large, suspension-style pack bridge over the Selway. At the north end of the bridge is a marked junction with a trail leading along the east side of the river to North Star Ranch, still 2 miles downstream. Across the bridge, the route heads into heavy timber and brush to emerge at Running Creek Ranch short moments later.

The first of three privately owned tracts you will find along the river, Running Creek Ranch consists of a handful of cabins and outbuildings as well as a steep airstrip cut out the forest. An old hound dog greeted me here as I walked along the fence and a trio of kittens kept watch from the comfort of a covered porch nearby. The trail stays just outside the fenceline until reaching a signed junction with the Running Creek Trail (532ML) some 100 yards upstream of its confluence with the Selway River. Were it not for the well-constructed pack bridge, Running Creek would present an impossible ford until midsummer.

The route ventures into open surroundings once again and continues beside the river, passing rock outcrops of largely igneous origin. The complementary ruddy and purple colors of the weathered rock are visually pleasing; the surrounding semiarid foothills are strangely picturesque and a far cry from the ancient cedar forests found elsewhere in these mountains. After passing a junction with the abandoned Archer Point Trail (546X), the route contours around the next major bend in the river and crosses a series of timbered benches opposite the North Star Ranch. Cross-river views of the North Star inholding take in a short airstrip and a few large buildings set back against wooded foothills on a bench overlooking the river. Of the four parcels still under private ownership in the Selway-Bitterroot, this one is perhaps the least intrusive.

The route reenters forest as it draws to within 1 mile of Goat Creek. Across the river are occasional traces of an old trail (521X) to 4,198-foot Elevator Mountain—a steep and rocky path that fell into disuse years ago. A signed junction with the Archer Mountain Trail (529S) appears just before you cross the pack bridge over Goat Creek. Beyond this point the river pursues a northerly bearing, passing through stands of mountain hemlock and western red cedar, to reach the long USFS airstrip at Shearer.

As a wooden sign indicates, stock users must bypass the airfield. Those traveling on foot might just as well continue through the clearing to the Shearer guard station and corral, located in the trees at the far end of the landing zone. Aircraft occasionally touch down at the Shearer airstrip, but use here is not as heavy as that at the Moose Creek Ranger Station. One individual tried unsuccessfully to force its closure by "salting" the airfield so that big game would tear up the landing zone in their search for the mineral. The stock bypass trail and several others leading from the corral link up just past the guard station structures. From here the route leads quickly to Elk Creek, where a makeshift footbridge provides a dry crossing.

Less than a mile beyond Shearer you come to another bridge—this time over Ditch Creek—before entering a parcel owned as part of the Selway Lodge. A solar-powered electric fence enclosure surrounds the lodge airstrip, which in turn is surrounded by tall grass and wildflowers. (Gates provide access through this privately owned section, but please remember to close them behind you.) The trail shuffles alongside the airstrip momentarily, then leaves the lodge property and crosses a second pack bridge over the Selway River. At the eastern end of the bridge a marked junction with the Gardiner Peak Trail (520S) offers the first of several especially scenic side trip opportunities.

Potential campsites appear in the form of clearings beside the trail, and at mile 16.3 you reach a long, sturdy suspension bridge spanning Bear Creek. This enormous tributary is sufficiently deep and swift to qualify as a river in its own right—and some older maps even refer to it as such! Some decent campsites are located near the marked junction with the Bear Creek Trail (516ML). This is a good spot to spend your second night out.

The trail stays out of sight of the river for short time until returning to its vicinity for a series of sweeping meanders entrenched in the deep canyon. In a few burned-over sections heavy, soaking foliage crowds the path; elsewhere, you traverse ledges several hundred feet above the watercourse. An excellent pack bridge crosses the moss-covered chasm of Pettibone Creek at 18.5 miles. On the hillside above this crossing are several signs indicating the junction with the Pettibone Creek Trail (633S).

More of the same follows in the miles ahead as the river's course shifts to a northwesterly heading. Easy stream crossings await you at both Cow and Glacier creeks, but as the trail closes in on Dog Creek it begins a hot, elevated traverse that is more difficult than most people expect. Perilously steep terrain forces the route ever higher above the canyon floor until the river seems almost forgotten. The terrain here is quite rugged, with numerous outcropping rock shelves emanating heat throughout the afternoon and the open ponderosa forest offering precious little shade.

This long suspension bridge provides a dry crossing over the Selway River near Running Creek.

After crossing Hell and Hopwood creeks in rapid succession, the trail maintains its contour for another mile before dropping steadily down the ridge and entering shadier forest near Moose Creek. Signs mark the junction with the heavily used East Fork Moose Creek Trail (421ML) at this point. A short jaunt to the Moose Creek Ranger Station, situated in the trees nearby, is well worth the effort.

The Moose Creek Ranger Station is the largest USFS administrative complex in the Selway-Bitterroot Wilderness. Its many outbuildings, corrals, and other structures stand on the northeastern end of a sprawling landing field and serve as a major staging area for smokejumpers and backcountry trail crews operating on the Moose Creek District during the summer months. Everything from Cessnas to twin-engine DC-3s to Ford tri-motors have touched down here over the years—a fact that has aroused the ire of many a wilderness traveler unaccustomed to the hustle and bustle of the outpost. They generally land in early morning or late afternoon to avoid cross-canyon turbulence during the hottest hours of the day.

From the junction the route continues southwest into heavy forest, then swings around the southern end of the airstrip. Views from this location reveal a wide mountain valley with 7,386-foot Bailey Mountain standing sentinel in the background. The trail drops along the hillside, passing a cutoff trail to the ranger station and a junction with the Moose Ridge Trail (562ML), which crosses the Selway River on another large pack bridge located just upstream. You reach a signed junction with the Big Rock Trail (693ML) just across the pack bridge spanning Moose Creek.

The Selway doglegs west below the Moose Creek confluence. Here, as the river makes its way through the burned-out canyon, it encounters no fewer

Pack bridges such as this one over Goat Creek span most of the larger Selway River tributaries.

than seven major rapids in the next 5 miles. Excellent views of every one of them are available without even leaving the trail, which traverses exposed bedrock and tackles steep canyon walls with lots of ups and downs (class IV + Ladle and Little Niagara rapids are undeniably the most impressive examples). It is hard to believe that anything could hold fast in a current this strong, but those submerged rocks and protruding boulders heavy enough to stay in place create a plume of blue-green oxygenated water that trails off for a hundred yards or more downstream.

Reentering green forest near Halfway Creek, the trail passes a marked junction with the old Halfway Creek Trail (447W) on its way to Cedar Flats. The flats are shaded, accessible, and well suited for camping; however, these are among the most heavily used sites along the trail. If vacant, Cedar Flats are a good place to spend your third or fourth night on the Selway.

The route reaches a marked junction with the trail up Meeker Ridge (458S) shortly before crossing Meeker Creek, then continues on to Three Links Creek at 37 miles. Two junctions branch from the main river trail at this point. The Mink Peak Trail (438ML) crosses the river via pack bridge and ventures into the enigmatic country south of the Selway while the Three Links Trail (405ML) follows its namesake creek upstream and into the Selway Crags region of the wilderness. A third trail (606S), dim and poorly defined, takes off northeast toward Sixtytwo Ridge and the old Bear Wallow Lookout site. The few marginal campsites found along Three Links Creek appear badly torn up and overused by horse parties.

Much to surprise of most newcomers to the Selway River, a second extended uphill pitch begins west of the Three Links confluence. This time you make a steady pull upslope until the tread hovers on the hillside several hundred feet above the canyon floor. Traversing the hot, south-facing sidehill, the route passes high over Dry Bar and then descends steadily to Pinchot Creek. The lower reaches of this drainage show evidence of recent large-scale erosion, but the stream itself is easy enough to cross. Some excellent campsites are located in this general vicinity.

The trail stays reasonably close to the river for several more miles and presses on toward Ballinger Creek. Another bridge provides a dry crossing here. Located only 7.6 miles from the Race Creek Trailhead, Ballinger Creek is a logical choice for your final night on the trail.

Overhanging rock and blasted-out ledges provide more overlook points as you travel through forest of alternating age and thickness. The Selway flows slow and deep in these lower reaches, with whitewater runs near Power, Cupboard, and Renshaw creeks being the only rapids of significance. Additional campsites near Cupboard and Renshaw creeks supplement those exposed on sandbars by receding waters in late summer. After passing Renshaw Creek, the route rendezvous with the primitive Otter Butte Trail (623W) before continuing past Teepee Creek.

The foot of Fog Mountain deflects both river and trail from a westerly course to a southwesterly direction as it closes the remaining distance to Race Creek. You leave the designated wilderness behind at Packer Creek and follow the trail through more bottomland forest to your waiting vehicle.

Thus ends the 50-mile odyssey in the same quiet, unassuming manner in which it began.

The Selway River meanders through a deep canyon near Dry Bar.

Side trips: If you decide to spend more than six days on the trail, consider making a side trip or two. There is no shortage of possibilities. Most of the ridgeline hikes originating from the river trail, such as those to the fire lookouts atop Gardiner and Shissler peaks, are rather strenuous affairs. Those for whom the dry ridgelines hold no appeal might instead consider side trips into the Bear, Moose, or Three Links drainages, all of which offer more shade and much easier hiking.

Option: The net loss in elevation between Paradise and Race Creek makes going downstream the preferred direction of travel, but you can always try the hike in reverse. There is also the option of floating the Selway River, but permits for floating are quite difficult to obtain.

Afterword

On July 23, 2000, I completed the last of the hikes featured in this guide-book—Flat Creek, located at the far southern end of the wilderness. Just over a week later, passing thunderstorms touched off a series of wildfires across the Bitterroot and adjoining national forests in what was later billed as the worst wildfire season in fifty years. In the weeks that followed, flames consumed more than 250,000 acres in the Bitterroot National Forest alone. Among those acres were Flat Creek and the Little Clearwater drainage, which were razed in the Lonely Fire that consumed 19,900 acres.

No guidebook can forecast the likelihood of catastrophic fires like those that blackened huge swaths of the Bitterroots in the summer of 2000. It is therefore important to recognize that a guidebook's accuracy has its limitations. The descriptions included in these pages represent snapshots of what these trails were like when I hiked them. I have tried to present an accurate account of the conditions you are likely to encounter and to capture a sense of time and place in each of the descriptions (often by including personal statements of the "when I hiked this trail on July 31, 1993," variety).

The wildfires of 2000 reinforced the notion that all guidebooks are, by their very nature, works in progress. On a number of trails—Blodgett Canyon, Mill Creek, and Flat Creek, among others—you will notice significant discrepancies between what you read in the text and what you see on the ground. But the effects of fire are transitory, and in a matter of only a few years, new growth will rise to take the place of the old. Thus does wildfire change the complexion of the landscape without altering its underlying character.

Appendix A: For More Information

LAND MANAGEMENT AGENCIES

BITTERROOT NATIONAL FOREST
Forest Supervisor's Office
1801 North First Street
Hamilton, MT 59840
Phone: (406) 363–7117
www.fs.fed.us/r1/bitterroot/

Darby Ranger District
712 Highway 93 North
Darby, MT 59829
Phone: (406) 821-3913

Stevensville Ranger District
88 Main Street
Stevensville, MT 59870
Phone: (406) 777-5461

West Fork Ranger District
6735 West Fork Road
Darby, MT 59829
Phone: (406) 821-3269

CLEARWATER NATIONAL FOREST
Forest Supervisor's Office
12730 Highway 12
Orofino, ID 83544
Phone (208) 476-4541
TDD Phone: (208) 476-0129
www.fs.fed.us/r1/clearwater

Lochsa Ranger District—Kooskia Office
Route 1, Box 398
Kooskia, ID 83539
Phone: (208) 926-4275

Lochsa Ranger District—Powell Office
Milepost 162, Highway 12, ID
Mail: Powell Office—Lochsa Ranger
District
Lolo, MT 59847
Phone: (208) 942-3113

LOLO NATIONAL FOREST
Forest Supervisor's Office
Building 24, Fort Missoula
Missoula, MT 59804
Phone: (406) 329-3750
TDD Phone: (406) 329-1048
www.fs.fed.us/r1/lolo/

Missoula Ranger District
Building 24A, Fort Missoula
Missoula, MT 59804
Phone: (406) 329-3814

NEZ PERCE NATIONAL FOREST
Forest Supervisor's Office
Route 2, Box 475
Grangeville, ID 83530
Phone: (208) 983-1950
www.fs.fed.us/r1/nezperce/

Moose Creek Ranger District
HCR 75, Box 91
Kooskia, ID 83539
Phone: (208) 926-4258

Red River Ranger District
P.O. Box 416
Elk City, ID 83525
Phone: (208) 842-2245

National Interagency Fire Center
3833 South Development Avenue
Boise, ID 83705
Phone: (208) 387-5457
www.nifc.gov

OUTFITTERS & ADVOCACY ORGANIZATIONS

Idaho Outfitters & Guides Association
P.O. Box 95
Boise, ID 83701
Phone: (208) 342-1919
E-mail: ioga.org
www.ioga.org

Montana Outfitters & Guides Association
P.O. Box 1248
Helena, MT 59604
Phone: (406) 449-3578
E-mail: moga@mt.net
www.moga-montana.org/

Wilderness Watch
P.O. Box 9175
Missoula, MT 59807
Phone: (406) 542-2048
E-mail: wild@wildernesswatch.org
www.wildernesswatch.org

The Wilderness Society
900 Seventeenth Street NW
Washington D.C. 20006-2506
Phone: (202) 833-2300
www.wilderness.org

USGS TOPOGRAPHIC MAPS

Missoula Blueprint Co.
1613 South Avenue West
Missoula, MT 59801
Phone: (406) 549-0250

Map Distribution
U.S. Geological Survey
Box 25286, Federal Center
Denver, CO 80225
www.mapping.usgs.gov

WEATHER INFORMATION

Accuweather
www.accuweather.com

Intellicast
www.intellicast.com

The Weather Channel
www.weather.com

Appendix B: Selected References

BACKCOUNTRY ETHICS, SAFETY, AND SURVIVAL

Harmon, Will. *Leave No Trace.* Falcon Press, 1997.

Harmon, Will. *Wild Country Companion.* Falcon Press, 1994.

Moynier, John. *Avalanche Aware.* Falcon Press, 1998.

Preston, Gilbert. *Wilderness First Aid.* Falcon Press, 1997.

Schneider, Bill. *Bear Aware.* Falcon Press, 1997.

Telander, Todd and Woodmencey, Jim. *Reading Weather.* Falcon Press, 1997.

Torres, Steven. *Mountain Lion Alert.* Falcon Press, 1998.

GEOLOGY

Alt, David and Hyndman, Donald W. *Northwest Exposures—A Geologic Story of the Northwest.* Mountain Press Publishing Co., 1995.

HIKING

Arkava, Morton L. *Hiking Trails in the Bitterroot Mountains.* Pruett Publishing Co., 1983.

Arkava, Mort. *Hiking the Bitterroots (2nd ed).* Self-published, 1998.

Maughan, Ralph and Jackie Johnson. *Hiking Idaho.* Falcon Press, 1997.

Morrison, Sheila G. *29 Bitterroot Trails.* Self-published, 1982.

FISHING

Konizeski, Dick et al. *The Montanans' Fishing Guide Vol 1: Montana Waters West of the Continental Divide (5th ed).* Mountain Press Publishing Co., 1998.

MOUNTAINEERING

Caffrey, Pat. *Climber's Guide to Montana.* Mountain Press Publishing Co., 1986.

Lopez, Tom. *Exploring Idaho's Mountains.* The Mountaineers/Seattle, 1990.

HISTORICAL INTEREST

Faneslow, Julie. *Traveling the Lewis & Clark Trail.* Falcon Press, 1998.

Kresek, Ray. *Fire Lookouts of the Northwest (3rd ed).* Ye Galleon Press, 1998.

Moore, Bud. *The Lochsa Story—Land Ethics in the Bitterroot Mountains.* Mountain Press Publishing Co., 1996.

ROCKCLIMBING

Green, Randall et al. *Rockclimbing Montana.* Falcon Press, 1997.

Torre, Rick. *Bitterroot Climber's Guidebook.* Self-published, 1998.